THE ENIGMA OF EVIL

Can We Believe in the Goodness of God?

THE ENIGMA OF EVIL

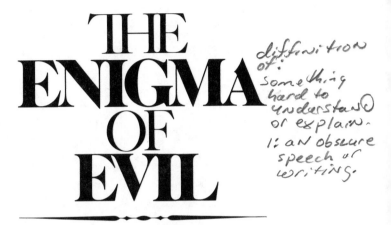

diffinition of: something hard to understand or explain. 1: an obscure speech or writing.

Can We Believe in the Goodness of God?

John W. Wenham

Community Church
609 Thomas Street
Fond du Lac, WI 54935

Academie Books Grand Rapids, Michigan
Zondervan Publishing House

THE ENIGMA OF EVIL
Copyright © 1985 by The Zondervan Corporation
Grand Rapids, Michigan

First published in 1974 by Inter-Varsity Press under the title *The Goodness of God*

ACADEMIE BOOKS are published by Zondervan
Publishing House, 1415 Lake Drive, S.E.,
Grand Rapids, Michigan 49506

Library of Congress Cataloging in Publication Data

Wenham, John William.
   The enigma of Evil.

     Reprint.   Originally published: The goodness of God.
Downers Grove: Intervarsity Press, 1974.
     Bibliography: p.
     Includes indexes.
     1. Theodicy.   I. Title
BT160.W45   1985   231'.8   85-2361
ISBN 0-310-29871-7

Biblical quotations are from the Revised Standard Version of the Bible (copyrighted 1946 and 1952, Second Edition 1971, by the Division of Christian Education, National Council of the Churches of Christ in the United States of America) unless otherwise stated.

Printed in the United States of America

85 86 87 88 89 90 / 10 9 8 7 6 5 4 3 2 1

CONTENTS

A GOOD GOD ?

'Look at the goodness of God,' says the Christian teacher. But when we look into the Bible things *seem* far from good. The book contains many horrors. There is tyranny, cruelty, mutilation – eyes gouged out, hands lopped off – deceit, licentiousness, war. Not only war, but God-sent war. Assyria, one of the cruellest nations of history, is called the rod of God's anger. God is angry and wreaks vengeance. A man here is struck blind, another dumb, another is covered with leprosy, another falls down dead, another dies in agony, another goes mad. Whole populations are devastated by plague or famine or flood or 'fire and brimstone'. With God's full permission, the Devil and a host of other powerful and malevolent spirits stalk the earth, tempting and tormenting men, even to the extent of depriving an innocent man of health and wealth and family. There are cursing psalms. There are terrible pictures of hell, in which a man craves water to cool the tip of his tongue, and in which the smoke of torment arises for ever from a lake of fire. There is war on earth and war in heaven and war in the human heart.

Lord Platt, writing to *The Times*[1] about the New English Bible, said: 'Perhaps, now that it is written in a language all can understand, the Old Testament will be seen for what it is, an obscene chronicle of man's cruelty to man, or worse perhaps, his cruelty to woman, and of man's selfishness and cupidity, backed up by his appeal to his god; a horror story if ever there was one. It is to be hoped that it will at last be

[1] 3 March 1970.

proscribed as totally inappropriate to the ethical instruction of school-children.'

'Look at the goodness of God,' says the Christian teacher. But when we look at the world of solid reality, as seen in history and in the contemporary world, things *seem* far from good. There is the long-continuing tale of man's inhumanity to man. Every age has known oppression and torture and 'the sighing of prisoners': Spain had its Inquisition, Britain its Atlantic slave trade, Germany its gas chambers, Russia its Siberian labour camps. A world torn by war now lives under the protecting threat of the hydrogen bomb. But it is a world still swept by fear and lust and greed and racial tension. It is a world where the ordinary man feels himself the pawn of irresistible, impersonal forces which govern his life. Is it conceivable that a kindly Providence of unlimited power presides over it? How can God look on in silence as the bombs rain down on defenceless cities, as widows and orphans cry to heaven for protection? How can God endure the age-long grinding poverty of the Eastern multitudes?

Further than this, human wickedness does not by any means appear to be the sole cause of human misery. Babies are *born* deformed, both physically and mentally. They *inherit* diseases; they *inherit* tendencies to insanity. Why does he allow apparently purposeless torture to the sick, producing at times not purification, but agonized bitterness? Why does he allow one of his faithful servants to endure torment on the border-line between sanity and insanity? Is this world of preying animals, of parasites, of viruses, of bacteria, the work of a good Creator? Is it God's design which allows a quantum of energy from outer space to cause some hideous mutation in an unborn child? Men find themselves in a world of earthquake and typhoon; in a world accident-prone, where bereavement and inconsolable grief may strike without warning. It is a world united only in expectation of death; a world, to many, without purpose or hope, against which there is a deep, despairing hatred.

A good God?
That is the question.

It may seem strange to regard the most difficult aspects of Christian belief as a useful starting-point for an enquiry into the character of God. Yet, as R. E. D. Clark has so forcefully pointed out, 'it is a generally accepted principle in science that it is only through the study of the unusual, the odd and the seemingly inexplicable, that man can be led onwards towards new knowledge. The scientist whose mind revolves only in the grooves of well recognized theory has little chance of discovering important new principles. An important element in the scientific method is the focusing of attention upon the things that science cannot explain, or has difficulty in explaining. In this way only can it be discovered whether known principles will cover all the facts, or whether new principles remain to be discovered . . . it will often happen that the good theory, based upon phenomena that once seemed queer and out of the ordinary, will help us to understand the ordinary and commonplace.'[2] This book started as a defensive exercise – as an attempt to answer some very difficult questions about the Bible; but it led on into a deeper understanding of what the goodness of God really means, and so it has become a positive exposition of the character of the living God, the One with whom we have to do.

In an earlier book, *Christ and the Bible*,[3] it was argued that the Gospels give a very full and clear account of the attitude of Jesus to the Old Testament. (If the Gospels give us no true idea of him, we have no adequate basis for calling ourselves Christians.) He taught that its history was true, its teaching authoritative and its form of words inspired. He regarded God as its author, so that what it said, God said.

Many thoughtful people, who (like Lord Platt) have only a superficial knowledge of the Old Testament, are likely to find this conclusion extremely perplexing. Indeed they may greet such a proposition with incredulity and horror. 'You cannot believe in the tribal god of the Old Testament, and it is

[2] R. E. D. Clark, *The Universe: Plan or Accident?* 3rd ed. (Exeter, 1961), pp. 7 f.
[3] J. W. Wenham, *Christ and the Bible* (London, 1972). In this book it is also argued that he not only authenticated the Old Testament directly, but that indirectly he authenticated the New Testament as well. The reliability of the sayings of Jesus in the Gospels is also discussed.

monstrous to implicate Christ in such a belief.' Yet the evidence that Christ did so believe is apparently inescapable. Christians, it seems, must either come to terms with it or virtually empty of content their affirmation of faith in Christ as their teacher.

This book is written for Christians, and is not intended in the first place for non-Christians who find difficulty in believing because of the problem of evil – though it is hoped that such may find something of value in it. It is intended for Christians, but it is not intended for Christians who are looking for glib answers. Easy answers could not possibly be right; answers which fit the facts could only be profoundly disturbing. The intention is to show that, in his attempts to understand the ways of God, the Christian must eschew easy answers – in particular those answers which dismiss the uncomfortable features of the Bible. We must look at *reality* – look at it hard – till at last we realize that there is no way out; till we realize that we are children, that we are fools, that we are at heart conceited, stiff-necked rebels, who will get everything wrong, unless we are prepared to give up telling God what he should be like and what he should do; till we realize that we can know only what God is pleased to tell us. We must listen and try to understand.

God and his revelation need no defence. Apologetics, in so far as it is valid, consists of two things: clearing away of misunderstandings of the revelation and showing the weaknesses of alternatives to it. These things we shall try to do as best we can, but we shall have failed to convey our message if any reader thinks that he has been given all the answers and that he now 'comprehends' God. An important lesson to get across is that sinful, finite man sees in a glass darkly. In the Christ portrayed in the Bible he indeed sees a great deal, but there are infinite tracts that he does not see nor understand. This book will have fulfilled its purpose even if at the end of the road its readers feel that they must reject many of its fallible and ignorant explanations, providing it has caused them to take Christ as their teacher more whole-heartedly, and to realize that any other authority (be it their own ideas or those of any other human being) is worthless in comparison.

The argument is as follows: Chapter 1 shows that the problem cannot be solved by cutting out the disagreeable parts of the Bible, for it is not just an Old Testament problem, it is also a New Testament one; and it is not just a New Testament one, it derives pre-eminently from Jesus himself. Jesus, New Testament and Old Testament all hang together. Furthermore, should one be tempted to liberalize the Bible by the use of critical scissors, one has a further problem which is not amenable to such easy solutions: the problem of Providence. Every Christian, liberal or conservative, has to face the problem of evil, and of the way God governs his world. It is impossible to get rid of the facts of history. This problem, which comes from the world of solid reality and which brooks no evasion, can provide a point of departure for looking at the biblical problem afresh.

Chapter 2 attempts to ease the biblical problem at its most difficult point, by looking again at Jesus' teaching about hell. Chapter 3 looks at some inadequate solutions which deny the perfection either of God's sovereignty or of his goodness.

Chapters 4 to 6 argue that the problem of Providence and the problem of the Bible are closely parallel, and that nine principles which enable us to tackle the former enable us to tackle the latter also. Taken seriously these principles – freedom, deterrence, punishment, delayed retribution, corporate solidarity, limitation to suffering, sanctification through pain, atonement, finitude – go far to explain the Bible difficulties.

Chapter 7 tries to show that the recording of the sins of its saints enhances the Bible's value rather than detracts from it, and also that the limitations of the Bible's laws reflect God's wisdom, not his imperfection. Much of the trouble arises not from the Bible's lack of morals, but from the severity of its morals. This severity is seen in the way that the sins of the saints are mercilessly exposed, and also in the severity of some Old Testament laws. It is shown that misunderstanding arises from a failure to recognize that wise legislation for a fallen race is not concerned with highfalutin theories of what life should be like in a perfect world, but with the realities of life as it is. In this the Bible is sane as well as severe.

In the light of these principles the two most difficult

problems – God's command to eliminate the heathen from the Promised Land and the biblical curses – are then examined at some depth in chapters 8 and 9, and are found to take their place in one consistent portrayal of God's activities.

The last chapter shows how the goodness of God may be seen in all its fullness in the perfect blend of kindness and severity revealed in Jesus Christ. So it is that a study of the moral problems of the Bible takes us to the heart of biblical theism, and therefore to the heart of the modern religious debate. In an Additional Study, 'The Doctrine of the Good God', it is shown how biblical theism provides a God-given touchstone for evaluating all attempts to improve upon the Bible's teaching. All man-made improvements are seen in fact to be deformations. The Bible, undiluted and unadorned, takes us to the only God, the God who is, the God who has revealed himself in word and deed, the God with whom we have to do.

1 A SERIES OF
STUMBLING-BLOCKS

Let us go back and hear this difficulty spelt out in more detail. It is often put in some such way as this: If we accept the idea that the whole Old Testament was written under the inspiration of God and that its history and doctrine are true, surely this involves us in quite unworthy beliefs as to the character and conduct of God? The 'heroes' of the Old Testament are utterly sub-Christian. Abraham is a polygamist, Jacob a coward, a liar and a coveter, Samson a sensualist, Jephthah apparently killed his own daughter. David (a 'man after God's own heart') was a murderer and an adulterer. The God of the Old Testament seems arbitrary and cruel and unjust. He is a God of vengeance, a 'jealous' God. He turns Lot's wife into a pillar of salt; he bids Abraham offer his son in sacrifice; he sends serpents to bite the disobedient Israelites; he causes the ground to swallow up Korah, Dathan and Abiram; at the call of his servant Elijah he sends fire from heaven to wipe out a hundred soldiers; to vindicate Elisha before the jeering children, he sends a bear to tear forty of them. He seems to have his favourites, preferring the despicable Jacob to the virile Esau. He hardens Pharaoh's heart and then plagues him for standing firm in face of calamity. Perhaps the most appalling of all, he commands the utter extermination of every man, woman and child in Canaan by the Israelites; he not only commands it, but the Old Testament takes great pains to rub in the fact that their disobedience to this command was one of the main causes of their subsequent miseries. Add to this the impossible idea that God put a lying spirit in the mouth of the prophets of Israel; that he inspired the sentiments of the imprecatory psalms, with their 'Happy shall he be who takes your little ones and dashes them against the rock!' – and the net result is utterly incompatible with Christian conceptions.

The only sane position for the Christian to take, it is said, is to regard the Bible as the story of man's emergence from primitive, false conceptions of God to a mature, enlightened understanding. It is one part of the whole story of evolution, the marvellous story of the progressive development of a universe under the guiding hand of God. The Bible is a true enough account of what men have *thought* about God. But in parts it gives a very untrue account of what God is actually like. The lower conceptions must continually be tested by the higher.

This point of view was provocatively and entertainingly stated by Bernard Shaw in *The Adventures of the Black Girl in her Search for God*, written during the liberal heyday. He says:

> Now the study of this history of the development of a hypothesis from savage idolatry to a highly cultivated metaphysic is as interesting, instructive, and reassuring as any study can be to an open mind and an honest intellect. But we spoil it all by that lazy and sluttish practice of not throwing out the dirty water when we get in the clean. The Bible presents us with a succession of gods, each being a striking improvement on the previous one, marking an Ascent of Man to a nobler and deeper conception of Nature, every step involving a purification of the water of life and calling for a thorough emptying and cleansing of the vessel before its replenishment by a fresh and cleaner supply. But we baffle the blessing by just sloshing the water from the new fountain into the contents of the dirty old bucket, and repeat this folly until our minds are in such a filthy mess that we are objects of pity to the superficial but clearheaded atheists who are content without metaphysics and can see nothing in the whole business but its confusions and absurdities.[1]

There are wide differences of opinion as to how the divine activity in this process is to be conceived. Shaw advocated a crude pantheism. Others will allow a series of direct personal encounters between selected individuals and the personal God, who has been made known to us by Christ. Yet they all have

[1] G. B. Shaw, *The Adventures of the Black Girl in her Search for God* (Edinburgh, 1932), pp. 69 f.

this in common, that the modern reader is required to distinguish between those parts of the Bible which rightly purport to give an account of God and those parts which wrongly do so. Some may call the process progressive revelation, but much of what is represented as revelation is no such thing. The book of Deuteronomy, for instance, prefaces the command to slaughter the Canaanites with the words of Moses: 'Now this is the commandment, the statutes and the ordinances which the Lord your God commanded me to teach you.'[2] Moses (adherents of this school will argue) doubtless thought that this was God's will; but of course it was no such thing. A God of love could and would have taught nothing so cruel. It is the task of the discerning reader to detect such errors in Scripture and to distinguish carefully between supposed revelation and genuine revelation.

Most Christians would state this view in a more moderate form. But, however moderately stated, it has a twofold difficulty. In the first place, *how are we to know what to jettison and what to keep?* With Bernard Shaw it was simple enough. He virtually scrapped the lot, apart from a few snippets which he misinterpreted.[3] Others would argue that reason and conscience (since they have been given us by God) are a sufficient guide. Yet many have discovered by experience the fallibility of both. They have found that, as their study has progressed and their spiritual life has deepened, their views as to what should be accepted and what should be dismissed have changed. Things which they once thought repellent and unworthy of the Word of God, they now find to be deeply instructive. Things which they once thought ridiculous, they now find to be important. This is the experience which Coleridge had in his study of Plato. He found himself utterly baffled by the apparent lack of consistent meaning in considerable parts of the *Timaeus*. He could not, however, give a

[2] Dt. 6 and 7.
[3] He said of the disciples: 'There are moments when one is tempted to say that there was not one Christian among them' (*Black Girl*, p. 72). Shaw's idea of a Christian was far removed from that of the New Testament, therefore he rightly perceived that there was very little of what he chose to call Christianity in it. Had he been a bit more thorough, he would have discovered that there was none at all.

contemptuous verdict because all that he could comprehend impressed him with a reverential sense of the author's genius. He also remembered numerous passages, now fully intelligible, which had formerly been no less unintelligible. He concluded that the ignorance lay in himself.[4] If this is the case with a great human thinker, may not the process be even more far-reaching when we are dealing with divine revelation? Indeed, since God is God and man is man, is it not a logical impossibility for man to fashion any criterion whereby to determine the limits of God's Word? God's thoughts will always be higher than man's thoughts. Man cannot make himself the judge in divine things. No criterion can possibly be right, unless God himself has given that criterion.

But, it is said, is not Jesus Christ himself that very God-given criterion? The Christian does not judge the Bible out of his own head. His judgments are based upon his knowledge of the loving Fatherhood of God, as shown in the teaching of Christ, the Incarnate Word of God. But here lies the second difficulty: *Jesus accepted the Old Testament as true, authoritative and inspired.*[5] Therefore it is impossible to use the Jesus of history as a yard-stick for criticizing the Old Testament. The only sort of Jesus who can be used for such a purpose is a fictitious character. It seems wise then to see what the New Testament (and Christ himself) have to say on these matters which cause offence.

THE STUMBLING-BLOCK OF THE NEW TESTAMENT

It is plain at once that it is fallacious to regard this as essentially an Old Testament problem, and to set the 'bloodthirsty' Old Testament over against the 'gentle' New Testament. Possibly the phenomenon is more crude in the Old Testament than in the New, but of the two the New Testament is the more terrible, for the Old Testament seldom speaks of anything beyond temporal judgments. The death of Uzzah for a seem-ingly trifling infringement of the Mosaic law is indeed a fearful thing, but there is no suggestion that the penalty is eternal damnation; whereas the Son of man in the Gospels pro-

[4] S. T. Coleridge, *Biographia Literaria*, ch. 12, para. 2 (Everyman's, pp. 134 f.).
[5] This is discussed at length in *Christ and the Bible*.

nounces eternal punishment. To the Old Testament writers the impending 'wrath' is usually a judgment on the historical plane; to the New Testament writers it is usually a judgment beyond the grave – though even here a sharp contrast is not to be imagined. It is the New Testament which records the sudden death of Ananias and Sapphira, the sudden blindness of Elymas and the terrible end of Herod Agrippa, whom an angel of the Lord smote and who 'was eaten by worms and died'; and the destruction of Jerusalem is pictured as a divine judgment in the New Testament as clearly as was the destruction of Babylon or Nineveh in the Old.[6] But the *stress* is on the after-life, so that we find in each of the four Gospels, in Acts, in Paul's letters, in Hebrews, James, Peter, John, Jude, and the book of Revelation, strong and clear teaching about the judgment and the wrath to come.

Omitting for the moment our Lord's words, here are a few examples of New Testament teaching:

John the Baptist: 'You brood of vipers! Who warned you to flee from the wrath to come? . . . he will clear his threshing floor . . . the chaff he will burn with unquenchable fire.'

John the Evangelist: 'He who does not obey the Son shall not see life, but the wrath of God rests upon him.'

Acts: 'And as he argued about justice and self-control and future judgment, Felix was alarmed.'

Paul in his letters: The foundation of his great doctrinal exposition in the Epistle to the Romans is the terrible passage on the wrath of God: 'You are storing up wrath for yourself on the day of wrath when God's righteous judgment will be revealed. For he will render to every man according to his works: . . . for those who are factious and do not obey the truth, but obey wickedness, there will be wrath and fury. There will be tribulation and distress for every human being who does evil . . . on that day when . . . God judges the secrets of men by

[6] Many biblical references are included in the Notes for the benefit of those who wish to study the matters discussed more fully; but to save overloading the page with reference-numerals these are frequently grouped together, a paragraph at a time: 2 Sa. 6:7; Mt. 25:41–46. Acts 5:1–11; 13:11; 12:21–23. Mt. 23:34–38; 24:15–21; Mk. 13:14–20; Lk. 21:20–24.

Christ Jesus.' 'Let no one deceive you with empty words, for it is because of these things that the wrath of God comes upon the sons of disobedience.' 'The Lord is an avenger in all these things, as we solemnly forewarned you.'

Hebrews: 'For if we sin deliberately after receiving the knowledge of the truth, there no longer remains a sacrifice for sins, but a fearful prospect of judgment, and a fury of fire which will consume the adversaries. A man who has violated the law of Moses dies without mercy at the testimony of two or three witnesses. How much worse punishment do you think will be deserved by the man who has spurned the Son of God? . . . It is a fearful thing to fall into the hands of the living God.'

'For you have not come to what may be touched, a blazing fire, and darkness, and gloom, and a tempest, and the sound of a trumpet, and a voice whose words made the hearers entreat that no further messages be spoken to them. For they could not endure the order that was given, . . . But you have come . . . to a judge who is God of all . . . See that you do not refuse him who is speaking. For if they did not escape when they refused him who warned them on earth, much less shall we escape if we reject him who warns from heaven . . . let us be grateful for receiving a kingdom that cannot be shaken, and thus let us offer to God acceptable worship, with reverence and awe; for our God is a consuming fire.'

James: 'Judgment is without mercy to one who has shown no mercy.'

1 Peter: 'For the time has come for judgment to begin with the household of God; and if it begins with us, what will be the end of those who do not obey the gospel of God? And

> "If the righteous man is scarcely saved,
> where will the impious and sinner appear?" '

2 Peter: 'Swift destruction . . . their condemnation has not been idle, and their destruction has not been asleep . . . the Lord knows how to keep the unrighteous under punishment until the day of judgment . . . these will be destroyed in the same destruction . . . for them the nether gloom of darkness has been reserved . . . by the same word the heavens and earth that now exist have been stored up for fire, being kept until the day of judgment and destruction of ungodly men.'

Jude: 'Sodom and Gomorrah . . . serve as an example by undergoing a punishment of eternal fire.' 'Behold, the Lord came with his holy myriads, to execute judgment on all, and to convict all the ungodly of all their deeds of ungodliness which they have committed in such an ungodly way, and of all the harsh things which ungodly sinners have spoken against him.'

The book of Revelation bristles with judgments depicted in the most lurid colours. We will merely extract a few vivid phrases: 'the wine of God's wrath, poured unmixed into the cup of his anger', 'tormented with fire and sulphur', 'the smoke of their torment goes up for ever and ever; and they have no rest, day or night', 'the angel swung his sickle on the earth and gathered the vintage of the earth, and threw it into the great wine press of the wrath of God'. 'From his mouth issues a sharp sword with which to smite the nations, and he will rule them with a rod of iron; he will tread the wine press of the fury of the wrath of God the Almighty'; 'the second death, the lake of fire.' [7]

Surely it cannot be said that the severity of God is primarily an Old Testament problem. These references are but a fraction of the total, but they show beyond all cavil that the problem of the judgment of God finds its acutest expression in the New Testament.

THE STUMBLING-BLOCK OF THE TEACHING OF CHRIST

Further, if it is fallacious to try to drive a wedge between the Old and New Testaments, it is equally fallacious to attempt to show a contrast between the teaching of our Lord and the teaching of the New Testament writers. The temptation to do this has been very strong, and the taste for a sentimentalizing of Jesus has been indulged to such an extent during the past

[7] Mt. 3:7–12; *cf.* Lk. 3:7–17. Jn. 3:36; *cf.* 1 Jn. 5:12, 16. Acts 24:25. Rom. 1:18–2:16; Eph. 5:6; 1 Thes. 4:6. Heb. 10:26–31; 12:18–29. Jas. 2:13. 1 Pet. 4:17 f. 2 Pet. 2:1–3:7. Jude 7, 14, 15. Rev. 14:10–20; 19:15; 20:14.

hundred years that a totally erroneous mental picture of him
has very largely become the common property of theologians,
preachers, church folk and non-Christians. The majority of our
contemporaries genuinely think that Christ taught that God
was the loving Father of all mankind, who would make everything come out all right for everyone in the end, no matter
what they did. The belief that Jesus taught the love of God as
no-one before had ever taught it, and that by his life and
actions he displayed love as no-one before had ever displayed
it, is true. In him there was no hint of hardness, or of lack of
sympathy, or of unwillingness to spend himself to the limit on
behalf of those in need. Yet he did not teach that all would be
well for everyone in the end, no matter what they did. With
great earnestness he called on everyone to repent and with
great compassion he invited those weighed down with cares and
sorrows to come to him for rest. Yet this very Jesus uttered the
most terrible warnings, not once or twice, but again and again.

Speaking with no trace of harshness and with a wealth of
compassion and concern, he frequently spoke of judgment. He
warned men of perdition and destruction, of the danger of
losing their souls. Christ spoke of sins which would not be forgiven. He spoke often of hell. Frequently he spoke of fire in this
connection. Sometimes he spoke of eternal fire or eternal
punishment. He spoke of it as a place of wailing and gnashing
of teeth. Sometimes he spoke of outer darkness. Sometimes he
spoke of torment. To feel the full weight of this teaching of
Christ, the relevant passages [8] should be looked up and written
out. To do this is to receive an awesome and indelible impression which remains with one for life.

In sheer number these statements are inescapable. In in-

---

[8] The most important references are: *Judgment*: Mt. 10:15; *cf.* 11:21–24;
Lk. 10:12–15. Mt. 12:36, 41, 42; *cf.* Lk. 11:31, 32. Jn. 5:26–29; 12:48.
Perdition, destruction, losing one's soul: Mt. 16:26; Mk. 8: 36, 37; Lk. 9:25.
Mt. 22:2, 7; Lk. 13:3, 5; Jn. 12:25; 17:12. *Sins not forgiven*: Mt. 6:15;
12:31; *cf.* Mk. 3:29; Lk. 12:10. Jn. 8:24; Mt. 7:23. *Hell*: Mt. 5:29, 30;
10:28; *cf.* Lk. 12:5. Mt. 23:33–36; Lk. 11:50, 51. *Fire*: Mt. 5:22; Jn.
15:6. *Eternal fire, eternal punishment*: Mt. 18:6–8; *cf.* Lk. 17:1, 2; Mk. 9:42–
48. Mt. 25:41–46. *Wailing and gnashing of teeth*: Mt. 13:30–42, 49, 50;
24:50, 51; *cf.* Mt. 25:26–30; Lk. 13:24–28. *Outer darkness*: Mt.
8:12; 22:13. *Torment*: Lk. 16:22–28; Mt. 18:34, 35 ('jailers': Greek
'torturers').

tensity they are fearful. We are here faced with the ultimate horror of God's universe, before which we stand aghast, longing to escape, but as in a nightmare unable to move. We cannot escape, for we know *who* said these things, we know his tenderness, we know the authority of his words and we know that this is the language (be it more or less symbolic) which *he* regarded as best fitted to describe the price of impenitence. It is Love who speaks like this, it is God himself. It is the final test of our repentance towards God and our faith in Jesus Christ that we accept our creatureliness and our sinfulness when faced with this teaching; that we really, sincerely acknowledge that *our* thoughts are limited by ignorance and perverted by sin; that we accept (however reluctantly and protestingly) *his* teaching and we reassert (however falteringly) our trust in his love.

THE NEW TESTAMENT UNDERLINES THE OLD

It is worth noticing too how often specific Old Testament difficulties are taken up, reaffirmed and then embodied in the teaching of the New, several times by our Lord himself. Instead of softening the harsh outlines of the Old Testament, the New Testament actually engraves them more deeply. Again and again the most unpleasant characters and the most unpleasant incidents of the Old Testament are adopted by the New without apology and without mitigation, sometimes to repeat an old lesson, sometimes to teach a new lesson more severe than the first. On other occasions where there is no specific reference to the Old Testament, we come across parallels of thought which remind us that our Old Testament difficulty is a difficulty common to both Testaments.

It is not only in the Old Testament that Rahab, Samson and Jephthah are regarded as examples of faith, but also in the New. The offering of Isaac may present difficulties to the modern reader of the Old Testament, but the New Testament accepts it as a supreme example of both faith and works. Is the God of the Old Testament a jealous God? So is the God of the New – 'Shall we provoke the Lord to jealousy?' (1 Corinthians). Is the God of the Old Testament a God of vengeance? So is he in the New – 'Vengeance is mine, I will repay,' re-echo Romans and Hebrews. 'The Lord is an avenger,' says 1

Thessalonians. Does the law of Moses demand death without mercy for the transgressor? 'How much *worse* punishment', asks the New, 'will be deserved by the man who has spurned the Son of God?' Does God send a lying spirit to deceive the false prophets of Israel? Paul says of the impending apostasy, of those who refuse 'to love the truth and so be saved': 'Therefore God sends upon them a strong delusion, to make them believe what is false, so that all may be condemned who did not believe the truth but had pleasure in unrighteousness.' Does the Old Testament thunder out its anathemas? Paul (the author of glorious passages on love) can write: 'If any one is preaching to you a gospel contrary to that which you received, let him be accursed;' 'if any one has no love for the Lord, let him be accursed.'[9] Are we going to find the imprecatory psalms repudiated in the New Testament? On the contrary, we find them honoured with a frequency of quotation rather above the average.[1]

The Old Testament apparently glories in the fall of the enemies of the people of God. The book of Revelation gathers up in a single chapter a wealth of Old Testament imagery and phraseology and pours it out in a tremendous description of the fall of Babylon the Great, in the course of which a voice from heaven says:

> 'Render to her as she herself has rendered,
> and repay her double for her deeds;
> mix a double draught for her in the cup she mixed.
> As she glorified herself and played the wanton,
> so give her a like measure of torment and mourning.
> Since in her heart she says, "A queen I sit,
> I am no widow, mourning I shall never see,"
> so shall her plagues come in a single day,
> pestilence and mourning and famine,
> and she shall be burned with fire;
> for mighty is the Lord God who judges her.'

[9] Heb. 11:31 f.; Jas. 2:25. Heb. 11:17; Jas. 2:21. 1 Cor. 10:22. Rom. 12:19; Heb. 10:30; 1 Thes. 4:6. Heb. 10:29. 2 Thes. 2:11 f. 1 Cor. 13; Rom. 12:9–21; Gal. 1:9; 1 Cor. 16:22.
[1] See pp. 157 f.

From the earth comes the cry:

> 'Rejoice over her, O heaven,
> O saints and apostles and prophets,
> for God has given judgment for you against her!'

And the multitude in heaven cries with a mighty voice:

> 'Hallelujah! Salvation and glory and power belong to our
>   God,
> for his judgments are true and just;
> he has judged the great harlot who corrupted the earth with
>   her fornication,
> and he has avenged on her the blood of his servants.'

Once more they cry,

> 'Hallelujah! The smoke from her goes up for ever and ever.'[2]

Several of the most striking references to God hardening hearts or blinding eyes are taken up in the New Testament, sometimes in the context of a discussion of divine election, as in Romans: 'The scripture says to Pharaoh, "I have raised you up for the very purpose of showing my power in you, so that my name may be proclaimed in all the earth." So then he has mercy upon whomever he wills, and he hardens the heart of whomever he wills.' In the same context Malachi is quoted: 'Jacob I loved, but Esau I hated.' Hebrews similarly recalls of Esau that 'he found no chance to repent, though he sought it with tears'. The Gospel of John says of some who listened to Christ: 'Therefore they could not believe. For Isaiah again said,

> "He has blinded their eyes and hardened their heart,
> lest they should see with their eyes and perceive with their
>   heart,
> and turn for me to heal them." '[3]

[2] Rev. 18:6–19:3.
[3] Rom. 9:13, 17 f.; Mal. 1:2 f.; Heb. 12:17; Jn. 12:39 f. This passage from Is. 6:10 (together with Is. 29:10) is also alluded to in Rom. 11:8:

> 'God gave them a spirit of stupor,
> eyes that should not see and ears that should not hear.'

The Flood, the destruction of Sodom and Gomorrah and the various disasters in the wilderness seem to have made a particular impression on the apostolic church, partly doubtless because our Lord himself used them to illustrate his teaching on judgment and perdition. He refers to the Flood in two passages and to Sodom in four. He compares the death from serpent-bite with the perishing wrought by unbelief.[4] In every case there is no softening of the Old Testament teaching, but the historical judgments are taken as illustrations of the even more solemn judgments of the age to come.

THE STUMBLING-BLOCK OF PROVIDENCE

These considerations go far to show the consistency of the biblical position – the moral difficulty of the Bible is not merely a problem of the Old Testament, nor even of the New Testament, it is a problem common to the teaching of the Old Testament, of the New Testament and of Christ himself. But so far our conclusions have been largely negative and at first sight far from helpful to the defender of the Christian Faith. We have done little more than add to the well-known difficulty of the Old Testament two further and even more serious difficulties – the moral difficulty of the New Testament and the moral difficulty of Christ's teaching. But we must go yet one step further into the abyss before we can hope to see light. We must recognize that there is not only the moral difficulty of the Bible, there is also that whole complex of difficulties in the world about us to which we referred at the beginning, which we may describe as the moral difficulty of Providence.

Here is a difficulty which faces every Christian, whether he regards the whole Bible to be true or not; and it is a difficulty even harder to evade than the biblical one. It cannot be airily dismissed by any superficial formula. The problem is with us and forces its attention upon us every day of our lives. It is another stumbling-block of the first magnitude.

Yet this further stumbling-block may not be altogether a disadvantage. In spite of its apparent difficulty, it seems to

[4] Mt. 24:37, 38; Lk. 17:26, 27; other New Testament references are Heb. 11:7; 1 Pet. 3:20; 2 Pet. 2: 5. Mt. 10:15; 11:23, 24; Lk. 10:12; 17:28–32; cf. Rom. 9:29; 2 Pet. 2:6, 7; Jude 7; Rev. 11:8. Jn. 3:14; cf. 1 Cor. 10:5; Jude 5, 11 (Korah's rebellion).

have a place in the whole picture which we are building up. For the important point to notice is this: *the moral difficulties of Providence are very much akin both in degree and extent to the biblical difficulties.*[5] Therefore, if the difficulties in the one case are not insuperable, it is reasonable to suppose that they may not be insuperable in the other.

That the degree and extent of evil to be seen in the Bible is much the same as that to be seen in the world is fairly clear. As far as human sin and its results are concerned the Bible portrays the world faithfully: fear, lust, greed, callousness, cynicism, racial tension, oppression, imprisonment, war and torture are all there. Deformity, disease, innocent suffering, bereavement and death are there too, as are natural disasters and the great impersonal forces of world history, and animal pain. The scale of the one matches the scale of the other. (The modern threats to the survival of the race, for instance, remind one of Noah's flood.) What the Bible lacks and a modern

---

[5] This is a particular case of the principle so clearly enunciated in Joseph Butler's famous *Analogy*. The full title of Butler's work was *The Analogy of Religion, Natural and Revealed, to the Constitution and Course of Nature*; and in it he showed that there is a close similarity between the dealings of God as recorded in the Bible and the dealings of God as observed in his providential ordering of the world. Butler (whose book was published in 1736) was replying to objections urged against the Christian Faith by the Deists. The Deist believed (like the Christian) that the universe and man had been created by God, and that God had given to both laws governing their own nature; but (unlike the Christian) he considered that man's own inner constitution and the orderly world about him provided all the raw materials and all the potentialities needed for him to work out his own salvation. The Deist saw no need for, and did not believe in, the redemptive doctrines which lie at the heart of the Christian Faith. Butler set out to show, and showed most effectively, that the difficulties which the Deist found in the Christian Faith were also to be found in Nature, and that therefore if the difficulties did not invalidate their beliefs in the one case they could not rightly do so in the other. In this, as he says in the introduction, he was following an idea of Origen who fifteen centuries before had 'with singular sagacity observed, that *he who believes the Scripture to have proceeded from him who is the Author of Nature, may well expect to find the same sort of difficulties in it, as are found in the constitution of Nature*'. He worked out the analogy with regard to belief in a future life, God's government by rewards and punishments, our state of probation, the credibility that revelation must contain things appearing liable to objections, the appointment of a Mediator, and the redemption of the world by him. As an over-all system of apologetics Butler's work is open to grave objection, but on this particular point he too shows singular sagacity.

scientific study of the world supplies is a knowledge of some of the 'natural' forces which govern mental and bodily disease and heredity and physical catastrophes. What scientific study lacks and the Bible supplies is some knowledge of the 'spiritual' forces which govern the world; and the Bible also gives some glimpses of the world to come. The only difficulties that are peculiar to the Bible are those which seem to suggest that God is either the author of some evils or that he approves of them.

Now if the same sort of difficulties which we find in the Bible are also to be found in Providence, it follows that attempts to make the Bible acceptable to the modern palate by deleting all that appears 'savage' and 'blood-thirsty' will land us in insuperable difficulties over the question of Providence. We can see with our own eyes that God allows war, famine, disease, torture and misery – and that on a colossal scale. Though it is profoundly difficult to understand, it is thoroughly consistent with what we see in the Bible. It is in fact easier to accept the God of the Bible than it is to accept a liberalized God whose character has ceased to be terrible. The God of liberal theology is not only out of touch with the Bible, but also with the world as we find it.

This recognition of a certain grim consistency within the Bible, and of a grim consistency between the Bible and the world of Nature, is not likely to make the Christian Faith any more palatable to those outside – at least for the time being. But it does serve a very useful purpose if it helps to solve the domestic controversy within. It shows the most promising way of tackling both problems, and makes it clear that nothing will be gained by running away from the Bible. If Christianity is true at all, the position of strength will be found in a bold assertion of faith – faith in the living God who has spoken in Jesus Christ; faith in Jesus Christ as teacher; faith in the Scriptures which he authenticated; faith in the perfect love of God which he revealed. In the end the full biblical doctrine will speak more deeply to the needs of the unconvinced than will any diluted version of Christian teaching.

The ultimate horror of God's universe is hell. The other difficulties of the Bible and of Providence are real enough, but however appalling they may be, their seeming harshnesses and injustices are only temporary, cut short at death. The terrors of hell, on the other hand, belong to the world which lies beyond death. For a single being to endure pain hopelessly and unendingly, or even to pass out of existence and forfeit for ever the joys of heaven, is more terrible than any temporal suffering.

BIBLICAL IMAGERY

It would have been easier to have evaded the subject of hell altogether on the just ground that it is far too big a topic for adequate treatment. Had this book been simply an academic exercise, it would have been sensible to have argued: 'This is a book for Christians; Christians are committed to the teaching of Christ; Christ taught the existence of hell with a wealth of terrifying images; it is best to let these images speak for themselves, leaving further comment to those who can discuss the issues at length.'

Yet this is not a mere academic exercise, it is an attempt to grapple with the heart's cry of contemporary man who wants to know what to believe about God. If the biblical imagery is left undiscussed, there is no guarantee that he will interpret first-century images correctly. Twentieth-century man does not and cannot come to the Bible with an empty mind. The very word 'hell' comes to us laden with literary and artistic associations of many centuries. Platonic philosophy clearly had a great influence on Christian thought and Greek mythology on Christian art. Satan is still currently represented in the likeness of Pan, a pagan deity with tail and horns, rather than as the prince of this world and the angel of light of the Bible.

Modern scholarship, whatever its faults may be, has tried very hard to see the New Testament through first-century eyes, and it is now recognized that medieval thought, though believed at the time to be in complete harmony with the Bible, was in many respects quite alien to it. A large number of serious students think that the doctrine of hell as traditionally taught comes in this category. It seems highly desirable therefore that this question should not be side-stepped. Unfortunately the subject is so vast that it will not be possible even to summarize the discussion in such a way that the reader can come to a considered judgment on it. The most that can be done is to outline the alternatives and to give references to books where the matter is more fully discussed.

TRADITIONAL ORTHODOXY

'Traditional orthodoxy' (as we shall call it, but without begging any questions) is said to have had its first official formulation at the Second Council of Constantinople in 553. Among its acts are the nine Anathemas of the Emperor Justinian against Origen, the last of which runs: 'If anyone says or thinks that the punishment of demons and of impious men is only temporary and will one day have an end . . . let him be anathema.'[1] Traditional orthodoxy was based on a number of seemingly plain scriptures, mostly derived from Jesus' own teaching in the Gospels. Jesus spoke of the rich man in Hades, tormented by the flame, wishing the beggar Lazarus to dip the tip of his finger in water to cool his tongue, but told of the great chasm between them which no-one could cross. Jesus also spoke of unquenchable fire, of the undying worm and the wailing and gnashing of teeth of Gehenna. Most strikingly of all, he used precisely the same adjective in the same sentence

[1] *Nicene and Post-Nicene Fathers*, Second Series, Vol. 14, *The Seven Ecumenical Councils*, p. 320. The anathemas of Justinian were adopted by an earlier synod in Constantinople in 543. There is some question whether these anathemas were adopted by the ecumenical council of 553, or whether they were interpolated into its acts later.

when speaking of 'eternal (or everlasting) life' and of 'eternal (or everlasting) punishment'. Having declared that on the day of judgment the Son of man would say to those at his left hand, 'Depart from me, you cursed, into the eternal fire prepared for the devil and his angels', he concludes his solemn statement with the words: 'They will go away into eternal punishment, but the righteous into eternal life.'

The same teaching, but spelt out in even stronger terms, is given in the Revelation of John, where it is said of those who worship the beast that 'the smoke of their torment goes up for ever and ever'. Later on it says: 'the devil who had deceived them was thrown into the lake of fire and sulphur where the beast and the false prophet were, and they will be tormented day and night for ever and ever.'[2] This expression 'for ever and ever' is repeatedly used in Revelation for the reign of God and of the saints; it seems logical therefore to infer that the torments of the lost are as unending as the bliss of the redeemed.

TRADITIONAL ORTHODOXY'S TREATMENT OF THE DIFFICULTIES

To traditional orthodoxy the doctrine was of course difficult. To reconcile the idea of torment which goes on for ever and ever with the love (or even the justice) of God is not easy. The easy thing is to do the opposite and paint the doctrine as revolting and incredible. But the traditionalists contended rightly that philosophical arguments concocted by sinful humans as to how a holy God should order the world to come cannot be relied on. They are liable to prove too much, for similar arguments, if used about the way God orders this present world, would lead to a denial of God's existence. For a Christian one simple sentence of revelation must in the end outweigh the weightiest conclusions of man-made philosophy.

As to the duration of hell, it seemed to the traditionalists that they had not just one straightforward sentence of revelation, but a whole collection of them, which only the incorrigibly perverse could hope to explain away. A minor classic on the traditionalist side was M. Horbery's *An Enquiry into the Scripture Doctrine concerning the Duration of Future Punishment*, first published in 1744 and reprinted in 1878. He wrote: 'It is hard

[2] Lk. 16:19–31; Mk. 9:43, 48; Mt. 8:12; 25:41, 46; Rev. 14:11; 20:10.

to say, how any Doctrine can be taught more plainly . . . how could he have done it in plainer Words, or in a more emphatical Manner?' A modern writer, W. Hendriksen, says: 'The passages . . . are so numerous that one actually stands aghast that in spite of all this there are people today who affirm that they accept Scripture and who, nevertheless, reject the idea of never-ending torment.'[3]

AUGUSTINE AND AQUINAS

Even so, thoughtful Christians, who were often themselves men of sincere piety and who cared deeply for their fellow-men, did their best to reconcile their belief in the sovereignty and goodness of God with the concept of unending torment (and of unending sin which it implies). Augustine, who has been the greatest single influence on Christian thought since New Testament times, was the arch-opponent of the Manichean religion, which taught a dualist doctrine of the eternal coexistence of good and evil. He had to rebut the charge that unending torment involved the eternity of evil. He did this by maintaining that, whereas unpunished sin was an evil, sin properly punished was a good. Thus the existence of souls undergoing their just punishment throughout eternity was a good and not an evil, and in consequence God and the saints would enjoy unsullied and unending bliss in spite of the existence of hell.[4]

Similarly Aquinas, in the supplement to his *Summa Theologica* (the most famous of all medieval works of theology), argued the justice of the punishment and the happiness of the saints in contemplating it. He is recorded as saying: 'This is

[3] M. Horbery, *An Enquiry into the Scripture Doctrine concerning the Duration of Future Punishment* (London, 1878), pp. 55 f.; W. Hendriksen, *The Bible on the Life Hereafter* (Grand Rapids, 1959), pp. 197 f. Other modern treatments from the standpoint of traditional orthodoxy are L. Boettner, *Immortality* (Philadelphia, 1956); J. A. Motyer, *After Death* (London, 1965). Weighty works of the nineteenth century include E. M. Goulburn, *Everlasting Punishment* (London, 1880); E. B. Pusey, *What is of Faith as to Everlasting Punishment?* (3rd ed., Oxford, 1881); S. D. F. Salmond, *The Christian Doctrine of Immortality* (3rd ed., Edinburgh, 1897).

[4] John Baillie, *And the Life Everlasting* (London, 1934), p. 244, speaks of 'his bland assurance that the universe is no less admirable and beautiful a place for having a chamber of horrors eternally present within it, so long only as each horror of pain perfectly matches and balances each horror of sin'.

also becoming to Divine justice, that . . . they be tormented in many ways and from many sources.' 'Everything is known the more for being compared with its contrary, because when contraries are placed beside one another they become more conspicuous. Wherefore in order that the happiness of the saints may be more delightful to them and that they may render more copious thanks to God for it, they are allowed to see perfectly the sufferings of the damned.' He then added a further justification (frequently used by other writers also) why the punishment of mortal sin is eternal. By sinning 'one offends God Who is infinite. Wherefore since punishment cannot be infinite in intensity, because the creature is incapable of an infinite quality, it must needs be infinite at least in duration.'[5]

MODERN WRITERS

Nearly all the leading thinkers of the Reformation period continued in the same tradition, as have most scholars since that time who have held strictly to the truth and consistency of the Bible. A good representative of the nineteenth century was Charles Hodge, a lucid writer of great influence. In intention his approach is strictly and exclusively biblical. His most important points (which interestingly are made in this order) are:

1. It is an almost invincible presumption that the Bible does teach the unending punishment of the finally impenitent, that all Christian churches have so understood it . . . what the great body of the competent readers of a plain book take to be its meaning, must be its meaning.

2. The doctrine of the perpetuity of the future punishment of the wicked was held by the Jews under the old dispensation, and at the time of Christ. Neither our Lord nor his Apostles ever contradicted that doctrine . . . They themselves . . . taught that doctrine in the most explicit and solemn manner.

3. We are incompetent judges of the penalty which sin deserves. We have no adequate apprehension of its inherent guilt, of the dignity of the person against whom it is committed, or of the extent of the evil which it is suited to produce.

4. How do we know that the reasons . . . which constrained God to allow his children to be sinful and miserable for thousands of years, may not constrain Him to permit some of them to remain miserable forever?

[5] Aquinas, *Summa Theologica*, Part 3, English Dominican trans., 1922, pp. 169, 107, 203.

5. We have reason to believe . . . that the number of the finally
lost in comparison with the whole number of the saved will be very
inconsiderable.[6]

A welcome feature of modern discussions is the human concern which begins to be shown. Earnest attempts are made to
mollify the doctrine, either (like Hodge) by arguing the com-
parative fewness of the lost (B. B. Warfield also speaks of them
as a 'relatively insignificant body'), or by arguing that the
degree of suffering might be much milder than it was usually
painted. Horbery quotes Archbishop King with approval as
saying: 'in Hell there may be some whose Condition is prefer-
able to not being.' A popular writer, H. Silvester, while
formally repudiating the idea of annihilation and espousing an
eternal hell, declares: 'Hell cannot be "side by side" with
heaven. Heaven is being, hell towards not-being.'[7] This notion
in fact sounds like a repudiation of the traditional doctrine,
since a movement of indefinitely long duration towards non-
being would seem to be a slow process of annihilation, which
must eventually reach its term.

These attempts to soften the doctrine of unending suffering
have themselves come in for criticism. In principle, it is said, it
makes no difference whether it is one person or billions who
suffer, or whether the anguish is intense or mild; it is a human
being living in sin, in a state which can properly be called
torment, without hope, for ever and ever. To ordinary human
logic it looks like an ultimate dualism in which the perfection
of God's creation is permanently marred by a hideous blot.
Furthermore, it is more than doubtful whether the Bible indicates that the number of the finally lost will be 'very inconsiderable'. Jesus spoke of the 'many' who were on the way
to destruction and of the 'few' who were on the way to life, of
the 'many' who were called and the 'few' who were chosen.[8]
Equally it is more than doubtful whether attempts to play

[6] C. Hodge, *Systematic Theology* (London, 1873) III, pp. 870—880.
[7] B. B. Warfield, art. 'Predestination', in *Hastings Dictionary of the Bible* IV,
p. 63. Horbery, *op. cit.*, p. 154, n. 1. H. Silvester, *Arguing with God* (London,
1971), p. 90. U. E. Simon, *The End is Not Yet* (Welwyn, 1964), p. 207, makes
the important point: 'Heaven must not be viewed as the counterpart to
Hell. Our fondness of symmetrical arrangements, if apt to suggest a God-
Satan, Heaven-Hell, Good-Evil parallelism, must be resisted.'
[8] Mt. 7:13 f.; 22:14.

down the intensity of the pains of hell are justified, since Jesus himself used terms of horror to describe them.

Such considerations have prompted intensive efforts to find alternatives to the teaching of traditional orthodoxy. These fall into two categories, which may be labelled 'universalism' and 'conditional immortality' respectively. Universalism teaches that all men will finally be saved. Conditional immortality (so called because it maintains that man is not naturally immortal, but that he may become immortal on condition of faith in Christ) teaches that the unrepentant, when they have suffered the due penalty of their sins, will pass out of existence.

UNIVERSALISM

However much we might wish universalism to be true, it seems impossible to reconcile it with many passages in the Bible. To those who regard the Bible as self-contradictory a plausible case (but no more than plausible) can be made out for Paul being a universalist on the basis of certain well-known texts, such as: 'As in Adam all die, so also in Christ shall all be made alive' and 'at the name of Jesus every knee should bow'. Paul teaches an ultimate reconciliation of all things to God, but only after judgment has been carried out, which will mean 'wrath and fury . . . tribulation and distress for every human being who does evil'; 'they shall suffer the punishment of eternal destruction and exclusion from the presence of the Lord.'[9] From the rest of the Bible there is little that can even plausibly be quoted in favour of universalism.

Universalism is usually argued in terms of man as a free being living for ever within the influence of God's infinitely patient love. In his selfishness and pride man may long resist God's gentle attraction, but in the end Love will win his free and full response.[1] Yet this enormously important truth (if it were a truth) is nowhere to be found in the Bible, and is in fact

[9] 1 Cor. 15:22–28; Phil. 2:10; see also Rom. 5:18; Eph. 1:20–23. Col. 1:20; Rom. 2:1–10; 2 Thes. 1:9.
[1] This is attractively argued by J. A. T. Robinson, *In the End, God* . . . (London, 1950), chapters 8 and 9 – one of his most powerful pieces of writing. J. H. Leckie's *The World to Come and Final Destiny* (Edinburgh, 1918) is a careful and thorough work which finally inclines towards universalism.

contradicted by it. It is in effect a doctrine of purgatory, but a purgatory regarded as the destination, not only of the baptized who die in venial sin (as taught in medieval theology), but of all those who die unfit for heaven.

But the Bible nowhere teaches the existence of a place for slow purgation after death. On the contrary it teaches that at the end of the age, at Christ's second coming, there will be an immediate and instantaneous change for those who are in union with Christ, so that they become like him;[2] whereas those who do not belong to Christ will have to face their judgment in their sins. This instantaneity has far-reaching implications, for what happens to those who are alive at Christ's coming establishes in principle what happens to all men: they are judged on the basis of their condition when their earthly life ends. The doctrine of a purgatory of unlimited duration has in fact affinities with those Eastern religions which teach an age-long transmigration of souls, rather than with the Bible.

If purgatory as an intermediate place between heaven and hell is denied and the purifying process is put in heaven (as apparently is done in the Church of England Doctrine Commission's report of 1971: *Prayer and the Departed*),[3] the biblical doctrine is even more seriously undermined. Heaven ceases to be a place of perfect purity and joy, and it becomes a place where toiling sinners continue (for God alone knows how long) on the moral treadmill, failing, suffering, trying again. One of the great consolations of the Bible is its insistence that the moral struggle does not go on for ever, but that it ends for the whole human race on the day of judgment.

CONDITIONAL IMMORTALITY

The other alternative, the possibility that the lost will eventually pass out of existence, needs much more serious attention. Conditionalists (as those who uphold conditional immortality are called) look for the resurrection of all men, followed by a just sentence according to the deserts of each, which will mean anguish (but not unending torment) for those

[2] 1 Cor. 15:51 f.; 1 Jn. 3:2.
[3] *Prayer and the Departed*: Report of the Archbishops' Commission on Christian Doctrine (London, 1971).

outside Christ, finally terminating in the second death. Some (though not all) believe that there is no conscious existence of a soul-without-body between death and resurrection, but that at death all pass into a soul-sleep in total unconsciousness. This would mean that the first consciousness of the redeemed after death would be of Christ's welcome into paradise, that is to say, into heaven.

The conditionalist tries to establish his case by raising fundamental questions. For example, does the Bible teach that the soul is immortal? Does it not rather teach that the soul that sins will die?[4] Do not the most frequently used terms, 'death', 'destruction', 'perishing' and the metaphor of the fire which consumes vegetable matter, suggest an end? (The description of Gehenna is based on the garbage dump in the Valley of Hinnom outside Jerusalem, where the slow fires ceaselessly burnt and the worms steadily consumed the rotting rubbish.) Does not the Bible rather teach that man is mortal, and that sin is a self-destructive force whose final wages are the complete destruction of body and soul? Is not immortality part of the gift of eternal life bestowed on those who come to partake of the divine nature through union with Christ?[5] Is not the universalist's insistence on the eternity of all souls a move in the direction of pantheism, and the traditionalist's insistence on the eternity of sinning souls a move in the direction of dualism? These are some of the questions conditionalists tend to ask.

Some, such as L. E. Froom, challenge the factual accuracy of Hodge's claim that unending torment has virtually been the sole doctrine of mainstream Christianity, derived from a monochrome belief in first-century Judaism. They admit that from the sixth century to the Reformation unending torment was the accepted orthodoxy with few dissenting voices, and that after the Reformation it continued to be dominant in the

---

[4] Ezk. 18:4; Rom. 6:23, *etc*. It is sometimes said that the Bible does not teach the immortality of the soul, but that it assumes it. But that so important a truth should not be explicitly taught is strange. The onus of proof is on those who say it is assumed.

[5] The Lord alone has immortality (1 Tim. 6:16); well-doers seek immortality (Rom. 2:7); immortality is brought to light through the gospel (2 Tim. 1:10); those in Christ will put on immortality (1 Cor. 15:54); they have become partakers of the divine nature (2 Pet. 1:4).

major churches at least till the nineteenth century, though with a growing volume of dissent. They deny that unending torment was so generally accepted by first-century Jews that Jesus' hearers would necessarily have interpreted his teaching in this sense without some specific denial on his part. They maintain that conditional immortality was generally accepted in the early church until its thinkers tried to wed Plato's doctrine of the immortality of the soul to the teaching of the Bible. This unequal yoke, they say, spawned two bastard off-spring: universalism (as taught by Clement and Origen of Alexandria) and unending torment (as taught by Tertullian and Augustine).

As to the key biblical texts, which seem so inescapable, they claim that the unquenchable fire and undying worm mean only fire which is unquenchable and worms which are undying until their work of destruction is complete. Eternal punishment has been dealt with by them in two different ways. Some argue that eternal punishment is everlasting in its effects (like the 'punishment of eternal fire' which destroyed Sodom and Gomorrah, mentioned in Jude 7), but not in its pains. It is an everlasting punishment, but not an everlasting punishing. Others argue that the concept lying behind the Greek word *aiōnios* is that of contemporary Jewish thought, which spoke of the two contrasting ages: 'this present age' and 'the age to come'. Eternal life is the life of the age to come and eternal punishment is the punishment of the age to come. The former has been made available by the coming of Jesus and the in-auguration of his reign; the latter will be administered by Jesus when, as Son of man, he utters the final judgment. Christ's reference to 'eternal life' and 'eternal punishment' is not primarily concerned with the everlastingness of the two destinies, but with the finality of what happens when the advent of the New Age is consummated. These two views are not mutually exclusive and both could be held together.

Conditionalists also deny that the highly symbolic Revela-tion of John intends us to picture a final state which includes continuing sin and suffering. The smoke of torment which rises for ever represents the memory of the triumph of God's righteousness, not a continuing burning of tortured flesh. As to the parable of the rich man and Lazarus, it is noted that the scene is Hades, not Gehenna (Hades is one day to be cast *into* the lake of fire),[6] and that the passage is pictorial rather than literal. It would be precarious for any school of thought to draw literal conclusions from it about the topography of the next world.

If it is said that conditionalism devalues the terror of the biblical deterrents, since 'to believe in annihilation is only to believe what the atheist believes' and many tormented people might welcome annihilation, conditionalists would reply in these terms. (1) The atheist has no conception of the wonder and blessedness of heaven. (2) He therefore has no conception of what it means to forfeit heaven – to forfeit the very purpose for which he was made. (3) He has no realization of what will be involved in the dread of awaiting judgment and in the anguish and remorse of standing naked in the presence of God to see his true self revealed and to hear the Judge say: 'Depart.' (4) It is doubtful if anyone really desires annihilation. Man clings tenaciously to life, and it is arguable that the prospect of annihilation is the most dreadful of all fates. Certainly it is the most final of all tragedies. If the purpose of the Bible is to paint the horror of just judgment and final destruction its language is not exaggerated.[7]

TRADITIONAL ORTHODOXY NOT TO BE SURRENDERED LIGHTLY

This line of argument is attractive and can be set out with great learning and has now gained the adherence of a wide spectrum of Christian thinkers. It seems wise, however, to set out five caveats to caution those who might be tempted to abandon the traditional view too easily.

1. Beware of the immense natural appeal of any way out

---

[6] Rev. 20:14.
[7] Conditionalists regard their doctrine as providing a more effective deterrent than the traditional teaching, on the ground that the latter is incredible to those who hear and is simply not believed. The point was put by a writer quoted (though with disapproval) by Horbery (p. 274): 'We only imagine we believe it . . . Nothing that is over-strained, or seems exaggerated, strikes the Mind. Let a Schoolmaster tell his Scholar that his Father will hang him if he doth not study; he laughs at the Menace. It is too much disproportion'd both to his own Demerits, and the Idea he entertains of his Father's Equity.'

that evades the idea of everlasting sin and suffering. The temptation to twist what may be quite plain statements of Scripture is intense. It is the ideal situation for unconscious rationalizing.

2. Beware of the pervasive and insidious influence of the present liberal *Zeitgeist* on all our thinking. The modern world and the modern church have little use for a disciplined submission of the mind to the revelation of God, with the result that 'Christian' thought has been penetrated at a thousand points by ideas contrary to its God-given faith. Such a doctrine as unending torment would inevitably be a natural point for merciless attack in a climate of opinion committed to the elimination of everything offensive to modern sentiment.

3. Note that the modern revival of conditionalism was pioneered mainly by Socinians and Arians, who rejected such fundamental doctrines as the deity of Christ, and that today it constitutes an important element in the teaching of Jehovah's Witnesses and Christadelphians.[8] Be wary of such bed-fellows.

4. Note that the adoption of conditionalism, even if it can be accepted as a possible interpretation of the Bible, does not solve all the difficulties. It can never be easy to accept the idea that God will decree the annihilation of beings made in his own image, nor that he will decree pain which will be of no benefit to the sufferer.[9] It may, however, be claimed that these difficulties are similar in character to those posed by other temporal judgments and may be considered along with them, and that they do not introduce a problem of a different order of magnitude such as is presented by the idea of unending pain.

[8] The Seventh-Day Adventists also hold this belief, but they are in a different category from Jehovah's Witnesses and Christadelphians, since they stand essentially in the broad stream of traditional evangelicalism, having eccentricities which may be regarded as more or less peripheral.

[9] Sometimes it is said: 'It is inconceivable that God should work for the healing of a human being and then, having failed in his efforts, should cut his throat.' This is to misconceive the normal process of judgment. It may not be necessary to think of God ordering the infliction of chastisements *ab extra* at the last judgment, but rather of every person suffering the natural, self-destructive consequences of his own wrong choices. When the metaphor is used of the severe beating and the light beating (Lk. 12:47 f.), it could simply mean that the unrepentant will inevitably suffer degrees of painfulness according to the degrees of their guilt. It might be nearer the mark to think of their end as a merciful euthanasia than as a callous execution.

5. Beware of weakening zeal for the gospel. The gospel
should be preached with passionate urgency. One who has
believed that the alternative to faith in Christ is unending
misery in hell may well find that the sudden loss of confidence
in this doctrine will leave him deflated, with the edge of his
evangelistic zeal impaired. The evangelist R. A. Torrey in the
conclusion to his study of this question wrote this:

> Shallow views of sin and of God's holiness, and of the glory of Jesus
> Christ and His claims upon us, lie at the bottom of weak theories
> of the doom of the impenitent. When we see sin in all its hideous-
> ness and enormity, the Holiness of God in all its perfection, and the
> glory of Jesus Christ in all its infinity, nothing but a doctrine that
> those who persist in the choice of sin, who love darkness rather
> than light, and who persist in the rejection of the Son of God, shall
> endure everlasting anguish, will satisfy the demands of our own
> moral intuitions . . . the more closely men walk with God and the
> more devoted they become to His service, the more likely they are
> to believe this doctrine . . . If you in any wise abate the doctrine,
> it will abate your zeal. Time and again the author has come up to
> this awful doctrine and tried to find some way of escape from it,
> but when he has failed, as he always has at last, when he was
> honest with the Bible and with himself, he has returned to his work
> with an increased burden for souls and an intensified determination
> to spend and be spent for their salvation.[1]

Such a challenge merits the most earnest searching of heart as
well as the most conscientious searching of Scripture. If
Torrey's view is rejected, another view must be found which
evokes at least as great a zeal for the glory of God and the
salvation of men.

THE NEED FOR FRESH STUDY

Yet, having said all this, a long tradition of belief within the
Christian church is not decisive. Errors creep in and they die
hard, especially when they have been elevated to the status of
orthodoxy. At the first whiff of supposed heresy the godly are
liable to shut their ears and to rush upon the well-meaning
offender. Yet in the matter under consideration the problem is
a real one, *and a biblical one.* Plato envisaged everlasting punishment,[2] but the problem was not acute for him, since he had no

[1] R. A. Torrey, *What the Bible Teaches* (London, n.d.), pp. 311–313.
[2] Plato, *Laws* 904 f.

knowledge of the God of Christian revelation. It is because of his knowledge of the God of the Bible, the God of justice and love and omnipotence, that the Christian is troubled. He finds it difficult to imagine *that* God tolerating ceaseless torment.

A study of the literature reveals a remarkable failure by the 'traditional orthodox' to get to grips with the solid arguments put up by the conditionalists. This is partly due to a vicious circle, in which suspicion of heresy has made it difficult for conditionalists to find reputable publishers, which has resulted in their books being unread, which in its turn has resulted in their views remaining unduly suspect. H. E. Guillebaud, best known for his book on the atonement, *Why the Cross?*, included in that work a note on eternal punishment, in which he appears to take the traditional view for granted. He then gave himself to a more thorough study of the moral problems of the Bible. This resulted in two manuscripts, one of which was published in 1941, just after his death, under the title *Some Moral Difficulties of the Bible*. The other manuscript dealt with the doctrine of hell, and came to conditionalist conclusions. But no publisher could be found for this until 1964, when it was printed privately under the title *The Righteous Judge*. A few years later B. F. C. Atkinson, a Greek scholar and author of several books on biblical subjects, published (also privately) a work entitled *Life and Immortality: An Examination of the Nature and Meaning of Life and Death as they are revealed in the Scriptures*. This was the fruit of a lifetime of study and is a remarkable piece of sustained argument. Even more remarkable is the vast work of L. E. Froom, *The Conditionalist Faith of our Fathers*, amounting to 2,476 pages of well-organized, lucid exposition, put out by Seventh-Day Adventist publishers.[3]

These books are not above criticism, nor on the other hand can they fairly be ignored. They cover a great deal of difficult

---

[3] H. E. Guillebaud, *The Righteous Judge*; B. F. C. Atkinson, *Life and Immortality* (both obtainable from the Rev. B. L. Bateson, 26 Summershard, South Petherton, Somerset, TA13 5DP, England, priced 25p and 50p respectively, plus postage. L. E. Froom *The Conditionalist Faith of our Fathers*, 2 vols. (Review and Herald Publishing Association, Washington, D.C., 1966, 1965). Of an earlier generation, the books of J. A. Beet are well argued: *The Last Things* (London, 1897, revised 1905); *The Immortality of the Soul* (London, 1901).

and controversial ground (they are not always in agreement with one another) and are admirably suited to initiate a thorough debate. It is important that the stigma of heresy should not be attached to this point of view at least until there has been full and free discussion. Discussion there must be if Christians are to be renewed in a common mind for the faithful proclamation of the gospel.

It needs to be stressed that our summary of the debate in this brief compass (with none of the detail argued out) provides no basis for decision on so grave and complex an issue. The aim has been to discourage those who hold traditional orthodoxy from surrendering it lightly, while encouraging the serious consideration of the case for conditional immortality. If after renewed study traditional orthodoxy should succeed in making out its case, it would (at least superficially) make the task of defending the teaching of Christ more difficult than with conditional immortality, but *relatively* it could only make the acceptance of the hard facts of Scripture and Providence easier. For if we feel bound to accept the endless misery of one human being, we cannot raise great objection to the quickly passing miseries of man's earthly existence, however many they may be and however agonizing at the time. But as far as the thesis of this book is concerned, we shall consider ourselves under no obligation to defend the notion of unending torment until the arguments of the conditionalists have been refuted. We shall assume that the realities of judgment are at least as awful as conditionalists maintain and shall try to see how these fit into the pattern of other judgments found in the Bible and in history.

And let it be quite clear that these realities are awful indeed. Jesus and his disciples taught again and again in terrible terms that there is an irreversible judgment and punishment of the unrepentant. Warnings and loving invitations intermingle to encourage us to flee the wrath to come.

3 SOME INADEQUATE SOLUTIONS

If the Bible's greatest difficulty has sometimes been made intolerable by exaggeration, other difficulties have been made insoluble by over-simplification. No solution can be right which denies either God's complete sovereignty over his creation, or God's perfect goodness.

DENIAL OF GOD'S SOVEREIGNTY

It is common ground to Christian believers that God made everything, that he sustains everything, that he knows everything, that he is everywhere. We know that even the direst crimes of history are done with divine knowledge and permission. As Jesus himself said: 'You would have no power over me unless it had been given you from above.'[1] But the Bible goes further than this. It not only makes God one who permits evil, it also represents him as one who controls it. Almighty God is the *Pantokratōr*, the All-Ruler. However else we may try to explain the difficulties which are all around us, we are not allowed to invoke God's incompetence.

God's omnipotence would seem to be a necessary outcome of the fact of his Creatorhood.[2] To think of God creating out of nothing all the minute particles of our vast universe (to say nothing of its non-material wonders) and then not having

[1] Jn. 19:11.
[2] Divine creating must be sharply distinguished from human creativity. Human 'creativity' fashions something new out of materials that are given. It is an activity *within* the divinely created order, whereas creation out of nothing is an exclusively divine activity through which something comes *de novo* into the created order from outside.

perfect knowledge and control of them seems absurd. Austin
Farrer, however, in his book *Love Almighty and Ills Unlimited*,[3]
imagines just this.

> He made a half-chaos of self-moving, brainless forces to be the
> bottom and soil of his creation, out of which higher forms should
> arise. But then a semichaos, if it is to be itself, must be a field of limit-
> less accident; and accident is by definition an uncalculated effect.
> It may be foreseen, provided against, discounted, or profited by;
> it cannot be intended or arranged. It would be meaningless to say
> that God himself planned the detail of a chaos, or of a semichaos
> either, in its chaotic aspect.

This notion of a field of limitless accident is not biblical.
There is no suggestion in the Bible that God is the celestial
chess-player, awaiting the unknown move, who by 'infinitive
contrivance draws some good out of every cross-accident'. On
the contrary, God knows every detail: 'the hairs of your head
are all numbered'; 'he determines the number of the stars, he
gives to all of them their names'; there are no accidents: not
one sparrow 'will fall to the ground without your Father's
will'. God 'accomplishes all things according to the counsel of
his will'.[4] God's perfect design for this world was made before
creation. This world is an orderly whole, a cosmos not a chaos. ✓
Not a quantum of energy moves outside his plan.[5]

With many, it is true, the biblical axiom that God rules the
world has been allowed to become something shadowy and in-

[3] A. Farrer, *Love Almighty and Ills Unlimited* (London, 1962), p. 164.
[4] Mt. 10:30; Ps. 147:4; Mt. 10:29; Eph. 1:11.
[5] It is true that the physicist has to come to terms with an element of randomness, for example in the breakdown of radioactive atoms. The behaviour
of a particular atom cannot be predicted, but the behaviour of a whole
population of atoms can be predicted statistically. It is hotly debated as to
whether this randomness is an ultimate factor in nature or whether further
knowledge will show that the behaviour of each atom is causally determined. To one who has been scientifically trained it is extremely difficult to
believe in an ultimate arbitrariness, and it is not a notion which comes
easily to a theist. But it is well to remember that all this discussion is concerned with the realm of the ultra-small, whereas the Bible is concerned
essentially with God's dealings with men. It is wise not to be dogmatic over
deductions either from Scripture or from scientific observation which are
incapable of empirical verification, and therefore perhaps we should not
rule out the *possibility* that an element of arbitrariness at the atomic or sub-
atomic level might be consistent with God's detailed control of man's world.
But in any case the Bible is clear that God is ruler of all things.

distinct and has been pushed into the background of their thoughts. In their well-meaning attempt to avoid implicating God in evil they have deprived him of his control of the world; this applies to happenings both great and small. Take, for instance, the Nazi persecution of the Jews. However perplexing it may be, it is an inescapable fact that God did not step in as the millions were driven into the gas chambers. God's in-activity creates a tremendous problem to those who believe that he is in control, but at least they are convinced that his justice and wisdom and love will be finally vindicated. But to those who do not believe that he is in control, his passivity suggests the appalling possibility that God did not intervene, not because he did not want to, but because he could not do so. If this is so with the big things, it is so with the little crises of our individual lives. It profoundly affects everyday Christian living, for it means that we cannot turn to him confident of his power to intervene if he wishes to do so; we cannot *entrust* any-thing to him. If God wishes to control evil, but cannot do so, we are reduced to Dualism, with a god of good waging in-conclusive war against a god of evil. In such circumstances the would-be Christian, deprived of the ability to trust, cannot be expected to put up much of a fight. 'Faith' without trust be-comes a shadowy thing, no longer a power to overcome the world.

In this respect the intuition of the ordinary person who holds God responsible for what happens and says, 'Why has God done this to me?' is sounder than that of the liberal theologian who wishes to exonerate God of responsibility. It is in fact cold comfort to say to a heart-broken person whose only child has been killed or whose husband has been fearfully injured: 'This is not God's doing or God's will; we live in a disordered world in which evil has been let loose; we must expect these things where sin reigns; but keep trusting God.' Yet what meaningful trust is left if we cannot entrust a child or a husband to him? How infinitely more comforting, more biblical and more glorifying of God it is to cry with Amos in defiant faith: 'If disaster falls . . . has not the Lord been at work?'[6] Though moral evil is contrary to God's will, he permits both it and its consequences. Indeed he not only permits its consequences, he

[6] Am. 3:6, NEB.

sends them – for wholly good and loving reasons, even when those reasons are hidden from us.

Furthermore, even if God could be absolved of the responsibility for inactivity by his impotence, he could not be absolved of the responsibility for having allowed the situation to arise, for when he created the world he must have known the potentialities that he was creating. Or, if he did not know what he was doing, we must add ignorance and folly to his impotence and inactivity.

To deny God as the All-Ruler is to deny the God of the Judaeo-Christian tradition, which is of course to deny the God of Jesus Christ. This whole process of blurring the image of God as Creator, Sustainer, Ruler, Judge, Father, Lover, must be reversed. The image of the personal God as perfect in power and righteousness and wisdom and love must be brought back into sharp focus. This God is the living God with whom we have to do, even in the minutest particulars of our lives. To dissolve our Christianity into a misty religiosity, however attractively dressed up, is to lose touch with the real God.

DENIAL OF GOD'S GOODNESS

Because it is difficult to believe in creation and to deny omnipotence, some have therefore sought to deny God's goodness. There are those who have been unable to escape the belief that a mighty and intelligent being has made the world, and yet they cannot accept his goodness. Tormented themselves by anxieties and tensions, they try to picture the maker of the universe. In moments of desperation they feel that only a sadistic monster could have designed, created and kept in being such a living hell. But no Christian can allow lodgment in his mind of any dark speck upon the character of God. If God is good at all, and has implanted some sense of goodness in us, it is scarcely thinkable that there should be any trace of evil in him. Certainly no Bible writer imagines that God would or could do anything wrong.[7] To allow one speck of evil in God

[7] The fact that God is frequently said to have repented of, or been sorry about, some action of his (*e.g.* Gn. 6:6; Ex. 32:14) is not of course a contradiction of this. God's 'repentance' is not because he has changed, but because the situation has changed. His wholly good and unchanging nature shows itself in his changing attitude towards changing circumstances.

is to cross the great watershed which separates biblical theism from pantheism.

It needs of course to be recognized that the Bible does not attempt to deal with the one apparently unanswerable problem: 'Why did God ever make a world in which there was even a possibility of evil?' Before the creation God was perfect and self-sufficient, needing nothing to render his being or his bliss complete. When the travail of the world's sorrow is over all will be perfect once again. That God, acting under no compulsion, should have allowed, even temporarily, sin and suffering is the unanswered and (to the limited human mind) unanswerable problem. Yet, though philosophically nonplussed, the Christian has a way of dealing with the problem which is personally satisfying. He is unashamedly glad that God did not remain in his solitary perfection. He is glad to be alive, glad to have known human love, glad to have tasted the love of God, glad to have the promise of eternity with him.

To the Bible God's power and goodness are both axiomatic. God is love. The whole Bible story is the story of that goodness and love.

The outline of the biblical drama stands out with immense clarity. 'In the beginning God created the heavens and the earth . . . And God saw everything that he had made, and behold, it was *very good*.'[8] God, the supreme Person, made a good world and he made man as the crown of his creation. Man was made for fellowship with God, to love him person to Person. Man misused his powers of understanding and his powers of choice and was thrust out from Paradise. And so the long tale of tragedy began, a war to the death with no final victory till the closing chapters of the book of Revelation.

In the front of the stage we see the bitter human struggle; the fall brings pain, sorrow, murder, the break-down of sexual relations, the corruption of man's innermost imagination and the destruction of his society. This is all pictured as the outworking of an evil principle in man's nature and as a divine judgment upon his sins. The race is fragmented into hostile national groups, struggling for supremacy and struggling for

[8] Gn. 1:1, 31.

survival.[9] In the midst of the universal darkness, God sets on foot a work of saving love. Man is not left to the pitiless forces of natural selection in a world where might is right. In place of natural selection, God begins his work of election. God chooses the weak things of this world to confound the things that are mighty. God sets his love on an insignificant Semite, living in a town in Iraq, and makes a covenant with him, Person to person. God first trains this man Abraham; then his family; then, over a period of more than a thousand years, the nation of Israel that is descended from him. He takes a people ground down by cruel slavery, in the eyes of the world helpless and despised, and makes of them his own covenant nation. Through this people of God's love the conquest of sin is to be achieved.

In New Testament times we find this people scattered throughout the civilized world, still persecuted and despised, yet looking eagerly for the coming of a Messiah. The central scene of the drama reveals the Tri-Personal nature of God, whose love is manifested when God the Son comes into the world, as the Second Man. Taking human nature upon himself, Jesus comes as mediator between God and man, to be man's representative, and by suffering death in his place, to overcome sin and death for ever. Empowered by God the Holy Spirit, the church sets forth to proclaim to all nations the offer of forgiveness of sins and eternal life to everyone who will repent of his sins and put his trust in the divine Redeemer. The story ends with the new heaven and new earth, where death is no more, and where tears and sorrow and pain are gone for ever.

This is the story of man and of God's dealings with man as seen in the front of the stage. Man was made good; he forfeited his goodness and his happiness by sin; God has taken steps to restore the perfection of human nature. Sin, with its attendant suffering, is a hideous evil, allowed temporarily by a wise and loving God, but it is to be wholly overcome on the Last Day.

But this does not represent the full breadth and depth of the Bible's story. We are given glimpses of deeper purposes and

[9] Gn. 3–11.

more widely-ranging activities of God's love which take us beyond an exclusive concentration upon man alone. We see that human beings are not the only intelligent inhabitants of God's creation. The Lord of Hosts has his myriad angels about him, his archangels, his seraphim, his 'living creatures', all enjoying his presence. We see, too, that sin did not begin with man. There are creatures of God, made by him 'very good', who have become malignantly evil. There has been a cosmic Fall, with far-reaching consequences, lying behind the Fall of man. Satan is fearful as a roaring lion and subtle as an angel of light. The child of God who lives in the world of the Bible knows himself to be a very little person in a great and awesome universe. Yet he is given a glimpse of the eternal counsels of the love of God, wherein, before the foundation of the world, the Son took for himself the role of the Lamb to be slain for sinners; wherein the Father pre-ordained to give his chosen ones to the Son as his bride.[1] It is against this background that man, though puny in his ignorance and twisted in his sinfulness, is seen to be the object of God's love.

There are indeed terrible evils in the world, but if we are to see things in proportion, we dare not dwell exclusively on them. There may be times when we feel the whole earth to be a vile place, and we never want to open a newspaper or watch a news programme again. Yet to think of it in these terms patently represents only a half-truth. Almost all of us have a host of memories, if we care to summon them, of exquisite and breath-taking pleasures – the joys of friendship and humour, of home and love, the joys of adventure, the joys of the natural world, the joys of mental discovery, of literature, of drama. It is more nearly true to say that 'every prospect pleases, and only man is vile'. If we once take sin seriously, and extract all the evils caused by sin from our view of the world, we have to admit that most of what is left looks like something worthy of a good and glorious Creator.

But, if God is both omnipotent and good, and God loves us, we have the answer to our question. Why do we suffer? *We suffer* (however strange and paradoxical it may seem) *because God loves us*. Our sufferings are part of a tremendous pro-

[1] Jn. 17:24; Eph. 1:4–14.

gramme devised and directed by Love himself. On the vast canvas of human existence the darkest areas take their place in a glorious design which Love is painting. This painting is now far advanced and it should be possible, with the aid of revelation, to see something of the good purposes which lie behind Love's ordering of the world.

4 GOOD FEATURES IN
AN UGLY WORLD:
FREEDOM AND ITS COST

As we have seen, the moral difficulties of the Bible run parallel
with the moral difficulties of Providence for most of the way, so
that it is possible to look at these together, leaving on one side
for the time being the difficulties peculiar to the Bible which
seem to suggest that God is the author or approver of evil. The
latter are not to be taken lightly, but they in fact add little to
the already enormous weight of the problem posed by God's
permission of so much wrong and suffering. Therefore if the
moral difficulties of Providence are not insuperable (and to the
Christian believer they are not, since by definition he has
accepted the Good News of the Love of God made known in
Christ, and he *knows* that there is *some* answer to the mysteries
of God's ways), then the parallel difficulties in the Bible are
not insuperable either. The treatment of these mysteries which
follows is believed to be on lines laid down by the Bible and
endorsed by the main body of Christian thinkers, but it is important to notice that the argument is still valid for any
believer who remains dissatisfied with this particular treatment, or who thinks that he can deal with the problems better.[1]

[1] Valuable on this subject are C. S. Lewis, *The Problem of Pain* (London,
1940) and H. A. E. Hopkins, *The Mystery of Suffering* (London, 1959). The
chapter on 'Evil' in R. E. D. Clark, *The Universe: Plan or Accident?* (3rd ed.,
Exeter, 1961) gives an illuminating summary of the light thrown by science
on the nature and causes of many current evils, vindicating the benignity
of the natural order and making a terrible indictment of human wickedness. J. Hick, *Evil and the God of Love* (London, 1966), though deficient in its
understanding of both creation and soteriology, is a useful introduction to
the philosophical debate. A useful Roman Catholic work is C. Journet,
The Meaning of Evil (London, 1963). Journet follows the Augustine/Aquinas

Whatever the answer, it remains true that if the one set of problems can be solved, so can the other. To put it crudely, if you can believe in God, you can believe the Bible – at least as far as moral difficulties are concerned.

We can see (in this and the next two chapters) nine things in God's ordering of the world which are profoundly good.

MAN A FREE AGENT

First, *it is good that man is a free agent, not a machine*. The problems of free will are notoriously difficult, but no Christian can hold that man is simply and solely a super-machine, nor even a super-animal. The Bible picture of Adam in the Garden of Eden shows unfallen man living in fellowship with God, endowed with the faculty of reason, able to choose between obedience and disobedience, enjoying free will in the fullest sense. After the Fall, man is still man, still in one sense free, but in another sense a slave.[2] He still freely goes his own way

---

tradition and leans heavily on J. Maritain. Another is E. F. Sutcliffe, *Providence and Suffering in the Old and New Testaments* (Edinburgh, 1953).

[2] It would take us into areas of immense complexity to attempt to explore when and where and how the Fall of man took place, but we must hold to an irreducible minimum of Christian belief on this matter. It is essential to hold that there is an absolute, ontological difference between man and beast, and that therefore there must have been some initial creative act that made the first humans, whether by a new creation or by the breathing of the breath of life into an already existing creature. Christian doctrine therefore demands an Adam and Eve of some sort. But if there was an initial creative act by a wholly good Being, it is easier to regard the first man as created sinless than as created sinful. Therefore, though severely limited, this Adam would have had a faith relationship with God unobstructed by sin. (The obvious historical parallel is Jesus himself, the last Adam, whose humanity, apart from its sinlessness, was precisely like ours.) Further, since it is undeniable that man as he is now (and as he is known to history) is no longer sinless, his present state presupposes a Fall at some point in past time.

But these two fixed points in the story of man, his creation and his fall, have far-reaching implications. It means that the development of the world simply cannot be understood in terms of a purely naturalistic evolu-iton. These two key events, which fall outside any naturalistic scheme, *actually happened*. The twentieth-century Christian is therefore still justified in taking the narrative of Genesis with all seriousness, picturing Adam and Eve as unique historical figures, who started in fellowship with God, but who then disobeyed him and brought death upon themselves and their descendants. It is in any case a popular fallacy to suppose that the advance of anthropology has made it progressively easier to fit the known remains of early man into a naturalistic scheme. The reverse is true (see E. K. V. Pearce, *Who was Adam?*, Exeter, 1970).

without external compulsion, but 'his own way' is governed by a nature sinful in its desires and perverted in its reasoning. To this innate sinfulness of fallen man the whole Bible (and the whole of history) bears devastating witness. But man is capable of restoration through Christ, the last Adam: 'If the Son makes you free, you will be free indeed.'[3] In Christ an emancipation is begun which will be made complete in heaven, when no veil will hide God's presence and no restraints on man's desires will be needed.

It is probably idle to speculate as to whether God has created or could create free, rational and perfectly good beings, who had immediate access to his unveiled presence, without the use of a probationary period. (The mention of fallen and unfallen angels suggests that they also had their probation.) But it is at least almost certainly true to say that the one perfect Man-in-Christ whom God is now creating could have been made no other way. The mode of man's creation involved the setting of man in an environment where he was removed from the immediate presence of the divine glory. If a man were placed in the full light of the unveiled majesty of God, it is hardly conceivable that he would have any freedom to choose to sin. So man is put in a world where God is not seen, but his glorious handiwork is seen and his voice is at times heard.

John Hick sees the emergence of man as a free being as a natural stage in the onward, upward, evolutionary process.[4] He pictures the developing hominid, hitherto completely identified with the world and with his mind towards it, beginning to become conscious of the divine presence. With the dawning of a consciousness of God comes the first experience of sin. Man begins to be conscious of his self-centredness and world-centredness which militate against his attempts to respond to God. The essential point is that there is no coercion about this sense of God's presence; man may either respond to it or he may continue to go his own way. Hick sees the whole story of

[3] Jn. 8:36.
[4] J. Hick, *Evil and the God of Love*, pp. 313–323. See also his illuminating discussion of F. W. Schleiermacher (pp. 237–240) and A. Farrer (pp. 273–276), who both argued the need for an 'epistemic' distance between God and men. For the view that Adam was a special creation at the beginning of the neolithic period, see E. K. V. Pearce, *Who was Adam?*

mankind as the story of the gradual triumph of the unseen love of God in the hearts of free men. This is an attractive theory, but it hardly does justice either to the Bible or to the all-pervasive sense of guilt which is still characteristic of the human race. The divine presence so conceived is ambiguous to such a degree that the Fall is more or less excusable – it meant merely that man, when he first became faintly aware of the unseen Presence, still continued in the self-centred and world-centred life that had hitherto been natural to all living creatures. Indeed it makes the Fall (the entry of sin into the world) a fall upwards, a step forward in the progress of the race. It seems to presuppose gratuitously that there was no moment when God actually spoke to the first man and woman. Yet the Bible from beginning to end presupposes the horror of man's deliberate transgression, of his alienation from God (of whose presence he is nevertheless inescapably aware) and of his guilt.

The story of the Garden of Eden seems perfectly to describe the required situation – man not overwhelmed by the presence of God, yet perfectly aware of right and wrong, and left free to go his own way or God's way. Once man has rebelled the situation is radically altered. Man's condition is changed and God's activity changes. Man's freedom has itself been seriously compromised, but God's providential care of his world is now supplemented by his work of judgment and redemption. Sin is a dynamic force in the world destroying man's freedom, but even more dynamic is the saving power of God which is re-creating it. But it must be observed that the whole drama of redemption is continued in essentially the same environment: a world in which God is unseen, yet known by his creation, and in which he speaks to man at various times and in various ways by his prophets and finally by his Son. Man's probationary freedom is preserved and his character is developed because he has to live his life by faith. If he is to be true to his own nature as one who is made in the image of God for fellowship with God, he has to live 'as seeing him who is invisible'. This is not to act contrary to evidence, or without evidence – the evidence is clear and the knowledge of God can be evaded only by wilful suppression[5] – but it is to act without coercion. The incarnation

[5] Rom. 1: 18–21.

takes place in this same environment. Jesus himself grows up as a real man, in communion with his Father by faith, not by sight. 'Although he was a Son, he learned obedience through what he suffered; and being made perfect he became the source of eternal salvation to all who obey him.'[6] The creation of man and the invention of such a world as a nursery for the making and perfecting of God's free children seems almost incredibly ingenious – indeed truly marvellous!

The endowing of man with freedom of choice involves the possibility (in God's foreknowledge, the certainty) of sin in all its horror. Yet this freedom seems to have been a necessary prerequisite to a deep knowledge of God. The devotion of a free, rational being is higher and more beautiful than that of an animal, remarkable though the love between humans and animals may be. But this human freedom involved the possibility of cruelty, unchastity, hatred and war – not only for the unbeliever, but for the believer also. Thus we are told frankly of the drunkenness of Noah, of the cowardice and deceit of Abraham, of the sensuality of Samson, of the folly of Jephthah, of the murder and adultery of David, of the denial of Simon Peter. All such things are horrible intrusions into God's world, yet in spite of them no converted man would wish to change his status to that of either an animal or a machine.

SUFFERING AS A DETERRENT

Second, *it is good that sin is linked with suffering as a deterrent.* In the circumstances of our present life, pain is not altogether an evil. It can even on occasions intensify pleasure, as for instance when intense thirst is relieved by drink. Normally physical pain is in the early stages a warning, and a valuable deterrent against the misuse of things which are in themselves good. It is a good thing that the child quickly withdraws its fingers at the touch of something hot. It is one of the functions of pain in general to cause the sufferer to lie down and keep warm and so cause an economy of effort which allows the body to use its maximum resources to combat that which is causing the pain. It is only in its latest stages that pain becomes destructive.

Physical pain, however, is only one ingredient (and usually

[6] Heb. 5:8, 9.

not the most dreadful) in suffering. We may suffer also from fear, anxiety, sorrow at loved ones going wrong or losing faith or dying, remorse, envy, humiliation, a sense of injustice or estrangement, unrequited affection, boredom, and frustrations of all sorts. The Bible begins with a paradise lost and ends with a paradise regained. In Genesis 3 disobedience is followed not only by pain, but by shame, fear, toil and death. In Revelation 21 there is the promise that God will be with his people in the New Jerusalem and that 'he will wipe away every tear from their eyes, and death shall be no more, neither shall there be mourning nor crying nor pain any more'. It is probably right to infer that on the biblical view all suffering is ultimately caused by sin of some sort, and that in an unfallen world there would not even be illness, old age and accident such as we experience. To the non-Christian this doubtless seems very speculative and hypothetical. Yet even to the non-Christian it must be clear that a very great proportion of the world's suffering is due to what Christians call 'sin'. Imagine, for the sake of argument, a world in which sin was abolished, but the painful entail of sin still remained in the form of illness, old age and accident. It would be a world without war, without fear, without greed, without lust, without laziness, a world warm with unselfishness, neighbourliness, gratefulness and courage. It would be a world in which psychological disorders had largely disappeared.[7] It would be a world in which resistance to physical disease had greatly increased.[8] There is no doubt that in a world where self-pity had disappeared and cheerful sympathy abounded, the pains of illness, accident and old age would be far less hard to bear. The connection between sin and suffering is very close.

[7] It has been truly said that 'more people are sick today because they are unhappy, than unhappy because they are sick' (H. A. E. Hopkins, *The Mystery of Suffering*, p. 72).

[8] Even now the most physical of ills are amazingly affected by a patient's mental state. For instance, a broken bone will knit more quickly if a patient is in good spirits. In one state of mind a strong man may be filled with nausea at the prospect of a pin-prick and faint as he stands in the queue for inoculation. In another state of mind the same man will put up with a rain of savage blows on his face and nose for the self-chosen joy of the boxing ring. For an explanation of this and its bearing on the question of animal pain in times of danger, see R. E. D. Clark, *The Universe: Plan or Accident?*, p. 215.

This, as we have already seen, is borne out by the Bible. In countless places, from Adam's first warning of death to the final warning of the Apocalypse, the theme stands out in Scripture. God not only forbids sin, he also makes its results painful. God has made the way of the transgressor hard. As the old preachers would say, God's early painful judgments are part of his 'blockade of the road to hell', part of his 'trumpet-call to the unconverted'. They are warnings lest a man allow himself to be destroyed in the last final Judgment. This divine blockade is a more powerful force than most of us realize. It is now considered old-fashioned to teach children moral tales about the rewards of virtue and the dangers of transgression. Strewwelpeter is out of date. Yet the conscious deterrents and the unconscious restraints upon wrong-doing are still very powerful. The likely effects of excessive drinking are plain enough to see: the hang-overs, the money shortage, the neglect of wife and family and the forfeiture of their full affection and respect, the decline in public esteem, the endangering of a job, and perhaps in the end *delirium tremens*. The miseries of broken homes can be seen on all sides. It is still true, by and large, that laziness is the enemy of a full and satisfying life. It is still true that money-loving people become slaves to their own greed; instead of gaining lasting happiness, they gain shrivelled and miserly souls. It is still true that national corruption must lead to a nation's decline. Fundamentally we are all Cains at heart, who would willingly kill our enemies, if there were no deterrents. The outward sanctions of society and the inner sanctions of our own conscience totally forbid the very idea of murder. But once remove all fear of social reprisal and all uneasiness of conscience, and our natural man would commit murder at the first flush of hatred. Were it possible to remove all deterrents, our society would become a sink of iniquity overnight. Golding's *Lord of the Flies* unforgettably pictures what might be expected to happen to ordinary children when cut off from the restraints of ordered society.

David Hume, it is true, argued that the pain mechanism in animals and men was not necessary to their survival and welfare:

Pleasure alone, in its various degrees, seems to human understanding sufficient for this purpose. All animals might be constantly in a state of enjoyment; but when urged by any of the necessities of nature, such as thirst, hunger, weariness; instead of pain, they might feel a diminution of pleasure, by which they might be prompted to seek that object, which is necessary to their subsistence. Men pursue pleasure as eagerly as they avoid pain; at least, might have been so constituted. It seems, therefore, plainly possible to carry on the business of life without any pain. Why then is any animal ever rendered susceptible of such a sensation?[9]

Hume, however, failed to distinguish between physical pain and psychic pain. There is possible an almost infinite range of experiences under a given amount of physical pain. To a person in an acute state of anxiety, an imagined (though non-existent) sensation of pain may cause distress to the point of terror. Conversely, a Himalayan climber, physically at the end of his tether, may experience a fierce, exultant joy. Theoretically it might be possible to create a hedonic scale, with the sublimest pleasure at the top and the most unbearable pain at the bottom. Hume's suggestion would mean dividing the scale in two and discarding the bottom half, so that only degrees of pleasure would remain. But in a world where our present experiences of pain were unknown, this would simply mean that the experiences now labelled 'more pleasant' and 'less pleasant' could then be regarded as 'pleasant' and 'unpleasant'. The possible range of contrast would be halved, but psychologically the position would be unaltered. The same argument would lead to a further halving of the hedonic scale, and so on *ad infinitum*, until all experiences reached a dead level of hedonic neutrality. The Christian is bound to believe not only that the link between sin and suffering is a good thing, but also that the degree of pleasure and suffering allowed in human experience has been wisely and lovingly designed. The unbeliever would be hard put to it to demonstrate that a world deprived of its most intense experiences would have been a better place.

[9] Hume's *Dialogues concerning Natural Religion*, Kemp-Smith's ed. (Oxford, 1935), pt. xi, pp. 252 f.

5 GOOD FEATURES IN
AN UGLY WORLD:
BENEFICENT RETRIBUTION

There is a *third* feature of the world which is not at first sight so obviously beneficial, but which is fundamental to human dignity and human freedom, and to a just and stable society; and so we shall need to spell it out more fully than the other eight.

SUFFERING AS RETRIBUTION

It is good that sin is linked with suffering as retribution. The value of pain as a deterrent is fairly obvious. But in the long run even more important is the value of pain as part of a retributory system which is essential to the welfare of mankind. Fundamental to the Bible, from cover to cover, is the notion that *God not only deters, but that he also punishes.* Sin in essence is the assertion of one's own will in opposition to God's will. The appropriate punishment is to undergo something contrary to one's own natural inclination and will, which pre-eminently is what suffering is. If divine retribution is not accepted, there is, I believe, no hope of saving a view of God anything like that of the Bible and no hope of understanding what is happening in the world. Since the whole idea of punishment is at a discount in modern penal theory, it merits careful examination.

It is clear that an imperfect society cannot function unless unpleasant consequences are as a rule made to follow anti-social practices. But how are these unpleasantnesses to be understood? Are they simply devices to deter the anti-social and to protect society, or can they rightly be called 'punishments'? As R. C. Mortimer (sometime Bishop of Exeter) and C. S. Lewis have written with clarity and conciseness on this subject, we cannot do better than quote them at some length.[1]

Mortimer first explains *what punishment is*:

My main theme is that the idea of retribution is essential to the idea of punishment. This, to me, seems to amount almost to a tautology; as much as to say that the idea of punishment is essential to the idea of punishment. What *is* punishment? It is the deprivation of one or more basic human rights – liberty, property, personal integrity – with or without the consent of the person punished. A man may be deprived of his life by hanging, or of some of his property by a fine, or of his liberty by being put in prison, or of his rights over his own body by being flogged. These are the forms which punishment takes.

But these deprivations do not of themselves and alone constitute punishment. A boy sent away to boarding-school may be said in some degree to suffer a deprivation of liberty; the patient on the operating-table suffers an assault on his body; a man paying his income-tax suffers a deprivation of property. Yet in none of these cases is the idea of punishment present. And this is not to be explained by saying that in all these cases there is an element of consent, of more or less voluntary submission. For, on the one hand, the completely involuntary, enforced confinement of a lunatic in a mental hospital is not a punishment. And on the other, genuine punishments may be and often are voluntarily accepted. Indeed, there is meaning in saying that a man may punish himself.

He then shows that the idea of *desert* is essential to justice:

The essential condition for turning any of these deprivations into a punishment is that it is, in some sense, deserved; that past wrong conduct has somehow merited the deprivation, that it is due. It is this idea of desert, of retribution or paying back which supplies the essential element of justice in punishment.

[1] R. C. Mortimer, 'Retribution', in *Crucible* (Jan. 1963), pp. 1 ff. (This is the Quarterly Review of the General Synod Board for Social Responsibility, Church House, Westminster, London SW1.) C. S. Lewis's essay was first published in Australia, but was made available elsewhere in a symposium, *Churchmen Speak*, ed. P. E. Hughes (Appleford, 1966); this is now out of print, but the essay is available separately as a pamphlet *The Humanitarian Theory of Punishment* by C. S. Lewis (Marcham Manor Press, Appleford, Abingdon, Berkshire). An account of the debate which followed the original article will be found in S. B. Babbage, 'C. S. Lewis and the Humanitarian Theory of Punishment' (*The Churchman*, 81 (Spring 1973), pp. 36–47). This account, in somewhat revised form, together with the original Lewis essay, will shortly be available as a further publication from the Marcham Manor Press.

Having described how Justice is traditionally represented as holding in her hands a pair of scales, he explains how retribution *restores the balance*:

> The underlying concept is that certain actions infringe the rights of others – of God, or of Justice herself, personified, or of other members of the community. The proper balance of rights has been disturbed, and it is the work of justice to restore the balance by exacting retribution.

He then shows how important is the recognition of a man's *responsibility*:

> But how do we set about arriving at a just punishment? The first and necessary presupposition is that men are in general and on the average responsible for their actions. For without responsibility there can be no desert. And if there is no desert, no punishment is due. A man's personal dignity demands that we assume he is responsible for his actions. Not so to assume is to think of him and treat him as a lunatic. Most criminals, I think, bitterly resent the imputation that they are not to be held responsible for their crimes because they could not help themselves. *It is to think of them as puppets, not as men.*

I have italicized the last sentence because this is the vital point. If erring human beings are to be treated as human beings, the ideas of responsibility, desert, justice and retribution must be maintained.

But notice, *retribution is not society's revenge*. In assessing the just desert of an offence the degree of damage done to the community will be an important consideration. But it is essential to see that social disapproval does not take on the quality of revenge, since this may itself lead to injustice:

> We must be very careful not to allow ourselves to reach the position held by a distinguished judge in the last century. Sir James Fitzjames Stephen wrote as follows, 'The infliction of punishment by law gives definite expression and a solemn ratification and justification to the hatred which is excited by the commission of the offence.' And again, 'it is highly desirable that criminals should be hated, that the punishment inflicted on them should be so contrived as to give expression to that hatred.' It was this kind of sentiment which produced the 19th century prisons with all their squalor and discomforts under which we now labour.

DETERRENCE AND REFORMATION

It is important to notice also that *retribution does not exclude deterrence and reformation*:

> In stressing the importance, indeed the necessity of retribution to the idea of punishment, I must not be taken as denying the due place and importance of the other two elements in punishment, the reformatory and the deterrent. On the contrary, I am convinced that the just punishment is that which, being due to the offence, takes the opportunity at the same time to reform the offender and deter others.

Yet *deterrence divorced from retribution can be a terrible weapon of injustice*. C. S. Lewis, in castigating what he calls 'The Humanitarian Theory of Punishment', brings home the practical implications of this divorce:

> Every modern State has powers which make it easy to fake a trial. When a victim is urgently needed for exemplary purposes and a guilty victim cannot be found, all the purposes of deterrence will be equally served by the punishment . . . of an innocent victim, provided that the public can be cheated into thinking him guilty. It is no use to ask me why I assume that our rulers will be so wicked. The punishment of an innocent, that is, an undeserving man, is wicked only if we grant the traditional view that righteous punishment means deserved punishment. Once we have abandoned that criterion, all punishments have to be justified, if at all, on other grounds that have nothing to do with desert. Where the punishment of the innocent can be justified on those grounds . . . it will be no less moral than any other punishment. Any distaste for it on the part of a Humanitarian will be merely a hang-over from the Retributive theory.

Equally sinister is reformation divorced from retribution:

> According to the Humanitarian theory, to punish a man because he deserves it, and as much as he deserves, is mere revenge, and, therefore, barbarous and immoral. It is maintained that the only legitimate motives for punishing are the desire to deter others by example or to mend the criminal. When this theory is combined, as frequently happens, with the belief that all crime is more or less pathological, the idea of mending tails off into that of healing or curing, and punishment becomes therapeutic. Thus it appears at first sight that we have passed from the harsh and self-righteous notion of giving the wicked their deserts to the charitable and enlightened one of tending the psychologically sick. What could

be more amiable? One little point which is taken for granted in this theory needs, however, to be made explicit. The things done to the criminal, even if they are called cures, will be just as compulsory as they were in the old days when we called them punishments.

This merciful-looking doctrine in fact *deprives the law-breaker of the rights of a human being*:

> The Humanitarian theory removes from punishment the concept of desert. But the concept of desert is the only connecting link between punishment and justice. It is only as deserved or undeserved that a sentence can be just or unjust . . . There is no sense in talking about a 'just deterrent' or a 'just cure'. We demand of a deterrent not whether it is just but whether it will deter. We demand of a cure not whether it is just but whether it succeeds. Thus when we cease to consider what the criminal deserves and consider only what will cure him or deter others, we have tacitly removed him from the sphere of justice altogether; instead of a person, a subject of rights, we now have a mere object, a patient, a 'case'.

Law paradoxically is a condition of freedom, and the reign of just law (that is, law which exacts fair retribution) is *the foundation of a stable and free society*:

> If crime and disease are to be regarded as the same thing, it follows that any state of mind which our masters choose to call 'disease' can be treated as crime; and compulsorily cured. It will be vain to plead that states of mind which displease government need not always involve moral turpitude and do not therefore always deserve forfeiture of liberty. For our masters will not be using the concepts of desert and punishment but those of disease and cure.

To abandon the principle of retribution is to *open the door to the persecution of minorities*. It would be easy, for instance, for a government to adopt the idea that religion is a neurosis:

> When this particular neurosis becomes inconvenient to government, what is to hinder government from proceeding to 'cure' it? Such 'cure' will, of course, be compulsory; but under the Humanitarian theory it will not be called by the shocking name of persecution. No one will blame us for being Christian, no one will hate us, no one will revile us. The new Nero will approach us with the silky manners of a doctor, and though all will be in fact as compulsory as the *tunica molesta* or Smithfield or Tyburn, all will go on within the unemotional therapeutic sphere where words like 'right' and 'wrong' or 'freedom' and 'slavery' are never heard. And thus when

the command is given, every prominent Christian in the land may vanish overnight into Institutions for the Treatment of the Ideologically Unsound, and it will rest with the expert gaolers to say when (if ever) they are to re-emerge. But it will not be persecution. Even if the treatment is painful, even if it is life-long, even if it is fatal, that will be only a regrettable accident; the intention was purely therapeutic. Even as in ordinary medicine there were painful operations and fatal operations, so in this. But because they are 'treatment', not punishment, they can be criticized only by fellow-experts and on technical grounds, never by men as men and on grounds of justice.

Just law is also the prerequisite of mercy:

The Humanitarian theory wants simply to abolish justice and substitute mercy for it. This means that you start being 'kind' to people before you have considered their rights, and then force upon them supposed kindnesses which they in fact had a right to refuse, and finally kindnesses which no one but you will recognise as kindnesses and which the recipient will feel as abominable cruelties. You have overshot the mark. Mercy, detached from justice, grows unmerciful. That is the important paradox. As there are plants which will flourish only in mountain soil, so it appears that mercy will flower only when it grows in the crannies of the rock of justice: transplanted to the marshlands of mere Humanitarianism, it becomes a man-eating weed, all the more dangerous because it is still called by the same name as the mountain variety. But we ought long ago to have learned our lesson. We should be too old now to be deceived by those humane pretensions which have served to usher in every cruelty of the revolutionary period in which we live. These are the 'precious balms' which will 'break our heads'.

There is a fine sentence in Bunyan: 'It came burning hot into my mind, whatever he said, and however he flattered, when he got me home to his house, he would sell me for a slave.' There is a fine couplet, too, in John Bull:

> 'Be ware ere ye be woe;
> Know your friend from your foe.'

Just retribution is man's friend, for the sanctity of just law is the basis of all social sanctities and just law is itself an expression of the goodness of God. The concern of the Bible for personal righteousness and social justice seems at first sight to find expression in the most violent and exaggerated denunciations and in the relating and warning of utterly horrific judgments.

But could not the Bible be right in this? Could it not be that a passionate concern for righteousness of this intensity and a realization of the certainty of retribution of this fierceness alone provide an adequate bulwark against human tyranny?

Its beneficence may also be seen in other directions. *Retribution reinforces the effectiveness of deterrents*. The deterrent element in punishment should be neither underestimated nor exaggerated. While it is demonstrably true that when the severity of punishment is increased beyond a certain point it has little or no increased deterrent effect, it is absurd to suggest that punishment does not deter. Where there is a high probability of detection, quite moderate sanctions are very effective. Education by deterrence is analogous to Nature's education of any other growing organism. A child learns respect for the laws of gravity by the 'punishments' resulting on its baby tumbles. Experimental rats have to learn to avoid the electric shocks which stand between them and their food. Similarly some incipient criminals, learning that crime does not pay, forsake crime and lead a law-abiding life. The deterrent effect of punishment may have some measure of compulsion in it and the retreat from crime may at first be unwilling, but the deeper enjoyment and satisfaction of law-abiding conduct may eventually change the unwilling convert into a willing one.

But education which rises no higher than this animal reaction to pleasant and unpleasant stimuli has not even begun to be truly moral. It will not produce characters which are prepared to stand for what is right against heavy odds, for the simple reason that 'pleasant' and 'unpleasant', rather than 'right' and 'wrong', are its categories of thought. 'Right' and 'wrong' belong to the conceptual world of justice and retribution. When, however, conscience is enlisted on the side of good conduct, the deterrent effect of punishment is greatly increased; the dread of incurring guilt and shame gives intensity and poignancy to the unpleasantness of what would otherwise be a merely material punishment. When this dread takes the form of seeing oneself standing filthy before God's shining purity, its deterrent effect is overwhelming. In other words, a belief in retribution is the deepest and most effective form of deterrent.

Similarly, *a belief in retribution is itself a force in reformation*. A

wrongdoer who has been taught to think of himself as the unwilling victim of heredity and environment or as an unfortunate case of psychological illness may indulge in self-pity,
or he may learn to deceive those who have detained him, but
he is not likely to come to the only reformation that is of
ultimate worth – a reformation of will. The first decisive step
towards genuine reformation comes when a man acknowledges
that his punishment is deserved. He sees himself as a responsible being who has done wrong, not as a pathological case
who has been the victim of circumstances. The thief on the
cross was on the way to reformation when he said: 'We are
receiving the due reward of our deeds.' The Prodigal Son was
on his way to restoration when he said: 'I will arise and go to
my father, and I will say to him, "Father, I have sinned".'[2]

But (even more important than its contribution to deterrence
and reformation) *retribution is a witness to the character of God.*
True reformation involves a transformation of will, and it is
idle to pretend that either deterrence or the correct administra-
tion of justice will in themselves effect such reformation. Most
crime derives from a criminal character in which a man has
little will or even desire to live up to his own highest standards.
It is an over-optimistic view of human nature which thinks that
any normal form of punishment is likely to produce the revolution of will which is required. The only force likely to effect
such a revolution is a manifestation of powerful, disinterested
love. But even this does not preclude the opposition of a Judas
or of hostile Pharisees. We cannot therefore assume that the
forces of reform will be successful, nor can we argue that
punishment should be withheld if success is not likely to be
achieved.[3] Justice should be done because it is just, even

[2] Lk. 23:41; 15:18.
[3] F. D. Kidner makes the interesting observation that in the Old Testament
'the idea of reforming a person by discipline is confined to the realm of the
family, human or divine (see, *e.g.*, Dt. 8:2–5; Pr. 3:11 f.; 13:24; 22:15),
rather than the courts'. He then goes on: 'while for crimes, the deterrent
value of a sentence is always spoken of as secondary to that of ridding
society of an evil – the evil of an unpunished offence, whose extreme form
is "the guilt of innocent blood". (Dt. 19:13; 21:9, where the offence is
homicide.) In Deuteronomy, where these themes are prominent, the ridding
or "purging" concern is voiced eleven times between Deuteronomy 13:5
and 24:7, but the theme of deterrence only four times (Dt. 13:11; 17:13;

(according to the Bible) if it means that life (in this world) is irrevocably forfeit. Witness to the righteousness of God is at least as important as the reformation of individual sinners. True reformation does indeed require more than retribution, but it does not require less.

THE DIFFICULTY OF ASSESSING JUST RETRIBUTION

The problem of what constitutes just retribution in particular cases is immensely complicated, for there exists a whole range of possible degrees of responsibility. In most wrongdoing there is a larger or smaller element of psychological maladjustment which is beyond the wrongdoer's direct control and which may sometimes be greatly helped by medical or psychological treatment. But what makes a man human is the fact that he is a responsible being, even though his responsibility may be diminished. He knows that he ought to do right, and that he deserves punishment if he does not do so. What is most demoralizing, even dehumanizing, is to treat him as wholly non-responsible, simply an innocent victim of heredity and environment. Mental or physical illness may of course reduce powers of moral choice to vanishing-point, so that in some cases a patient seems to be living a life which is scarcely above that of a vegetable. What is important is that whatever element of moral choice still exists should be respected. This is what decisively differentiates man from the beasts. If this is not

---

19: 20; 21: 21), in each case as a sequel to it: *e.g.* "So you shall purge the evil from the midst of you. And the rest shall hear, and fear, and shall never again commit any such evil" (19: 19 f.). The logical order seems, then, to put requital first, with the purging of corporate guilt as its primary purpose, and deterrence as its secondary one. To these must be added, where they apply, the elements of reform.' *Hard Sayings* (London, 1972), p. 35. Professor J. L. Ackrill, in a lecture on Plato's *Republic* given in Oxford, made this point with regard to the reform of children and adults: The old idea was to treat adults as adults. They could do anything; if they did something wrong they were punished. Children were treated as children – to be protected from what is harmful and reared and reformed in what is right. The modern idea is to reverse this. We treat adults as children and reform them. We treat children as adults and let them see and do anything and everything. The modern idea seems inconsistent. If we say someone's background and education is responsible for his present need of reform, it is inconsistent to let children taste and see everything good or bad. (This is not an exact quotation, but is based on lecture notes.)

respected the prisoner or patient is degraded to the status of an animal.

Again, responsibility cannot be thought of simply in terms of accountability for isolated acts. A man who is drunk may do things which he did not and would not choose to do. He has become irresponsible, but he is responsible for his irresponsibility. A man may be a compulsive gambler, literally unable to control himself. But his state may have been partly the result of culpable laziness or greed earlier in life. A man is answerable for his character even more fundamentally than for his acts.

Furthermore, as we shall see later,[4] there are mysterious corporate solidarities in human life, in which families and communities and nations and indeed the human race share responsibilities. We cannot shrug off inherited evil as though we were just helpless, blameless victims. We share responsibility for what we are.

In his final paragraph Mortimer shows the *fallacy of omitting to punish on grounds of humility*:

> Humane, humble people, conscious of their own shortcomings, are naturally reluctant to impose any punishment at all. They would rather forgive and let go free; only, in a fallen world that may not be. For the punishment of offences is conducive to the maintenance of order in society. And order in society is in accordance with the will of God. A total absence of punishment would lead to chaos, would in itself be unjust, and would result in more bad men and fewer good men.

He shows also the *fallacy of omitting to punish on grounds of fallibility*:

> How are we to know the degree of guilt, the degree of wickedness in any particular case, and therefore the severity of the punishment which is due? The only answer to that is, that men must do the best they can . . . Human finite knowledge cannot hope to equal the omniscient justice of God. It was presumption to suppose otherwise, or to refrain from doing anything because we cannot equal the divine perfection. It remains our human duty to seek to impose upon offenders the punishment which is as nearly as possible proportionate to the gravity of the offence and the culpability of the offender, the punishment which he owes in retribution.

[4] See pp. 74 ff.

To sum up. It is necessary to society that unpleasant results should follow anti-social practices. But without a belief in fair retribution, there is nothing to prevent deterrents and techniques of 'reformation' becoming instruments of tyranny. Just law, which operates on the basis of desert, treats men as responsible beings. In exacting fair retribution the foundation is laid for a stable, free and merciful society, in which deterrents are effective and reforming influences are strong.[5] It is not too much to say that punishments, unpleasant though they are to those who undergo them and to those who administer them, are vital to human happiness.

We have of course been uncovering some basic facts of human nature which sophistication had tended to push out of sight. Until deadened by sophistication the human conscience in fact warmly responds to just retribution. A child prefers to live in a world where the rules are kept, and where in ordinary circumstances punishments are swiftly and fairly administered. The unsophisticated cheer when the wicked Haman is hung on his own gallows and when Jehu looks up at the painted Jezebel and cries, Throw her down! The villain *ought* to come to a bad end, the hero and heroine *ought* to live happily ever after. We are denying our humanity when we try to argue that we have now learnt better.

Now what is true of particular human societies is true of human society as a whole as governed by God. Just law is an expression of God's character, and so it is that the theme of God's judgments permeates the Bible. The God of the Bible not only deters, he also punishes. He professes to treat men as responsible beings, according to their deserts, in spite (as we shall see) of appearances to the contrary. The extent of human transgression and the extent of divine judgment in this world tend to obscure the beneficent effect of God's retribution, but in fact God's judgments alone stand between us and a universal tyranny. If the effects of original sin were allowed to work themselves out unchecked, man's inhumanity to man would know no bounds. Such elements of stability, freedom,

[5] While retributive considerations must determine the approximate degree of a man's punishment, there is every reason why its precise form should take into account deterrent and reformatory considerations.

mercy and goodness as we enjoy, we owe to the operation of God's righteous judgments among us. It is indeed a good thing that sin is linked with suffering as retribution.

According to the Bible, the supreme retribution is death; and death, both physical death and eternal spiritual death,[6] is what sin *deserves*. Basically sin is preferring to go one's own way rather than God's way; to choose one's own self-centred, selfish, corrupting world rather than the unspeakable glory of life in the presence of the great, holy, loving God. That way can mean only damnation. *Anything* is better than that – it is better to lose your right hand, your right foot or your right eye, says our Lord, than that. You are not to fear those who can destroy the body, you are to fear him who can destroy both body and soul in hell. To forfeit the presence of God is to forfeit all. Sin gives birth to sins, and sins bring in their train a seemingly endless trail of sadnesses, uglinesses and horrors; but these are the out-workings of something deeper – the choice of self rather than God. To go the way of the Lord, to grow up, that is, into the likeness of Christ for which we were made, is life. To go against the will of God, that is to reject the likeness and the love of Christ, is death. This is not only basic to the teaching of the Bible, it is also sober, logical sense. *If* God exists and *if* man is made for the very purpose of enjoying God's love, his rejection of that love can mean only ultimate disaster. He puts himself under the wrath of God, for the wrath of God is the obverse of the love of God, it is love rejected.

There are certain corollaries of this teaching, which have an

[6] Physical death is of course a natural phenomenon characteristic of the whole animal world, and it may at first sound ridiculous to suggest that human death is caused by human sin. The warning to Adam and Eve that in the day they ate of the fruit of the tree they would die was a warning (at least primarily) of spiritual death; for when they did so eat they did not die physically that day, but were banished from the garden where they had been accustomed to talk with God. Yet physical death (with its grim features) does appear to be included in the judgment. It seems to be almost a 'type' or foreshadowing of the spiritual death which issues in the 'second' death, the death of the last judgment. The Bible gives instances of those (like Enoch, Elijah and the risen Jesus himself) who were taken into God's presence without senescence and physical death having power to claim them. It may be presumed that an obedient Adam and Eve would similarly have escaped death, both physical and spiritual.

important bearing on our attempts to see the problem of suffering in the biblical perspective. To sin means ultimately to forfeit heaven, and this is the greatest possible punishment which anyone can ever receive, *and this is the punishment which sin deserves*. Compared with this all other punishments, however terrible, are relatively insignificant. This needs to be borne in mind continually when we are inclined to blench at the severity of the judgments of the Bible and at the permitted horrors of the world. It is not permissible to treat sin lightly – to regard it as entirely natural and therefore entirely excusable; we must not say in any final sense: To know all is to forgive all. On the biblical view, nothing could be more terrible than to choose the way of sin, for this is to forfeit for ever the love of God.

Furthermore, because sin deserves death and we are all sinners, it means that all our mercies are *undeserved* mercies. Any apparent unfairness in God's treatment of us arises not because some have too much punishment, but because some of us appear to have too little. None of us will ever receive harsher judgment than we deserve. The fact of God's grace was understood in Old Testament times: he is 'a God merciful and gracious, slow to anger, and abounding in steadfast love and faithfulness, keeping steadfast love for thousands, forgiving iniquity and transgression and sin'; 'he does not deal with us according to our sins'; in Ezra's words: 'Thou, our God, hast punished us *less* than our iniquities deserved.'[7] In the New Testament God's undeserved grace is the unending theme. The marvel is, in the biblical view, not that men die for their sins, but that we remain alive in spite of them.

[7] Ex. 34:6 f.; Ps. 103:10; Ezr. 9:13.

6 GOOD FEATURES IN AN UGLY WORLD: APPARENT EVILS, REAL BLESSINGS

We have seen that retribution itself is a good thing – indeed that it is essential to any truly human existence and to the welfare of society – yet there is a *fourth* (at first sight somewhat paradoxical) principle to be noted.

RETRIBUTION OFTEN DELAYED

It is good that retribution (and rewards), though certain, are often delayed. The problem with the real world is that the correspondence between punishment and crime does not seem close enough; our unsophisticated hopes and expectations are so often not fulfilled. In this life the villain is not always punished, and the good do not always have a primrose path to tread. It is this lack of a one-to-one correspondence between virtue and its reward and between evil and its punishment which led John Stuart Mill to deny God's omnipotence. In his essay on Nature he wrote:

> If the law of all creation were justice and the Creator omnipotent, then in whatever amount suffering and happiness might be dispensed to the world, each person's share of them would be exactly proportioned to that person's good or evil deeds; no human being would have a worse lot than another, without worse deserts; accident or favouritism would have no part in such a world, but every human life would be the playing out of a drama constructed like a perfect moral tale . . . Not even on the most distorted and contracted theory of good which ever was framed by religious or philosophical fanaticism, can the government of Nature be made to resemble the work of a being at once good and omnipotent.[1]

[1] J. S. Mill, *Three Essays on Religion* (3rd ed., London, 1885), pp. 37 f.

Modern writers have reacted against the naivety of Victorian moralizing, because of the obvious falsity of any attempt to relate sin and suffering to one another in a one-to-one correspondence. But Mill was no less naive when he thought that such a correspondence would be an indication of divine goodness and omnipotence. The Bible itself makes no attempt to establish such an immediately direct relationship. On one occasion, when a man who had been born blind was brought to Jesus, they asked him whose sin had caused the blindness, the man's or his parents'. He said that it was neither. On another occasion he put the question: 'Those eighteen upon whom the tower in Siloam fell and killed them, do you think that they were worse offenders than all the others who dwelt in Jerusalem? I tell you, No; but unless you repent you will all likewise perish.'[2]

The fact that retribution does not usually follow an act of sin immediately is a positive good. (This is true at least of the mature who have learnt the basic difference between right and wrong, though it does not apply to those who have yet to learn, who are better served by immediate praise or blame.) In his failure to see this lay Mill's naivety. Yet the point is obvious. The penalty for ignoring the properties of heat is a painful finger. The effect is immediate and the reaction instantaneous. There is no ground for moral approbation in such spontaneous response. But in the case of moral decisions such a conjoining of sin and pain would entirely defeat the object of the sanctions. Self-interest would compel a man to act rightly. There would be no room for reason or choice. Character is trained by the deliberate maintenance of a selected objective in spite of immediate impulses to do otherwise. Delay in the apportionment of rewards and punishments therefore serves a twofold purpose. It allows the sinner a prolonged opportunity for repentance,[3] and it provides the believer with an opportunity for deepening his faith and purifying his motives. As the saint cries out 'Lord, how long?' God gently asks him what it is that he really wants. Is it freedom from suffering or is it the pleasing of his heavenly Father? Is it goodness for reward or goodness

[2] Jn. 9:1–3; Lk. 13:4, 5.
[3] See Gn. 15:16; Lk. 13:34; 2 Pet. 3:9.

for God's sake? The highest goodness asks for no reward save that of knowing that it is doing God's will. It is really self-evident that if acts are to be truly virtuous, rewards and pains must not be obviously proportioned to deserts. To do right solely because it is right would scarcely be possible if the act were at once rewarded and the choice never costly.

Therefore as a general rule we do not find judgment following immediately upon sin. The sudden deaths of Uzzah, Herod Agrippa, Ananias and Sapphira, and the sudden onset of leprosy upon Gehazi and Uzziah, are exceptional – severe, yet merciful, reminders to the onlookers of the reality of God's judgments. While sometimes (as with venereal disease) a specific disease may follow a specific type of sin, there are no grounds for believing that a particular illness is usually the result of a particular sin. In the case of the man born blind, as we have seen, our Lord said clearly that it was *not* the result of his sin or of his parents' sin. Yet the Bible emphatically and repeatedly teaches that judgment will eventually follow upon sin. It is this deeply-rooted faith in God's justice which is so sorely tried, yet never quenched, in the anguished cries of the tormented saints. So often it seems that the innocent are suffering, while the guilty are going free. But, provided justice is eventually done, is even this a bad thing?

This need for a temporary lack of correspondence between moral decisions and their rewards explains in part why Providence has the appearance of capriciousness. We all know how terrifyingly capricious so-called 'acts of God' may be – one earthquake may occur harmlessly in the desert, while another decimates a city. On a deistic view of the world, natural disasters are outside the control of God. They are part of a vast machine in which a man, if he is unlucky, may get hurt; they are not instruments through which a personal Creator deals with his creatures. On a pantheistic view of the world they are part of an impersonal spiritual process in which man shares and for which no personal Creator is responsible. The Bible, however, asserts that the constituent parts of Nature, though behaving in an orderly way in accordance with God-given laws, are completely under his control and are instruments in his hands through which he deals personally with men. Why on one particular occasion God's providences seem kindly and on another almost inconceivably severe may often be quite unknown to us, but that rewards and punishments do not usually follow immediately upon our actions is plainly a good thing, even though at the time it may be hard to believe. At the more superficial level, much of the spice of life comes in fact from its uncertainty; and at its deepest levels, some of the most sacred experiences come from its most agonizing and undeserved trials. Indeed, as with Jesus himself ('who for the *joy* that was set before him endured the cross'),[4] the deepest joys come when the deepest sufferings are accepted as the ordering of unfathomable love.

CORPORATE SOLIDARITY

Fifth, *it is good that the results of sin (and of goodness) are not confined to the doer.* In society and church alike we are heirs of the liberal over-emphasis on individualism. It has been customary to think of progress as a continuous movement away from the solidarity of the social group towards a life of unlimited personal freedom. In politics and economics we have seen the lamentable results of a *laissez-faire* doctrine upon social development. In the churches of Western Christendom we have seen a defective sense of corporate church life. According to the Bible personal responsibility and group solidarity are both fundamental. Man will never escape from his social ties. The natural man is 'in Adam', sharing with his fellow-men all the pains and penalties of a common humanity. The spiritual man is 'in Christ', sharing with the elect all the joys and privileges of a restored humanity. He worships God now in the Body, and he will still be in the Body as he worships God in heaven.

The recovery of the concept of corporate solidarity (which had a major place in traditional Christian theology, especially amongst Augustinians and the early theologians of the Reformation period) and the recognition of its truly biblical character have been one of the great achievements of modern biblical study. It has been discussed in an illuminating way by

[4] Heb. 12:2.

J. de Fraine in *Adam and the Family of Man*.[5] Some extracts will give an indication of what is meant:

> The individuals (especially the more conspicuous ones) feel themselves members of a psychic whole, which surpasses them on the one hand, and on the other acts through them and finds its being in them.
>
> As the soul is completely in each part of the body, so the entire group is completely in each individual who forms part of it. (This accounts for the abrupt oscillations in Hebrew literature between singular and plural in corporate contexts.)
>
> In every true society the individual members can fulfil the duties of other members and take their place by vicarious representation.
>
> The representative does not mean the same thing as in our modern idiom. He *is* truly that which he represents; all are present in him.
>
> As soon as Adam (the leader) sins, the group (the collective Adam) takes on the condition of sin; all the 'children of Adam', that is, all those who fall under the term 'man', become sinners when Adam sins. For whatever happens to the head of the group happens *ipso facto* to the body dependent upon it.
>
> The present moment could be conceived as recapitulating the whole past, just as it could be conceived as pregnant with the whole future. Quoting Cornelius Mussus, one of the fathers of the Council of Trent: Before our births, we were all in Adam when he sinned; when we are born, Adam is in us.
>
> Adam is 'an incarnation of all mankind' (W. D. Davies). de Fraine sees 'the Son of Man' as a corporate personality term.[6]

All this is highly mysterious, yet it is fundamental to the biblical outlook. Could we but grasp it, it would surely be the key to much that is strange in human psychology and in divine providence. Why is it that we feel so inescapably guilty for

[5] J. de Fraine, *Adam and the Family of Man* (New York, 1965). See also J. Pedersen, *Israel* (E.T., London and Copenhagen, 1926), I, pp. 46–60, 77–96; II, pp. 263–269, 378–392. A. R. Johnson, *The One and the Many in the Israelite Conception of God* (Cardiff, 1961). H. H. Rowley, *The Faith of Israel* (London, 1956), pp. 99–123. H. Wheeler Robinson, *The Christian Doctrine of Man* (Edinburgh, 1911), pp. 27–30. C. Ryder Smith, *The Biblical Doctrine of Salvation* (London, 1955), ch. 1. J. A. T. Robinson, *The Body* (London, 1952). D. E. H. Whiteley, *The Theology of St. Paul* (Oxford, 1964), pp. 45 f. For this concept as a force at the present day, see J. V. Taylor, *The Primal Vision* (London, 1963), ch. 8, 9.

[6] These quotations will be found on pp. 14, 30 f., 27 (*e.g.* Nu. 6:23; Ho. 11:1), 14 quoting O. Spann, 33 quoting S. Mowinckel, 143 f., 24 n. 30 quoting J. L. McKenzie, 275, 202 ff.

conditions of mind which we did not create but simply inherited? Can it all be explained away as repressive condition-
ing? It seems incapable either of being explained away, or of
being avoided by permissive upbringing. We *feel* guilty, because we *are* guilty. We are members of sinning humanity. *Part*
of the answer to the question, Why do the innocent suffer? is
simply that there are no innocents. There are of course enormous differences in degrees of culpability, but no child of
Adam is an innocent in the absolute sense, and (as we have
seen) we are not in any case to expect an immediate, exact
correspondence between sin and its punishment.

This corporate principle is no accident. It is a deliberate
part of God's wise design for the world. It is no accident that
the Bible devotes chapter after chapter to genealogies. For
good and ill we are bound up through heredity and environment with our ancestors. For good and ill our descendants will
be bound up with us. The sins of the fathers are visited upon
the children to the third and fourth generation, and with those
who love him God's mercy reaches to a thousand generations.
In this way alone is there the possibility of progress. In this way
alone can there be any real history. It is just conceivable that a
world could be made in which every man was his own Adam,
in which every individual was insulated from his neighbour,
unable to help him or harm him, unable to receive his help or
suffer his injuries. But it would be a dull and lonely place. As
it is, the corporate principle adds enormously to the richness of
human experience, and to its responsibility. By my good deeds
I can send out influences for good which will spread like ripples
on a pond in ever-widening circles. By my sins the innocent
will suffer. Indeed as human sin lays its polluting and destroying hand on the world of animals, plants and physical things,
it sets the whole creation groaning. But would I have it otherwise? It is, surely, the wisdom of God that has made things this
way.

It is as we see the cumulative effects of sin in society that we
see the horror of the evil in the heart of man. Man would hush
up his sins. God shows forth his glory and goodness by exposing
sin and bringing it into the light. The Christian would conceal
the scandals in the church. God lets them come out that all the

world may see the latent sin for the hideous thing it is. We turn our eyes away from the horrors of the Inquisition, the slave trade, the industrial revolution, the gas chambers, the atom bombs. But God forces us to look. The movements of the human heart, apparently as insignificant as a tiny strip of film, are by the brilliant light of the corporate principle cast in all their terror upon the screen of human history.

And human history will not last for ever.

SUFFERING IS LIMITED

Sixth, *it is good that suffering is limited in degree and in time.* The sum total of human misery is beyond computation, yet it is limited. When the torturer goes beyond a certain point his victim faints. Mental tension has its own breaking-point. Famine will dull the senses. The ravings of delirium seem like a half-forgotten dream when the fever has passed. Even pain may induce a sort of numbness. The limit to the degree of suffering possible may seem high indeed, but for every man there is a providential 'Thus far, and no farther'. There is reason to believe that no man's sufferings will ever be greater than those of Christ, since throughout his life he shared the pains and sorrows of others to the utmost, and finally on the cross suffered what was due for the sins of the worst of us. To bear on a cross the sins of the world represents the limit of human suffering.

And there is a limit in time. Not only is it certain that this life will end, but it is certain that from the perspective of eternity it will be seen to have passed in a flash. The toils which seem so endless will be seen to have been quite transitory and abundantly worth while. As St Paul could put it while still alive: 'This slight momentary affliction is preparing for us an eternal weight of glory beyond all comparison.' Or, to use Christ's analogy: 'When a woman is in travail she has sorrow, because her hour has come; but when she is delivered of the child, she no longer remembers the anguish, for joy that a child is born into the world.'[7] For the blessed the sorrows of time will be remembered no more in the joys of eternity. For those who have rejected the love of God there will be after the

[7] 2 Cor. 4:17; Jn. 16:21.

last judgment just retribution varying in severity according to individual desert, but (in my view) the sufferings will end speedily and mercifully in the second death.[8]

It is this loss of the eternal perspective which (from the Christian point of view) makes the unbeliever's life so sad and his sense of values so distorted. He clings pathetically to this life, sensing rightly that he has no stake in the joys of the life to come. To many humanists the inviolability of life is an absolute: to take a man's life is to take everything (though, perhaps paradoxically, they often press for legalized euthanasia). In the Bible death is also regarded with awe, as something *un*natural, as being the result of sin which has intruded into man's relation with God, and as being the prelude to man's final judgment. The Bible too is fully aware of its consequences for those bereaved, and shows practical compassion for widows and orphans. It sees long life as something to be valued. Yet at the same time the Bible is quite realistic. It recognizes that death is the one universal fact of life and that it must be accepted and lived with. It recognizes that the prolongation of life beyond a certain point can mean a burden of labour and sorrow. But even in the Old Testament, death is not the end. Death means the grave, Sheol; yet there are glimpses of what lies beyond – as for example with Enoch and Elijah, who were taken alive into God's presence, where there is fullness of joy for evermore, and with Daniel's explicit reference to the resurrection of both just and unjust.[9] To be a man, made by the living God in God's own image and in covenant with him, is to be in fact aware that there is a greater and more enduring world beyond this one; but, as far as direct Old Testament revelation is concerned, the whole stress is placed on the need for righteousness here and now, and little encouragement is given to the Israelite to become preoccupied with what happens afterwards. When we come to the New Testament, however, the death and resurrection of Christ transform the whole scene. The penitent thief is promised the joy of being with Christ in paradise. With the exaltation of

[8] See chapter 2, where both the 'traditional orthodox' and 'conditional immortality' views of future judgment are considered.

[9] Gn. 5:24; 2 Ki. 2:11; Ps. 16:11; Dn. 12:2.

Christ to the right hand of the Father and the believer's union with him in the heavenly places, the Christian's present life and future expectation are meant to be permeated with the joy and wonder and glory of heaven.

SUFFERING CAN PROMOTE SPIRITUAL LIFE

Seventh, *it is good that suffering can promote spiritual life*. It may seem insensitive, if not impertinent, for one who has experienced little pain (and has shown himself a coward in what he has experienced), and who knows nothing of the deeper kinds of suffering, to write on this delicate subject. He can only plead that he is not citing his own evidence but that of others, who have plumbed the depths of pain and suffering and who speak with knowledge and sympathy.

It is a paradox that although the mature Christian is committed to a fight to the finish against suffering in others, yet (at least in retrospect) he welcomes it in himself. Though the prospect may be frightening and the reality itself almost unbearable, Christian teaching and Christian experience both indicate that the path to the crown is by way of the cross. The saint is to be half soldier; through hardship he gains toughness, powers of endurance and comradeship; through suffering he learns sympathy and he grows in purity. At first sight suffering may appear to have the opposite effect, bringing impatience and fretfulness. But God thereby brings unsuspected evil to the surface in order gently to skim it away. Our Lord, we are told, 'for the joy that was set before him endured the cross'. He called his disciples happy when they were persecuted. However reluctant we may be to embrace it, we know that suffering rightly received is one of the Christian's supreme means of grace.[1] It is one of the means of keeping him dissatisfied with this world and sustaining his yearning for his true home in heaven. He can sincerely thank God that all his 'joys are touched with pain'. The true value of suffering can be grasped only by suffering. A spectator can be wildly astray in his assessment of the situation. He may sometimes be tempted to apologize for the pain which God allows, only to find himself

[1] Heb. 12:2; Mt. 5:10. H. A. E. Hopkins, *The Mystery of Suffering* (London, 1959), chap. 7 deals helpfully with this.

shamed by the sufferer's inner peace and deep thankfulness for his new experience of his Saviour's love.

It seems to be a general truth of life that the richest and most worth-while experiences are costly, involving toil and pain whether of body or mind. At quite a low level there are the exhilarations of exploration or of sports which demand physical courage and endurance, in which pain is gladly accepted. There is the anguish and pressure of spirit which so often accompanies the production of a work of art. There are the mental pains willingly embraced by those who try to help the needy. At the highest level are the horrific experiences which cause wounds which never fully heal and which no-one would willingly experience again without a tremendous spiritual struggle, and which nonetheless a godly man does not resent. Such experiences, if accepted, drain away human pride and create the truly humble, selfless man.

Suffering can also be a means of blessing to a whole community. Intense, and apparently undeserved, suffering can evoke spontaneous compassion and massive generosity. Paradoxically, it is the very fact that a disaster is undeserved and harmful to the sufferers which evokes the response. If suffering came only when it was obviously deserved, this element of corporate compassion would disappear. The seemingly haphazard element in suffering is therefore necessary to this fine aspect of social life and so to that extent must be reckoned a valuable thing.

It is also often the decisive means of grace to the unbeliever. As in the earthly ministry of our Lord it was often trouble that brought the needy to Jesus, so it is today. As every pastor knows, the earnest quest for God often begins at a time of acutely felt need. Then indeed is suffering a blessed thing. A Malayan Christian once told the author his story, of how as a young Communist he was tortured by Japanese soldiers – a revolting thing in the eyes of the world. But to his family it was a blessed thing, for that man in his need recalled the Christian texts which he had heard, and cast himself upon the love of Christ. Finding faith himself, he was able when released to bring the Good News to his family. The unbeliever, Paul tells us, is always trying to suppress the truth which in his heart he knows.[2] It is love, not cruelty, that makes a man painfully aware of his sin and of the depths of his need.

Keats surely uttered a profound truth when he called this world 'the vale of Soul-making'.[3] This is precisely what it is meant to be, and suffering plays a vital part in the process. A world designed for this purpose would be a poorer place if it had no suffering at all. It would be a world without adventure and without the soul-making qualities of courage, disinterestedness, loyalty and sacrifice which need to be developed in the one who is still imperfect.[4]

OUR SUPREME GOOD THROUGH SUFFERING

Eighth, *our supreme good has come through suffering*. We have seen something in God's world both of our dangerous freedom and our painful judgments. Yet while we do not boggle at the fact of judgments, we are at first appalled by their severity. It shocks us that leprosy should be Uzziah's punishment for usurping the place of the priests by offering incense in the holy place, or Gehazi's because of a theft and a lie. It shocks us when Ananias and Sapphira fall down dead – for lying to God; when Herod is eaten by worms – for not rejecting divine honours; when Uzzah is struck dead – for disobeying God-given regulations about carrying the ark.[5] We want to lop off the apparently excessive penalties at the bottom of the hedonic scale.

Now the significant thing is this: what seems so difficult and shocking to us, with our distorted sense of values, did not seem shocking to the One who lived in perfect communion with God the Father. We are shocked that in Noah's day the whole land was inundated and a whole population was swept off the face of the earth. It was the divine penalty when 'the Lord saw that the wickedness of man was great in the earth'. But Christ was

[2] Rom. 1:18.

[3] *The Letters of John Keats*, ed. M. B. Forman (London, 3rd ed. 1947), p. 336.

[4] This is finely argued by J. A. Baker, *The Foolishness of God* (London, 1970), ch. 3. See also J. Hick, *Evil and the God of Love* (London, 1966), pp. 340 ff. for an amusing description of the jelly-fish world which a pain-free structure might have produced.

[5] 2 Ch. 26:16–21; 2 Ki. 5; Acts 5:1–11; 12:23. For Uzzah see pp. 134 f.

not shocked. To him it was the pattern of judgment which will
be repeated at his Second Coming. We are shocked at the fire
and brimstone on Sodom and Gomorrah. But Christ was not
shocked. To him it was an object-lesson to all who sin against
the light that God has given them. We are shocked that the
Lord 'sent fiery serpents . . . so that many people of Israel
died', when they grumbled against him. But Christ was not
shocked. To him it was a true picture of the death-dealing
power of sin.[6]

It is a painful process trying to think our way into the mind
of Christ, for it is profoundly humiliating. Yet this we must do
if we are to accept in our hearts that God's ways are just and
loving. Christ entirely shares the biblical view, on the one
hand, that for a man to be cast into Gehenna, the second
death, is a punishment more dreadful than any temporal
suffering, however awful; and, on the other, that the people of
God in fact suffer less than they deserve, not more. He sees the
impending, horrible siege and sack of Jerusalem as a just judgment on a people who have rejected God's Messiah; he does
not question the justice of God's government of the world and
he shows no doubt that the corporate sorrows of mankind are
the deserved result of our corporate sins. But, at the same time,
he offers to all penitent prodigals the utterly undeserved
warmth of a Father's love. It is sometimes hard for us to
believe in God's justice and it might seem harder still to believe
in his love; yet it was in the context of the world's most heinous
sin that God demonstrated his love dramatically, unforgettably and finally.

It was in circumstances of calamity, not of serenity, that the
church's faith was born. This was brought home to P. T.
Forsyth during the First World War, which, with its filth and
its senseless carnage, was the first devastating blow to
nineteenth-century evolutionary optimism. It was a war which
no-one wanted and no-one could stop. Yet clearly it did not
come from a malign external power; it was an eruption out of
the depths of human nature itself. It revealed what was in man.

[6] Gn. 6:5; Mt. 24:37-39, cf. Lk. 17:26 ff.; Heb. 11:7; 1 Pet. 3:20; 2 Pet.
2:5; Mt. 10:15; 11:23 f.; Lk. 10:12; 17:29, cf. Rom. 9:29; 2 Pet. 2:6;
Jude 7; Rev. 11:8; Nu. 21:4 ff.; Jn. 3:14, cf. 1 Cor. 10:9.

It was in this situation that Forsyth uttered his burning lectures: *The Justification of God*.[7] He said:

> Our faith did not arise from the order of the world; the world's convulsions, therefore, need not destroy it. Rather it rose from the sharpest crisis, the greatest war, the deadliest death, and the deepest grave the world ever knew – in Christ's Cross.

No Christian dare doubt God's goodness in permitting the most grievous suffering, when he remembers the means which God chose for the overthrow of evil. It was in the depth of human agony that Christ 'bore our sins in his body on the tree'. Not only tortured in body and forsaken by his friends, but cut off from his Father and become 'a curse for us', he suffered what no other man has suffered. But in dying he won the decisive battle against human sin and against the cosmic hosts of wickedness which have enslaved the world. On the cross 'he disarmed the principalities and powers and made a public example of them, triumphing over them'. What an amazing thing that God should choose this little planet as the scene of his final conflict with evil! What a reassuring thing that he should have chosen suffering as the means to the accomplishing of his ends. What a source of strength to know that he does not ask of us more than he was prepared to give himself.

To the believer suffering is now seen to go beyond mere retribution. By the solidarity principle, not only did Christ suffer for the sins of his people, but those who are in Christ may also suffer voluntarily with him for the sake of others. Paul said: 'By Christ's death . . . God has reconciled you to himself . . . It is now my happiness to suffer for you. This is my way of helping to complete, in my poor human flesh, the full tale of Christ's afflictions still to be endured, for the sake of his body which is the church.' No man could share in Christ's atonement, which was unique and offered once for all, but believers have the privilege of striving and suffering for the cause of the gospel and for the reconciling of the universe to God. Up till now 'the whole creation has been groaning in travail', but it waits with assurance the day of deliverance which his love has

[7] P. T. Forsyth, *The Justification of God: Lectures for War-Time on a Christian Theodicy* (1917; reprinted London, 1948), p. 57.

promised.[8] There is much that the Christian cannot understand, but in the darkest hour he can trust.

THE BLESSINGS OF IGNORANCE

Ninth and finally, *it is good that we cannot know everything.* It is
possible to raise objections to each of the points which we have
made. Pain *does* sometimes seem merely destructive; the certainty of final retribution *is* a matter of faith, not of logical
demonstration; freedom, the corporate principle, the atonement *are* profoundly mysterious; our Saviour's teaching about
hell *is* awful in the extreme. In addition, there is permeating
both Testaments the whole concept of election, of God's choice
of particular undeserving individuals and of a particular undeserving nation, which is left unexplained. That God has wise
and loving reasons for all his actions we know, but he has not
been pleased to tell us why he made from the same human
stock 'one vessel for beauty and another for menial use' –
'vessels of wrath . . . vessels of mercy'.[9] We are simply allowed
in humiliation and adoration to contemplate the fact that any
apparent unfairness in God's treatment of us arises not because
some have too much punishment, but because some of us, by
virtue of the cross, appear to have too little.

God's world is a great mystery, yet paradoxically no supposedly comprehensive water-tight system of answers could
possibly be right. No creature could conceivably 'comprehend'
God – could, that is to say, encompass God's uncreated mind
within his created mind. The very paradox of God's incompre-
hensibility is part of the case for biblical theism. We can know
what God has been pleased to tell us, and no more. Had God
set out the evidence with invincible clarity, the moral element
of the world would have been destroyed. God has given us
plenty of evidence if we are willing to believe, and he has given
us plenty of perplexities if we want to buttress our disbelief.[1]

---

[8] 1 Pet. 2:24; Gal. 3:13; Col. 2:15; 1:13–29, NEB; Rom. 8:22.
[9] Rom. 9:21–23.
[1] To some the study of Bible difficulties means deeper faith; to others, alas,
it means deeper antagonism. As an old writer said, Bible difficulties 'bring
out into open avowal the enmity of men to the things of God'. R. Haldane,
The Authenticity and Inspiration of the Holy Scriptures (5th ed. Edinburgh,
1845), p. 10.

Man's happiness lies in accepting his creaturehood from the hands of his wonderful Creator. When one thinks about it, it is really absurd for a being as ignorant as man to *expect* fully to understand the whole complex web of purposes which go to make up his God-given experiences. The truthful answer to the question: 'Why has God allowed this?' must always be prefaced by: 'I cannot pretend fully to know.' In one single, apparently simple, act of God there may be a dovetailing of purposes which concern many people, including perhaps those involved, those who observe and those who come after. Retribution, discipline, warning and instruction may all be intended, so that any easy answer will inevitably be an over-simplification. God is perfectly consistent in his doings, but the circumstances in which he acts are never identical. History is real, and God has different purposes at different moments in history. Therefore it may be the will of God that one man should die in battle, another by fire or flood, another in his bed. It may be his will to give striking evidence of his power to Bethsaida and Chorazin, yet withhold it from Tyre and Sidon. Who is man to pretend to understand the infinite wisdom and complexity of the divine purposes? It is man's desire to be as God which has been his undoing.

Job, after long agonized discussions about his sufferings, remained unsatisfied with all the suggested answers. But, when he was at the end of his own resources, God revealed himself to him. He just showed him the marvels of creation. Job there and then saw his ignorance and folly and realized the sin of presuming to tell God his business.

'Then Job answered the Lord:
"I know that thou canst do all things,
    and that no purpose of thine can be thwarted . . .
I have uttered what I did not understand,
    things too wonderful for me, which I did not know . . .
I had heard of thee by the hearing of the ear,
    but now my eye sees thee:
therefore I despise myself,
    and repent in dust and ashes."'[2]

[2] Jb. 42:1-6.

Job accepted what his mind could not understand, but what his heart told him was true. To take refuge finally in the inscrutability of God is not evasion, it is the highest wisdom demanded both by reason and sincere piety. Job knew nothing of the cross, yet he believed God. How much more then is it true of a Christian that, when he sees himself as a creature and a sinner in the presence of his incarnate Creator crucified, he knows that he can neither understand nor doubt.

THE KINDNESS AND SEVERITY OF GOD

It is along some such lines as these that the Christian must come to terms with the problem of suffering. The closer he keeps to the full biblical pattern, the stronger will his position be. If he seeks refuge in a doctrine of semi-chaos, if he denies the Fall, if he stumbles over election, if he rejects the Devil, if he ignores the principle of solidarity, if he denies retribution, if he makes Christianity this-worldly, if he turns away from suffering as a means of grace, if he fails to see Christ's death as a 'full, perfect, and sufficient sacrifice, oblation, and satisfaction, for the sins of the whole world', he will lose out intellectually and spiritually. A full-orbed orthodoxy may not answer all the questions, but it gives satisfaction to the mind and rest to the heart.

But note the conclusions to which we are driven as to the character of God. We see in these apparently strange providences both the kindness and the severity of God, of which (as rendered by the RSV) Paul speaks in Romans 11:22. The saying with which the book opened, 'Look at the goodness of God', was in fact only a part-quotation. Paul's complete sentence, as given in the Authorized Version, runs, 'Behold therefore the goodness *and severity* of God.' Without the note of severity, we misrepresent the whole picture. God's perfect hatred of sin is a terrible thing. Our troubles arise not from the weakness of the Bible's morals, but from their severity. In fact they are felt to be difficulties by us, not because of our moral sensitivity, but because of our moral obtuseness. The incomprehensible marvel is that such a sin-hating God should love sinners with an unspeakable love, and should be himself prepared to make satisfaction for our sins, quenching his holy wrath in the pains of the self-offering of the blood of the incarnate Son. In a strange way the measure of his severity is the measure of his love, for we know that God's severity and kindness are inseparably bound together, proceeding from the depths of the same divine Being. It therefore follows that if the one is so much profounder than we imagined, so must the other be. It is because God loves us that he will spare no pains to rouse us from our sins, and, having roused us, to unmask each hideous sin in turn to spur us to the battle. Could we wish it otherwise?

It seems desirable at this point to pause and to try to dissuade the reader from going further until he has digested the foregoing argument. If he is really persuaded that a good God rules the world and if he has some understanding of the rationale underlying God's strange providences, he will find that most of the Bible's 'difficulties' have ceased to be difficulties. Some perplexities will doubtless remain, but it is important to recognize the proper way to treat them: they must be dethroned from their God-accusing status and be put into the humble category of God-given data – to be simply accepted. There are some things in life which we *must* accept. When a student was heard to say, 'I accept the Universe', he received the reply: 'You jolly well better had!' The only thing that we can do about the fact of the Universe is to accept it; similarly the only thing that we can do about the facts of Providence is to accept them.

In the last resort it is not our business to justify God to man. Inevitably man's justification of God is either going to make him appear too human, answerable to our fallible standards, or utterly beyond reason, unless regarded with the eye of faith which has already seen and felt his love and goodness. Our business at most is to justify man's language about God. To believers God's providences are not difficulties, they are unyielding, inescapable facts with which we must come to terms. If only we could see things straight, we should realize that it is stupid to say: '*I* don't approve of the way God has made his world'; or, '*I* don't approve of the way he manages it.' This attitude is in fact worse than stupidity; did we but realize it, it

is arrogance – man presuming to tell God what to do. Whether
or not it seems so to us, God's ways are good and wise and
loving, and he will not change them. We must seek his help to
change ours. We must school ourselves not to complain about
the facts, but to learn from them. The facts of Providence are
material from which we can come to understand more clearly
the loving wisdom of God's ways.

It should be carefully noted, however, that it is not necessary
to our argument that the reader should accept our particular
treatment of the problems of Providence. He may indeed be
able to deal with them better. But what seems inescapable is
that any principles which are adequate to meet these problems
will be adequate to meet the problems of the Bible. The reader
at this stage may still not be sure of the divine authorship of the
Bible, and so he may want to hold himself free to cut out such
parts as seem unacceptable. But he needs to think out what it
means that the facts of Providence cannot be cut out.

If the argument thus far has not been grasped, the rest will
not carry conviction. The biblical 'difficulties', even if they are
precisely parallel to the inescapable facts of Providence, will
still seem terribly difficult. If however the point is grasped,
supposed biblical difficulties will appear as a challenge to the
Bible's divine authorship only if these nine principles do not
seem to cover them.[3]

[3] The nine principles are not concerned with evil in the animal, plant and
physical world. An Additional Note on 'Evil in Nature' will be found on
pp. 196 ff.

7 SUB-STANDARD SAINTS AND IMPERFECT LAWS?

Thus far we have been considering the doings of God recorded in the Bible which run parallel with his providential ordering of history. The only difficulties that are peculiar to the Bible (apart from those concerned with judgments in the life to come) are those which seem to suggest that God is the actual author of evils or that he commends people and actions which fall short of his perfect standards. In this chapter we shall look at the sins of the Bible's saints and at the supposed imperfections of Old Testament law.

THE SINS OF THE SAINTS

The Bible is ruthlessly candid about the sins of its saints, and this is often regarded as an argument against the Bible's morality. It is in fact just the opposite; it is an illustration of its moral integrity. The Christian wants desperately to hide his sins, not only for his own comfort of mind, but so that God's name shall not be blasphemed on his account. But God usually rules otherwise. His name needs no defence, and he is not one to hide the truth when man needs to learn a lesson. While the disease is still only partially cured, God does not normally suppress the symptoms. So it is that the very heroes of faith who are commended in the New Testament are clearly delineated in the Old as men with dubious records.

Noah, Jacob, Jephthah, Samson

'By faith Noah . . . constructed an ark.' But Noah disgraced himself when drunk. 'By faith Jacob . . . blessed each of the

sons of Joseph.' But Jacob deceived his father and cheated his
brother. Jephthah and Samson and David were among those
'well attested by their faith'. But Jephthah was a mixed-up
young man. He was an illegitimate child, harshly dealt with by
his family, and driven out to live the life of a bandit outlaw.
Yet in spite of this unstable background he was a man of faith,
who became his country's saviour in its hour of need. It is sad,
but not surprising, that such a man should make a foolish vow
which he felt unable to break.[1]

The story of Samson is the story of a strong man, who never
mastered his passions and who paid the price of his sins by the
loss of his eyes. In view of the grossness of Samson's sexual life –
deserting his Philistine wife, going in to a harlot, loving
Delilah – some have tried to interpret God's use of Samson on
the lines of God's use of the heathen Sennacherib.[2] Sennacherib was impelled by his own lust for power to attack
Jerusalem, but God put his bit in his mouth and directed his
evil actions to his own good purposes. This is certainly true as
regards the unsubdued evil side of Samson's nature – his sinful
impulses were overruled and directed to God's purposes. But
Samson is not depicted as an unbeliever. Though his parents
are not presented as particularly well-taught or godly people,
Samson was nonetheless given to them after a visit from the
angel of the Lord, he was dedicated to God as a Nazirite and
the Lord blessed him as he grew up. From time to time the
Spirit came upon him and on more than one occasion (including the moment of his death) he called on the Lord. The
narrative nowhere condemns Samson for his morals, but the
whole is consciously painted in lurid colours, calculated to
shock the first readers as it has shocked every generation of
readers since. It is a case of a man of faith being used in spite of
his sins. Beneath his barbarity and sensuality we are allowed to
see a faith that was genuine, and a concern for the glory of God
which his sins and suffering could never altogether extinguish.
What figure in the Bible helps us more when we are horrified
and nonplussed at the appalling inconsistencies of some
Christians? When we see some man, who has been used to

[1] Heb. 11:7, 21, 32–39; Jdg. 11–12.
[2] Jdg. 13–16; 2 Ki. 19:28.

bring people to faith, disgracing his Master's name, we are tempted to write him off altogether – till we remember Samson, who was attested by his faith.

David

The story of David, which is told at such length and with such a wealth of detail in the books of Samuel and the first book of Chronicles, reveals one of the great men of history. Few men of action have been men of such deep feeling. His prowess became proverbial, and so did his devotion to Jonathan. He showed astonishing generosity to his bitterest enemy. He was famous for his music, but he is remembered most of all for his poetry. Indeed, if the headings in the Psalter are to be relied upon,[3] no-one's poetry has been more read, and is now being more read, than that of David. Through it all shines a glowing love for God and a tender concern for those in need. David was a great man with a great heart and a great faith, so much so that he is called 'a man after God's own heart'. Yet the whole story betrays mercilessly David's frailties. We are told that the sight of a beautiful woman led him to adultery and murder. (No ordinary Oriental potentate would have thought twice about such a thing, whereas David poured forth an agony of penitence in Psalm 51.) The life of David is no fairy-story in which all ends happily. His life knew sinning and suffering right to the end.

These Bible saints are commended for their virtues, and in particular for their attitude to God, which is the foundation on which all lasting virtue is built; but they are not exonerated for their vices.[4] The truth that the Christian needs to learn about himself is that indwelling sin remains in the regenerate, and the regenerate must on no account forget it. No apologetic for Christianity can possibly fill the bill unless it acknowledges this

[3] For some comments on the reliability of the headings of the Psalms, see p. 160.

[4] The commendation of the unjust steward's prudence in Lk. 16:8 is brilliantly explained by J. D. M. Derrett, 'Fresh Light on St. Luke 16', *New Testament Studies* 7 (1961), pp. 198 ff., reprinted in *Law in the New Testament* (London, 1970). See also his treatment of Lk. 18:1–8: 'The Parable of the Unjust Judge', *NTS* 18 (1972), pp. 178 ff., where again God's actions are likened to those of a bad man.

fact. In spite of its good men and good deeds the record of the church as a whole is disgraceful, nothing whatever to be proud of. It is by faith that we know the grace of God to be invisibly at work in the church. As a matter of sight the evidence is ambiguous. We believe God, and God has said that Christ is perfecting his saints that they may become his Bride of faultless beauty. By faith we discern his working, but for the unbeliever the good is so marred by the evil that he may readily question its significance.

Sins recorded, though not reproved

God's exposure of the sins of the saints is characteristic of the Bible. Usually the moral condemnation, whether stated expressly or merely implied, is perfectly clear. Sometimes, however, a character is portrayed who successfully carries out some exploit in the service of God, but who, in the course of doing so, descends to some action of questionable morality. It is important to remember that the Bible's morality is not necessarily compromised by the things it records, *even if it does not at that juncture condemn them*, and even if the evil act is overruled to achieve God's purposes. The fact that Samson's desire for one of the daughters of the Philistines was within the divine purpose does not detract from the Bible's abhorrence of Samson's morals. The Bible makes plain that Haman and his friends deserved the retribution which they received at the hands of the Jews, but we are in no way debarred from suspecting the purity of Esther's motives in requesting a second day of vengeance. We are told that Jeremiah lied on the king's instructions, but we are not told that he was right to do so. Joseph, at the height of his God-given prosperity, concentrated all economic power in Pharaoh's hands. This is simply stated as a fact – no judgment is passed. We are free to make our own judgment. 'David took more concubines', but this is not written for our emulation![5] Great care must be used when arguing a moral point from some isolated act of a biblical character. The moral precepts of the Bible as a whole must judge the rightness or wrongness of a particular example.

[5] Est. 9:13; Je. 38:27; Gn. 47:20; 2 Sa. 5:13.

THE IMPERFECTIONS OF OLD TESTAMENT LAW

'An eye for an eye' and the Sermon on the Mount

It is often thought that the injunctions of the New Testament are so evidently higher than those of the Old that they cannot emanate from a common source. This idea is the result of a simple, but far-reaching, confusion between civil law and moral law. Directions given by a wholly wise legislator for the government of a fallen and sinful community are by no means the same as the directions he would give as the standards by which a man should judge his inner life. The New Testament sets up standards of righteousness with no qualifications: 'You shall love the Lord your God with all your heart'; 'you shall love your neighbour as yourself'; 'you must be perfect, as your heavenly Father is perfect'. It makes attitude as important as action: hate is murder, lust is adultery. But when it comes to the framing of civil laws by which a community is to be governed, biblical legislation is based on overt acts, not on inner attitudes.

Thus, in the Sermon on the Mount, the would-be citizen of the kingdom of God is given instruction about his unseen motives and is forbidden to seek vengeance for personal wrongs and is told to do good to his enemies. Our Lord is not giving directions to the civil judges, telling them to stop punishing evil-doers. It remains fundamental to the welfare of any society that the evil-doer should be punished with scrupulous fairness and that the well-doer should be acquitted. This is the Old Testament principle of the *lex talionis* – an eye for an eye and a tooth for a tooth. A man should receive what he deserves, no more and no less. This is the complete answer to the evils of the blood feud, where families for generations live either in fear of vengeance or in plotting it. Vengeance is taken out of the hands of the family and put into the hands of the civil judge, who is in fact God's representative. 'Vengeance is mine . . . says the Lord.' The judge performs a sacred duty when he administers justice.[6] The 'eye for an eye' principle

---

[6] Rom. 12:19; 13:1–5. The whole passage, Rom. 12:14 – 13:10, which sandwiches instruction about the need to obey the government between instructions about living the life of love, magnificently illustrates the distinction between civil laws and standards for the actions and inner attitudes of the individual Christian.

could not have been intended in the normal way to be taken literally. If one man knocked out another man's tooth, the judge did not call upon some lackey to knock a tooth out of the offending party. He assessed and secured fair compensation. In the passage in question the enunciation of the principle is followed immediately by an example of fair compensation: 'When a man strikes the eye of his slave, male or female, and destroys it, he shall let the slave go free for the eye's sake. If he knocks out the tooth of his slave, male or female, he shall let the slave go free for the tooth's sake.' [7]

It is thus a misunderstanding of the Sermon on the Mount to imagine that our Lord is repudiating the principle of civil justice, or undercutting the authority of the Old Testament. The passage [8] in which he draws a series of contrasts between the things 'said to the men of old' and the things which 'I say unto you', is prefaced by a startlingly unequivocal introduction: 'Think not that I have come to abolish the law and the prophets; I have come not to abolish them but to fulfil them. For truly, I say to you, till heaven and earth pass away, not an iota, not a dot, will pass from the law until all is accomplished. Whoever then relaxes one of the least of these commandments and teaches men so, shall be called least in the kingdom of heaven; but he who does them and teaches them shall be called great in the kingdom of heaven.'

The whole passage is concerned with misinterpretations of the Old Testament, not with any supposedly sub-standard regulations. The *lex talionis* was being interpreted Shylock-wise, as though it gave every man the right to demand his pound of flesh when wronged. It was being used as an instrument of personal revenge. Our Lord says that the citizen of the kingdom is to have an utter disregard for his own rights, and is to go to all lengths in showing his emancipation from material

[7] Ex. 21:23–27.
[8] Mt. 5:17 ff. It should be noted that the form of words used is not: 'It is written in the law, but I say . . .'; it is: 'You have heard that it was said to the men of old.' Jesus appears to be referring to oral instruction received ('You have heard'), which was being falsely represented as the true meaning of the instruction originally given ('said to the men of old').

ties. He must love his enemies and harbour no desire for vengeance in his heart. That is a very different matter from telling a judge not to administer justice.

Marriage, divorce and prisoners of war

Similarly in the matter of sex there is a moral law and there are civil laws. The same divine standard of the moral law is to be found implicit in the Old Testament and explicit in the New. The divine purpose was that a man should leave his father and mother and cleave to his wife, so that the two should 'become one flesh'.[9] The complementary nature of man and woman is taught unforgettably in the account of Eve's creation, and the expression 'one flesh' vividly describes the divine ideal for marriage, which can be fulfilled only in monogamy. But the Fall laid its defiling hand on sex, as it did on every other relationship. Marriage brought subjection, and birth brought pain. In a few generations there was bigamy, and at least by the time of Abraham polygamy was firmly established. The evils of polygamy are shown up unmistakably in the domestic unhappiness of one leading figure after another – Abraham, Jacob, David, Solomon. Yet, in the circumstances in which they found themselves, God did not see fit to impose a civil law upon his people to require them to break with this practice. He was content to give regulations to mitigate its evils.[1] In education, lessons need to be learnt in a suitable order and at a suitable pace, if the best results are to be obtained. If a child is overloaded or driven too fast, he will learn less well. Abraham and his descendants had enough to learn in all conscience, and doubtless God knew that the time for this lesson was not yet. It was left to our Lord to make the Old Testament standard

[9] Gn. 2:24; Mt. 19:5; Mk. 10:7.
[1] Dt. 21:15 ff. The same may be said of slavery, which is dealt with helpfully by F. D. Kidner in *Hard Sayings* (London, 1972), pp. 30 ff. A form of slavery was tolerated in the Old Testament, but conditions were so strictly regulated that there should have been little practical difference between the treatment of a slave and of a hired labourer. If (as we have seen) the owner were so much as to knock out his slave's tooth, he was to be set free (Ex. 21:27). Foreign slaves were even welcomed to circumcision and all the blessings of the covenant (Ex. 12:44). But the very idea of one man owning another is evil and potentially corrupting.

explicit and to forbid his followers to take another wife as long
as a former partner was living.[2]

The Old Testament regulations for divorce were similarly
adapted to the needs of the time. In days when women's rights
were few and their hopes of redress were slender, the Mosaic
legislation was a powerful buttress against masculine cruelty
and infidelity. No man could dismiss his wife on the basis of
some passing whim. He needed to have just ground for
divorcing her; and he needed to draw up a proper document
as a 'bill of divorce', so that her rights were safeguarded if she
married again. Divorce was the evil result of evil hearts, but it
would have been unrealistic to have forbidden it altogether, as
long as hearts remained evil. Because of the hardness of their
hearts, Jesus said, divorce had been allowed, and he himself
continued to allow it (it seems) on the grounds of unchastity.[3]
But it was divorce that was humane and carefully regulated.

The directions for the treatment of women prisoners of war
have sometimes been criticized, yet (in a hard-hearted and
lustful world) they are in fact remarkably exacting and
humane. For the Israelite soldier in a conquering army there
was to be no rape. If he desired a beautiful woman, he was to
take her to his own home and allow her a month to prepare for
marriage. There was no question of her becoming a slave
concubine. If at the end of that time he desired marriage, he
was to take her as his legal wife. Should he subsequently cease
to take a delight in her, he might not sell her or treat her as a
slave; he was to let her go where she liked.[4] In a world where
there are wars, and therefore prisoners of war, such regulations
in fact set a high standard of conduct.

The death penalty

The Sermon on the Mount forbids not merely killing, but even
hating, whereas the Old Testament has a long list of crimes for

[2] With regard to the vexed question of what a polygamist is to do with his
wives after he has been converted, the New Testament goes no further than
to forbid the man who still has more than one wife to become a church officer
(1 Tim. 3:12; Tit. 1:6).
[3] Dt. 24:1-4; Mt. 5:31; 19:7; Mk. 10:4.
[4] Dt. 21:10 ff.

which the holy community must exact the death penalty.[5] This list differs widely from the English code in the first half of the twentieth century. It is a far longer list, though a far shorter list than that prescribed by our law in the early nineteenth century, when there were 200 capital offences on the statute book, including trivial thefts and assaults. It included not only murder and the abduction of a man to make him a slave, but also blasphemy, profanation of the sabbath, sorcery and incitement to apostasy.[6] It also included incorrigible juvenile delinquency. In addition to this, detailed instructions are given about the waging of war.[7]

Old Testament laws not immediately transferable to modern times

It needs to be clearly understood that a defence of the morality of Old Testament law in Old Testament times does not necessarily imply that these laws should be reimposed today. Christians were (and are) bidden to study the Old Testament diligently, but nowhere is it said that they should go into all the world and impose its entire law on every society. Indeed, it became clear to the church at a very early date that the teaching of Jesus implied that much of the law should not be imposed on the Gentiles. (This became a practical issue when the questions of circumcision and table-fellowship had to be faced.) Christians were in fact told to obey the law of the land where they lived, unless that law contravened the law of God. Since those days circumstances have greatly altered in many areas of life through the coming of new knowledge and new technological skills and (as regards warfare) through the invention of appalling new weapons. Whether or not the old directions are still relevant, and how precisely they should be

---

[5] The main material is in Ex. 21: 12–17; 22: 18–20; Lv. 20.

[6] Lv. 24:15; Ex. 31:14; Dt. 13. This squares, as we shall see in the next chapter, with the consuming severity meted out to those who practised heathen abominations. The supreme horror is that a priest's daughter should play the harlot, like the sacred prostitutes of heathendom. The penalty for this is to be burnt with fire (Lv. 21: 9). The case of Achan provides an instance of death with burning in the period immediately after Moses. It should be observed that it was not death by slow torture as in the Middle Ages, but 'all Israel stoned him with stones; they burned them with fire' (Jos. 7:25).

[7] Dt. 21:18–21; Dt. 20.

applied if they are relevant, are questions demanding careful
study in each case (and opinions may well differ even after
study has been made). We are therefore concerned at this juncture to show only that the commands attributed to God were
not unjust or unloving in their Old Testament context.

Reaction and realism

In the climate of our times one has to run the risk of appearing
to be appallingly reactionary to attempt even this. Yet it is my
deepening conviction that much modern discussion of violence
and war and death lacks realism, and because it lacks realism
it contributes to that very inhumanity of man to man which it
is seeking to avoid. The well-intentioned reformer who under-
estimates the difficulty of his task is on the road which leads to
disheartenment and cynicism and finally to acquiescence in
cruelty. Popular opposition to war is a natural and wholesome
reaction to something horrible, but in many cases neither the
rationale of the opposition nor its practical outworkings have
been thought through. The one who takes original sin seriously
knows that life is lived on a descending escalator and that it is
a tough job even to stand still. The ranks of the unregenerate
are continually being refreshed by an endless stream of new
recruits, and from their hearts continually erupt, as Christ said,
evil thoughts, fornication, theft, murder, adultery, coveting,
wickedness, deceit, licentiousness, envy, slander, pride, foolishness. It is for a world like this that the laws of the Old Testament are framed. It is a world where force, both physical and
psychological, plays a tremendous part, whether for good or ill,
and one of the primary purposes of Old Testament law is to
defend the weak in this world of force. Rejection of all force is
the recipe, first for anarchy and then for tyranny – since in the
end anarchy is even more terrifying than tyranny and will not
long be tolerated by any community.

Death the desert of sin

Now (as we have seen) the Bible presupposes that sin leads to
and deserves death. If this is conceded, much follows. It is
perfectly *just* that the death penalty should be applied to any
sinful human being, if God sees fit, before the usual term of life

is over. It is therefore perfectly just that God should have decreed the death penalty for certain particularly destructive sins. Whether less drastic arrangements could have been made without over-all loss to the human race is a matter for debate. But it is a debate in which there are innumerable imponderables to be weighed. We must ask to what extent different types of vicious tendencies would have been transmitted by heredity to the descendants of those spared the death penalty. What influence would the continuing presence in society of those with a bad moral record have had upon the rest of the community? What punishments would have been most effective as deterrents and what most conducive to reformation? Research is throwing some light on these questions as they apply to modern society, but any attempt to apply its findings to an altogether different culture must be hazardous. To prove beyond reasonable doubt that a perfect legislator could have done better for mankind than the Old Testament legislator would be (to put it mildly) difficult. This will become more evident when, at a later stage, we remind ourselves that alternatives to the dread death penalty are themselves inescapably, if genteelly, dreadful.

If death is recognized as a just penalty for certain crimes, it follows that the infliction of that penalty by the proper authority is itself a just act. A clear distinction must be made between the immorality of a sinful act and the morality of its retribution. In a sinful situation actions may be desirable which in another situation would be totally undesirable. The undesirable action (in this case taking part in an execution, that is, in the killing of a man) is the result of sin, but is not itself sin. All violence is caused by sin, but not all violence is necessarily sinful – it may even be the occasion of virtue when it calls for courage and self-sacrifice.

The just war

Of course, in real life, situations are not simple. The wrongdoer is never solely to blame, nor is the agent of retribution wholly righteous. Nevertheless it is our duty to administer justice to individuals as best we can. When it is a case of one community at odds with another community, the rights and

wrongs are usually even less clear-cut, though it would be
over-cynical to say that the balance of right is never on one
side. Thus when the citizens of a state find themselves at war
with another state, they are in a situation caused by sin; but
the Bible does not regard participation in war as *in itself* an act
of sin. It is, of course, an exegetical blunder to take the sixth
commandment, 'You shall not kill', as an absolute prohibition
of the taking of human life, since it is part of a body of legislation which gives specific instructions about the death penalty
and about the conduct of warfare.[8]

F. D. Kidner says of the wars which were not specifically
wars of extermination:

> In less extreme kinds of warfare the kings of Israel had a name
> among their enemies for mercy (1 Ki. 20:31). Their rules of war
> made certain minimal restraints explicit, and evidently others by
> implication. Against enemies who were not appointed for utter
> destruction there must be no 'scorched earth' tactics (Dt. 20:19 f.),
> and before a city was besieged it must be offered peace conditions,
> which compare favourably with the brutal terms of, for instance,
> the Ammonites in 1 Samuel 11:2. Not that we should exaggerate
> this moderation. If a city opted to fight, and was taken, all its
> males except the children were to be put to the sword (Dt. 20:13).
> Even this, however, may conceal an understanding that it applied
> to those who still would not surrender, since we find that in practice
> the Israelites took prisoners in normal warfare, and considered it
> unthinkable to kill them (2 Ki. 6:22).[9]

Although victories are celebrated with exuberance, the Old
Testament does not glorify war. 'The peoples who delight in
war' are to be scattered.

> In a biting attack on the great aggressor of the day, Isaiah shows
> up the viciousness and puerility of those who go to war as a boy
> might go birdnesting, to bring back trophies and to find amuse-
> ment in spreading terror (Is. 10:13 ff.). Amos, for his part, preaches
> against the small operators: the little nations which are as heartless
> as the big ones, stopping at no cruelty to keep their feuds alive or
> their boundaries expanding (*e.g.* Am. 1:11, 13). Even David,
> whose wars were not for the most part irresponsible, and who hated
> vendettas, was deemed unfit to build the temple, 'for you are a
> warrior and have shed blood' (1 Ch. 28:3). The ultimate goal in

[8] Ex. 20:13; 21:12 ff.; 23:22 ff.
[9] F. D. Kidner, *Hard Sayings*, p. 42.

the Old Testament is a world at peace, its weapons destroyed or re-made for gentler arts, and its fears forgotten (Ps. 46:9; Is. 9:5; Mi. 4:3; Zc. 8:4 f.).[1]

The Bible cannot, therefore, be invoked in support either of an unprincipled militarism or of an absolute pacifism which regards all violent action and all taking of human life as sin. The great majority of thoughtful Christians down the centuries have reluctantly rejected pacifism and have argued that a Christian man may bear arms in a (relatively) just war. But it is the duty of Christians in every age to assess their own particular situation afresh. If a largely godless state calls on its citizens to perfect themselves in the use of vile and sophisticated weapons of physical and psychological destruction, they may well have to say 'No' – and suffer the consequences. When it comes to the question of 'just revolution', which is a burning issue in many parts of the world, Christians have found it more difficult to discover biblical warrant for the idea; but even here the evidence does not seem to be decisive in cases where populations are suffering extreme injustice.

Lying and the lesser of evils

It is a general principle of biblical ethics that, where one moral law comes into conflict with another moral law, choice must be made of the lesser of evils. The right choice – the choice which as a choice is righteous in the sight of God – inescapably involves doing something which is intrinsically evil. The deed remains evil, even though the blame for the evil rests not on the doer but on others. Thus on rare occasions falsehood may be necessary. To quote F. D. Kidner again:

> The weight of the evidence suggests that where life is arbitrarily threatened (as in Ex. 1:15 ff. by Pharaoh, or in 1 Sa. 16:2 by Saul) God may sanction – and even suggest, as in the latter case – an evasive reply which is intended to mislead; and that in war the opposing forces must expect deception in tactics (as in the feigned retreat at Ai) and in speech (as in Rahab's answer about the spies, or Hushai's profession of allegiance to Absalom), as a corollary of the general breakdown of peaceable intentions. Yet even so, just as war is not regarded as excusing unlimited violence (*cf.*, *e.g.*,

[1] Ps. 68:30. Kidner, p. 40. The New Testament recognizes that the warriors as well as the martyrs had their part to play in preparing the world for the gospel (Heb. 11:32–38).

Dt. 20:19 f.; 2 Ki. 6:22), truth is not implied to be of no account
in such a crisis, any more than mercy is. The other abnormal case
is where people have so utterly rejected truth as to show themselves
unworthy of it. Ahab, who hated true prophecy, was lured to death
by a lying spirit from the Lord; and in Ezekiel 14:7 ff. God
announced that He would Himself deceive the insincere enquirer.
The New Testament enunciates the same principle in Romans
1:28 and 2 Thessalonians 2:11 f.[2]

Jael the Kenite

Jael the Kenite is a particularly interesting case of a person in
a difficult moral predicament. Deborah and Barak's commendation of Jael as the 'most blessed of women' has been the
object of misplaced criticism. 'What happened then was as
much an outrage against the ethics of her own time as against
ours today. The terrible deed done, Jael stood guilty of
violating the laws of hospitality, of falsehood, treachery, and
murder.'[3] Yet this is an incident of war, and the ethics of war
and the ethics of peace are by no means the same. War is
indeed a very ugly thing, resulting from human sin; but to kill
in war is not necessarily murder. And it is plainly illogical to
allow a man sometimes to kill his country's enemy, but never
to tell him a lie in the same cause.

In this instance Israel, against great odds, was attempting to
throw off a cruel oppression which had lasted twenty years.
The case of Jael is analogous to that of the brave women of
enemy-occupied territory who at the risk of their lives lied and
even killed in order to shelter escaping prisoners. The Kenites
had long been friendly with the Israelites and evidently knew

[2] *Hard Sayings*, pp. 20 f. Language which speaks of God *sending* lying spirits
highlights the fact that God's attitude to sin is not passive, allowing it to go
on undisturbed. God is active; he so orders circumstances that sin is brought
out into the open and is judged. From the standpoint of those who listened,
therefore, the lying spirits are said to have been *sent* by God, though from
the standpoint of the spirits themselves they were merely allowed to do what
they wanted to do. In the case of Micaiah (1 Ki. 22:23) the Lord's message
is given in the form of an account of a vision and can hardly be intended as
a literal account of happenings in heaven. (It is, incidentally, a useful rule
of thumb in biblical exegesis to remember that Westerners are more likely
to err by taking the Bible more literally than intended than vice versa.)
[3] Jdg. 5:24. 'Jael', *The New Bible Dictionary* (London, 1962), p. 596. That
we are right to regard the commendation of Jael as having divine approval
is supported by the representation of Barak as a man of faith in Heb. 11:32.

something of the religion of Israel.[4] Jael saw the dreaded army commander approaching alone on foot; she made up her mind in an instant as to which side she was on. She respected the God of Israel and hated the filthy gods of Canaan. In a situation where betrayal of her sympathies would mean instant death, she carried through her purpose with perfect coolness, and so effected the *coup de grâce* in the war of deliverance. Jael is not blessed for murder and deceit (which remain evil things even when unavoidable), but for her courage and for her allegiance to the true God.

Alternative punishments

Whether in fact the Old Testament laws were cruel in comparison with those of our supposedly humane society is not as self-evident as many think. The Old Testament relied mainly on payment of damages, strictly limited corporal punishment and capital punishment, whereas modern society relies mainly on fines and imprisonment. The nearest thing to imprisonment in Old Testament law was confinement to a city of refuge for unintentional homicide.[5] The question of punishment is such an emotive subject that one almost despairs of its rational discussion. Anyone who defends corporal or capital punishment even in the most tentative way runs the risk of being branded as a sadistic ogre. Yet my horror of long-term imprisonment is horror at the sheer suffering that it entails. Far from being insensitive, I hate undergoing pain and seeing pain inflicted. Even though reason leads one to believe that the suffering is not nearly as bad as it looks, I hate to see a fly wriggling on a fly-paper or a fish struggling on a hook, and get little pleasure from watching amateur boxers knocking one another about, despite the knowledge that they do it because they enjoy it!

One would hate, therefore, really to hurt someone physically by way of punishment, and would deplore any system of corporal punishment which was either sadistic in intent or excessive in degree, or which was used without due consideration of the offender's psychological needs. Even more

[4] Ex. 2:18; Nu. 10:29; Jdg. 1:16; 4:11; 1 Sa. 15:6; 27:10; 30:29; 1 Ch. 2:55; Ne. 3:14.
[5] Nu. 35:22–28.

would one shrink from joining the firing-squad and taking part in an execution. But would this mean having relatively little qualm about committing a man to prison for a decade? If one had no imagination and no compassion, it would of course be easy – no unpleasantness, no soiling of the hands, soon out of sight and out of mind. But in fact my slight experience of prisons and criminal asylums fills me with dismay. To substitute long imprisonment for execution may at first sight seem like mercy. But judged by the suffering to be endured it is, surely, the reverse of mercy.

Long imprisonment is a living death. A man is separated from his wife and family (often causing them prolonged, unmerited hardship), he is put in a single-sex institution where a normal sex-life is impossible, his companions are criminals, he is shut up to his own bad conscience, but in conditions ill-designed to effect repentance and reformation and with slender hopes of satisfactory rehabilitation after release. With unlimited money and with angels for warders (which, realists please note, will never be), some of these evils might be considerably mitigated, but nothing can do away with the fact that a human being is deprived of his liberty. This aspect of the matter is highlighted in our top security gaols, which may be clinically hygienic and immaculate in *décor*, but in which men of drive and brains and initiative rot out their days. It is true, of course, that the human spirit has a remarkable resilience even in appalling circumstances, and that life, however bad, is seldom one of unrelieved misery; some sort of mode of living is worked out in prison life, in which its lights and shades continue to be felt with pleasure and displeasure. It is often true too that the life out of prison of one who has fallen foul of society may already have lost many of the elements which make up a fully human life, so that in some respects life in prison may be less unpleasant than life outside. (Such men are often at least as much victims of a cruel society as its creators.) But it is a poor defence of long-term imprisonment to say that it is merely substituting one dehumanizing process for another.

If (*per impossibile*) some sort of calculus could be devised to assess the amount of suffering caused to offenders and their

families by our long-drawn-out, physically painless punishments, and compare them with the short, sharp pains of the
older punishments, I find it hard to believe that the new would
prove the lighter. Furthermore, even in the most enlightened
and affluent society, it is an enormous struggle to get adequate
funds and suitable staff to run our penal institutions (and in a
fallen society it seems unrealistic to believe that it will ever be
otherwise). But in the poor, largely rural society of the Old
Testament, the provision of humane, secure, long-term prisons
would have laid an intolerable burden on the community –
apart altogether from the suffering and corrosion of character
caused by the loss of liberty.

It is all very well to talk *in theory* about the enlightenment
and humanity of modern penal codes, but *in practice* the prisons
of the twentieth century have probably witnessed torments as
vile as those inflicted in any age and inflicted on a wider scale
than ever before in history. We think naturally of Hitler's concentration camps, of Japanese prisoner of war camps and of
the prisons described by Solzhenitsyn. One's mind is numbed
as one tries to compute what it all adds up to in human terms.
These examples (which come from three of the most 'civilized'
nations of the world) are, it is true, very bad cases, but they
are, alas, not isolated examples. Like the mushroom cloud of
the atom bomb they are symbolic of our age. The inescapable
fact appears to be that sin will take its toll of misery *somehow*.
The primitive barbarity and the cheapness of life in the ancient
Near East is dreadful to contemplate, but is our sophisticated
barbarity really less dreadful? No society can hold together
without punishment of transgressors, and punishment is by
definition unpleasant. Are we really in a position to say that we
could have devised for the Israelite people unpleasantnesses
more just, humane and practical than those prescribed in the
Old Testament law? I for one doubt it.

Principles of punishment in the Old Testament

But when imprisonment is eliminated from the list of possible
punishments, what is left? Virtually: fines or damages (which
cannot be exacted from the very poor); some form of temporary slavery (to which must be attached other penalties if the

slave runs away); corporal punishment and capital punishment. It is difficult, if not impossible, to think of a practicable
system which would have been suited to the ancient world
which would not have contained at least some element of
corporal and capital punishment.

If this is agreed, the question then is: What are to be considered just punishments for what crimes? A characteristic of
biblical law is the pre-eminence it accords to human, as
opposed to economic, considerations. In Israel offences against
life and the structure of the family are punished much more
severely than in other Near Eastern cultures. For instance, in
Babylonian law, breaking and entering, looting at a fire and
theft are punishable by death. But in Israel no offence against
property attracts the death penalty. Punishments for theft are
very mild by oriental standards, or even by our standards
(where the Great Train Robbers were more heavily punished
than murderers). By contrast, in Israel the death penalty is
mandatory for murder, because man is made in the image of
God,[6] whereas other legal systems permitted monetary compensation. Similarly the Old Testament is more severe on
sexual offences and disobedient children than other cultures.
The humanitarian aspect of the biblical law is also illustrated
by its abolition of substitutionary punishment. Substitution is
often allowed in cuneiform law, *e.g.*, if through faulty con-
struction a house collapses, killing the householder's son, the
son of the builder who built the house must be put to death;
or, a seducer must deliver his wife to the seduced girl's father
for prostitution. But Deuteronomy 24:16 explicitly forbids this
kind of substitutionary punishment: 'The fathers shall not be
put to death for the children, nor shall the children be put to
death for the fathers; every man shall be put to death for his
own sin.'

The Old Testament law does not in fact exact fines (*i.e.* payments for the benefit of the state), but only damages (*i.e.*
payments for the benefit of the injured party). It is a principle

[6] Gn. 9:5 f. I am indebted in this and the following paragraph to an un-
published paper by my son G. J. Wenham, and to M. Greenberg, 'Some
Postulates of Biblical Criminal Law' in *Y. Kaufmann Jubilee Volume*, ed. M.
Haran (Jerusalem, 1960), pp. 5 ff.

that punishment allows the offender to make atonement and be reconciled with society. After he has paid the penalty the offender suffers no loss of his civil rights. Degradation of the offender as a motive for punishment is specifically excluded by Deuteronomy 25:3, where the number of strokes is limited to forty, 'lest, if one should go on to beat him with more stripes than these, your brother be degraded in your sight'. The degrading brutality of many punishments under Assyrian law is in marked contrast to the Hebrew outlook.[7]

It is against this general mildness of Hebrew law that we have to view its shocking severity with regard to (a) religious offences such as idolatry and blasphemy, (b) sexual offences such as adultery and homosexual intercourse, and (c) juvenile incorrigibility – all of which attract the death penalty.

Death penalty for religious offences

At no point is it more obvious that the Old Testament directions are in harmony with the basic biblical principles than here, and at no point is it more obvious that they are not suitable for incorporation into the statutes of a secular society. In biblical teaching departure from the living God is the fundamental sin and is the way of death. For a holy nation, in covenant with the Lord, to depart from him is to invite death, and this is written into the statute book of the people of Israel, where idolatry, blasphemy, divination and profanation of the sabbath are made punishable by death.[8] This is not to be taken

[7] Mutilation was a common punishment in Assyrian law and is not uncommon in some other cultures. In the Old Testament the cutting off of the hand is prescribed in one instance for what must have been a very rare offence (Dt. 25:11 f.). This law may have been intended for didactic purposes rather than for implementation, in order to stress the gravity of injuring a person's reproductive organs. It is interesting that Jesus, speaking in metaphor, cites such mutilation as being less terrible than the fires of Gehenna (Mk. 9:43).

[8] Lv. 20:2; 24:13; Ex. 22:18; Nu. 15:32-36. The positive principle of course is that only the best is good enough for God. This too was given legislative embodiment in the demand for perfect, unblemished animals for sacrifice (Ex. 12:5) and for unblemished persons to make the priestly offerings (Lv. 21:17-23). The last-named law perhaps seemed hard on the unfortunate descendants of Aaron who happened to be crippled or hunchbacked or injured – was it not calculated to add bitterness to bitterness? Yet Israel was only too ready to give God what cost little, and the external embodiment of the principle of holiness was necessary. One of the great

as implying that individual faith can be established by compulsion, but it is an assertion of the corporate principle which constitutes Israel as one people, and of the objective fact that Israel had been chosen by God as his own people. Inner consent could not be made the subject of legislation, but outward denial (which would be destructive of the very basis of the community's existence) could be. It was Israel's corporate belief in her divine election and her adherence to the divine law which in fact kept her from absorption by the nations, and it is this which made her ready for Christ's coming. Such legislation was right and necessary for ancient Israel, but any attempts to thrust such a law upon a secular society would be tantamount to conversion by force. Therefore when the new Israel was sent to make disciples of all nations, it was sent to win the individual faith and allegiance of those whom God was calling out of the midst of every nation; it was not sent to establish theocratic states.

Death penalty for sexual offences: adultery

The death penalty was prescribed for various sexual offences. It included certain practices which are psychologically abnormal, such as homosexual intercourse and bestiality; it included incest, with death and burning for the extreme case – 'if a man take a wife and her mother'. But it also included fornication (in certain cases) and adultery.[9] The pattern of sexual life envisaged in the Old Testament law was that of comparatively early betrothal and of marriage responsibly undertaken, of devotion to home and family, with the possibility of carefully regulated divorce and of the extreme penalty for promiscuity and adultery.

Nowadays we have so come to take adultery for granted that

---

themes of the Old Testament is the duty of caring for the poor and the defenceless. This derives from God's care for them, and no instructed Israelite would think that such loss of physical advantages and social privileges implied loss of God's love. The oppressed and needy are encouraged to turn to God in prayer, knowing that he will hear them (Ps. 69:32 f.). In the New Testament it is made particularly clear that it is characteristic of God to make up to the deprived what they have lost superficially (e.g. Lk. 4:18; 1 Cor. 1:26–29; Jas. 2:5).

[9] Lv. 20:14; Dt. 22:21; Ex. 22:16 f.; Dt. 22:22.

we fail to realize how distorted our values have become. When a man steals another's valuable property, he is severely dealt with by the law. But when a man deliberately seduces and steals another man's wife and robs his children of their mother, he probably gets off scot free. Yet in terms of the harm done and the destruction of human happiness the first crime is venial in comparison with the second. Sexual impulses are not so uncontrollable as the novelists would have us think. In this, as in everything else, we are enormously influenced by the 'expected pattern of behaviour'. If marital infidelity is expected, the temptation will be difficult to resist. If, on the other hand, it is regarded as a heinous crime, few will succumb. Both theologically and sociologically adultery *is* a heinous crime. No code of laws which included the death penalty for adultery would be thinkable unless accepted by public opinion, but who is to say that a code of this sort, willingly embraced by the covenant nation, would not have made for a stable and happy society in enviable contrast to the instabilities and miseries of a lax one?

The woman taken in adultery

The Old Testament attitude to adultery is often regarded as more severe than that of Christ. When the woman who was caught in the act of adultery was brought to Jesus, he is reported to have said, 'Neither do I condemn you; go, and do not sin again.' From this it has often been inferred that he rejected the Mosaic command, and did not consider that adultery merited death. This passage has been minutely examined by J. D. M. Derrett,[1] who comes to a quite different conclusion. He shows that the question provided a neat trap for Jesus. If he contradicted the law of Moses and ruled against stoning, he would be in trouble with the ecclesiastical authorities; if he lent his authority to a lynching, which was contrary to Roman law, he would be in trouble with the civil

[1] J. D. M. Derrett, 'Law in the New Testament: The Story of the Woman Taken in Adultery', *New Testament Studies* 10 (1963), pp. 1–26, reprinted in *Law in the New Testament* (London, 1970). The passage Jn. 7:53 – 8:11 is not an original part of the Fourth Gospel, and probably should not be regarded as Scripture, but there is good reason to believe that it is based on accurate recollection.

authorities. Derrett shows that the point at issue was not whether adultery merited death (concerning which no Jew would have had any doubt), but whether the evidence was legally satisfactory.

The Old Testament law was weighted heavily in favour of the accused,[2] which meant that in the case of certain crimes, such as adultery, it was virtually impossible to obtain the necessary evidence. Two witnesses were required, whose evidence had to agree in every particular, and any witness would be disqualified if he did not try to stop someone who was about to commit a crime. It was therefore useless to set a trap in order to gain evidence, as the evidence would be disallowed. Nonetheless, every Jew from childhood knew that *in the eyes of God* adultery merited death. In this particular case the evidence had clearly been obtained by two witnesses deliberately planted for the purpose, who made no attempt to prevent the sin. What our Lord wrote in the sand was evidently enough to make the case disintegrate.

This is not, however, to say that he repudiated the death penalty prescribed by the Old Testament. He was in fact explicit (as we have already seen) in teaching that the way of sin is the way of death, and that unrepented sin will lead to eternal death. But his action in this instance does illustrate the fact that his earthly ministry was not, in a direct sense, one of judgment. As John's Gospel says: 'God sent the Son into the world, not to condemn the world, but that the world might be saved through him'.[3] At his second coming he will be judge; but at his first coming his task was to call men to repentance and to faith. The woman's accusers tried to make him take the role of judge before the time. In effect he refused to do so, and instead challenged them all, accusers and accused, to repentance. It is possible that in the case of this woman we are to

[2] This is an interesting result of the Old Testament teaching that vengeance belongs to God, who is the righteous Judge. In view of the fact that every man will be judged by God, the earthly administrator of justice can afford to be meticulous in the standards of proof that he demands. It is more important to avoid wrongful condemnation than wrongful acquittal, for the transgressor will not in the end escape his due. As Kidner remarks, 'Final judgment will correct the rough judgment of history' (*Hard Sayings*, p. 43).
[3] Lk. 12:14; Jn. 3:17.

gather from his words, 'Neither do I condemn you', not only that he did not condemn her to death, but that she had responded to his challenge; that she was forgiven, 'saved through him'.

Homosexual practices

There can be no doubt that those with homosexual tendencies have suffered grievously down the centuries through the sins and misunderstandings of others. Knowledge of the subject is growing, but it is still imperfectly understood and it would be particularly foolish to draw hasty conclusions about the present-day situation from the Old Testament laws. We shall not, therefore, presume to try to apply the Old Testament law to our modern problems, but simply look at the situation in ancient Israel. Two points may be made. First, it is necessary to see the severity of this law in relation to that of other laws. Although homosexual practices were regarded as gross and heinous contraventions of the created order, it is important to note that homosexual sins were not treated (as they were in the later Western Christian tradition) as being more heinous than heterosexual sins.

Secondly, it is necessary to see the severity of this law in the context of the solidarity principle. We have already laid a good deal of stress on this principle in biblical thought and seen how the sins and blessings of one generation affect subsequent generations. This factor seems to play an important part in at least some cases of homosexual orientation. There is often an arrested or distorted psychosexual development which is the result of an abnormal relationship with either or both parents. Dominating and over-protective mothers, and weak or absent fathers, are often found in the families of homosexuals. The resulting distaste for the other sex may prevent a free and natural heterosexual love from developing; thus there may rise a temptation to seek sexual expression homosexually.[4] The deficiencies of parents may of course be largely the result of the

[4] On this subject, see H. Kimball-Jones, *Toward a Christian Understanding of the Homosexual* (London, 1967). Recent research indicates that there is also a correlation between biochemical factors (of which the causes are unknown) and sexual orientation.

deficiencies of grandparents, and theirs of great-grandparents.
We are all caught up in a web which goes back many generations. Our responsibilities are corporate and a parent may inherit a situation over which he has little or no control and for
which he carries little direct blame. Yet the effect of disregard
of the law of God by many individuals over an extended
period of time will in the end bring dire social consequences. In
this case children may be deprived of normal sexuality and all
the blessings of a happy home and a family of their own.

Now it is important to notice that this particular grim end-
product is the long-term result of transgressing the divine order
of creation. In the biblical order God is head of Christ, Christ
is head of the husband, the husband is head of the wife and the
parents are head of the children.[5] In the home there should be
a combination of humble authority and unselfish love. When
men give up obedience and love to God, therefore, it will be no
surprise if women give up obedience and love to their hus-
bands, and children give up obedience and love to their
parents. What is particularly serious is that this derangement
of the created order tends to become cumulative in effect.
When the divine 'expected pattern of behaviour' begins to
break down, it becomes ever easier for latent unnatural tendencies, which might otherwise have done no harm, to develop
and, in this instance, to lead to homosexual practices. Old
Testament law, determined to preserve a *helpful* expected pattern of behaviour, provided that these practices should be
nipped in the bud. Judged by the amount of suffering endured
by many homosexuals, it could be argued that the occasional
execution of a compulsive homosexual in Old Testament

---

[5] 1 Cor. 11:3; Eph. 5:22 – 6:4. It is insufficiently realized how important
it is that there should be a mutual understanding where final authority in
the home is vested. Where there is no such understanding and there is a
difference of opinion on a matter of principle between husband and wife,
it becomes a battle of wills – with the stronger personality winning and
both parties unhappy. This unhappiness is particularly likely where the
woman is the stronger personality. She inevitably tends more and more to
dominate and be seen to dominate. Where the husband is recognized as
head, the wife, when she has exhausted all her powers of persuasion, will
place the responsibility squarely on his shoulders and back him up, leaving
events to prove who was right. A ship run by saints would still need a cap-
tain; a home, however harmonious it may be, still needs a head.

times, however tragic it might be, would have been merciful even to the man concerned. When it is seen in the context of the mission of the Chosen People to the human race, it would have been an irreparable disaster if Israel had been allowed to become so corrupted that it had had to be destroyed before the Messiah had come. Other corrupt nations could be (and were) swept away; Israel had to be preserved, even if it meant laws of great severity.

Death penalty for juvenile delinquency

One particularly distressing condition for which death is prescribed is the incorrigible delinquent: 'If a man has a stubborn and rebellious son, who will not obey the voice of his father or the voice of his mother, and, though they chastise him, will not give heed to them, then his father and his mother shall take hold of him and bring him out to the elders of his city at the gate of the place where he lives, and they shall say to the elders of his city, "This our son is stubborn and rebellious, he will not obey our voice; he is a glutton and a drunkard." Then all the men of the city shall stone him to death with stones; so you shall purge the evil from your midst; and all Israel shall hear, and fear.'[6] This may at first sight seem sheer heartless cruelty. But the stress is strictly upon incorrigibility – incorrigibility in the face of repeated warnings of the death penalty. In our own day we have psychopathic children for whom even modern medicine has no satisfactory treatment. From very early years the utterly miserable life-history of many of them is all too predictable: problem childhood, delinquency, Borstal, prison – which ends finally only at death. Doubtless it was the same in principle in those days. In such cases it is important to notice (what is in fact true in all cases of capital punishment) that *the temporal penalty does not necessarily correspond to an eternal one.* God alone knows what is going on in the souls of those who have some terrible twist in their nature. He has, we know, a special care for the weak and the needy, and we are told not to sit in judgment.[7] In such desperate cases as are here envisaged it was not likely to make for the poor lad's happiness (or for the happiness of those about him) that he should continue to live

[6] Dt. 21:18–21.   [7] Mt. 7:1.

and perhaps to propagate his kind. The wisdom of the ages is inclined to say, 'Whom the gods love die young.' Certainly in such a case as this, if death were to come 'naturally' we should all regard it as a merciful release. It is strange, and surely hardly logical, to regard it as inhumane when merciful release comes through the workings of a social code.

It may well be that this horrifying law was not intended to be invoked, except possibly in the most extreme circumstances. Few parents could bring themselves to initiate such a proceeding, though the elders might on rare occasions do so and consider it part of their duty to inquire publicly as to the parents' discipline of the child. As in the case of adultery, where the law stood as a witness to the sanctity of family life, so in this instance it stood as a witness to the sanctity of parental authority, even though it could scarcely be implemented in practice.

Diminished responsibility

It should perhaps be observed at this point that the Old Testament law makes no distinction between the crimes of the sane and the insane. In our day it is increasingly recognized that murderers are usually mentally sick and have diminished responsibility. It is then argued that they should therefore not be executed, but be committed to the care of psychiatrists. This sounds eminently fair and humane. But what is the result? Unless they resort to surgery (and forcibly alter a man's personality), the psychiatrists can usually do nothing. They can only provide – in a so-called hospital – imprisonment for (literally) life. The patients are certified as insane and they certainly cannot be safely allowed out in society, but they are seldom raving lunatics. They are in most respects normal people and may well be clear-headed, even deep-thinking and sensitive, people. They are capable of mental suffering.

Now according to the Bible the proper penalty for murder is death – death now, rather than at the natural end of life. In the biblical view murder is intrinsically a very grave crime, its guilt rests upon the land and its inhabitants. The blood of Abel cried to God from the ground, and the ground was accursed for his sake.[8] But though murder is a particularly grave crime,

[8] Dt. 19:19 f.; Gn. 4:10 f.

it is surely contrary to the whole thrust of the Bible to think that those who actually commit murder are necessarily exceptionally wicked. According to Christ, hatred is in principle murder; we are all Cains at heart; we are all Judases. When the final crisis came in the life of Jesus, it was the *ordinary* sins of *ordinary* people that combined together to crucify him – love of money, cowardice, lack of principle, fear of losing a job, love of power. The murderer is usually simply one who has been brought by the corporate sin of man (in heredity and environment) to a place of appalling temptation, and he has succumbed. That his life should be forfeit forthwith (rather than at the natural time of death) may be properly regarded as a decree not only of judgment but also of mercy. Murder is more than the land can bear, but it is also more than the mind and conscience of the murderer can rightly bear. By death the land is purged and by death the miseries of this sinful world are brought to an end for the murderer himself.

Such was the Old Testament way of doing things: swift death for grievous crimes. To us moderns it may seem crude and shocking and perhaps degrading. But was it, in all honesty, inhumane? It is difficult really to think so. Present-day attitudes to the death penalty certainly do not seem to be governed mainly by an assessment of the offender's likely sufferings. It is hard to find adequate rational grounds for its total rejection except on the basis of the quasi-religious belief that death is final and absolute and that to take a man's life is to rob him of all. But the Christian knows that death is not the end. To him sudden death is indeed a solemn prospect, yet to one who loves God it is not in itself something to be dreaded. To face death is to face a merciful Judge, knowing that, if a man repents of his sin, he may, with the penitent thief, have the certainty and joy of being with Christ in Paradise.

We may conclude this chapter with short studies on two more peripheral topics which have caused perplexity:

The offering of Isaac
Whether it was intended that the law concerning incorrigibility should be invoked or not, there is certainly one example of a

death called for with no intention that it should be carried out.

God told Abraham to offer up his son Isaac. Now God is God and man is man, and what a holy and wise God may do to one of his sinful creatures is not necessarily a criterion of what one sinner may do to a fellow-sinner. The reason is this. In any situation our knowledge of circumstances is literally infinitesimal, our actions are inter-penetrated with wrong motives and our estimate of their likely results quite unreliable. For one human being, therefore, to urge another human being to offer up his son in sacrifice would be hideous and disgusting. But for the all-knowing, all-loving God to ask one of his deeply taught servants to be prepared to make such an offering is a very different thing. Abraham was the friend of God, and his whole life was dominated by a divine call to a life of faith which was to issue in blessing to all mankind. The blessing was to be given through the seed of his son Isaac, who had been miraculously born to Sarah in their old age. Now God asks him to surrender the son upon whom his deepest affections were centred and in whom all the hopes of mankind lay. 'By faith Abraham, when he was tested, offered up Isaac, and he who had received the promises was ready to offer up his only son, of whom it was said, "Through Isaac shall your descendants be named." He considered that God was able to raise men even from the dead.'[9] It was in truth a supreme act of faith and obedience, but it had a predetermined happy outcome for Abraham and an inescapable lesson for all in after-generations who have had to face the issue of their willingness to surrender their most treasured hope to God. This story too abides as one of the most perfect pictures of the divine Father's giving of his only Son.

[9] Gn. 22; Heb. 11:17–19. It has been suggested that Abraham had brooded morbidly over the practice of child sacrifice in the contemporary world and had wondered whether he would be willing to do for the Lord what the heathen would do for their gods. It is not, however, at all certain that child sacrifice was a well-known practice in his day. Whether it was or not the Lord with one stroke raised Abraham's dedication to the highest possible point and then killed for ever the idea that he would accept a human sacrifice.

Cruelty to animals, damage to plant life

In somewhat lighter vein we may turn finally to a matter which has troubled some animal lovers. The Bible as a whole is most kindly towards animals, as is shown in C. W. Hume's little book: *The Status of Animals in the Christian Religion*:

> Neighbourliness towards animals was such a deeply rooted tradition among the Jews that it was taken for granted . . . In neither the Old nor the New Testament, therefore, is there to be found that contemptuous attitude towards subhuman creatures which went with the humanism of the Renaissance. If man's superior capacities confer on him a privileged position, privilege does not exempt him from responsibility: 'A righteous man regardeth the life of his beast, but the tender mercies of the wicked are cruel.' Man and the lower animals are thought of as constituting a single symbiotic community under God. 'Behold I establish my covenant with you, and with your seed after you, and with every living creature that is with you, of the fowl, of the cattle, and of every beast of the earth with you.' When Jonah, having prophesied that Nineveh should be destroyed within forty days, was sore because the city was to be spared after all, he was asked 'Should I not spare Nineveh, that great city, wherein are more than six score thousand persons that cannot discern between their right hand and their left hand, *and also much cattle*? In other words, he might at least have had a thought for the children and animals, even if he was going to be made look foolish. God's tender mercies are over all his works.[1]

It is therefore a shock to read of God's command to Joshua, after he had defeated the great northern confederacy under Jabin, king of Hazor, that he was not merely to burn their chariots, but that he was to hamstring their horses. If this means that the animals were to be lamed sufficiently to make them useless for battle, we might possibly see here an illustration of the restraint which was urged upon the Israelites in warfare. It will be remembered that they were allowed to eat anything they found on the trees, but they were never allowed to cut down trees used for food. They were allowed, even in the case of Ai, to spare the cattle.[2] In the case of horses they were allowed (if this interpretation is correct) to render the heavy arms of the army useless for a time, but they were not allowed

[1] C. W. Hume, *The Status of Animals in the Christian Religion* (London, 1956), pp. 4–7. Pr. 12:10; Gn. 9:9 f.; Jon. 4:11; Jos. 11:6.
[2] Dt. 20:19 ff.; Jos. 8:2.

to destroy the animals in such a way that they could never again propagate their kind. Alternatively, it might be that the horses, like the cattle, were not to be slaughtered immediately but could be kept for food – a valuable source of meat when there was no refrigeration. In fact, however, the true answer seems to be that the translators (who here follow the Septuagint translation) have misunderstood an obscure word, and that the horses were not to be hamstrung, but that the horses (along with the chariots) were to be destroyed.[3]

But plants and animals have not the absolute value of human beings made in the image of God. Even in the ministry of Christ pigs were drowned and a fig-tree withered in the course of his struggle for the souls of men. The battle with evil is a matter of infinite seriousness. What mere man dares presume to question our Lord's right to bring home his lessons in whatever way he wills? In his love and wisdom he may make himself known by words and deeds of compassion. In his love and wisdom he may, if he wills, teach lessons by the destruction of a herd of pigs or by the cursing of a fig-tree. Once grant that we need to learn that Christ has power over all the powers of hell, and that we need to learn the lessons of faith and divine judgment upon the impenitent – then who can question our Lord's right to teach his lessons this way? Both acts in fact made a deep impression on those who saw them.[4]

But in general the Bible shows restraint towards trees, and care for animals. This only throws into stronger relief the most burning of all Old Testament problems. Did God really order the extermination of whole populations?

[3] See M. A. Beek, 'The Chariots and the Horsemen of Israel', *The Witness of Tradition* (Leiden, 1972), pp. 8 f., who refers also to J. H. Kroeze, *Het Boek Jozua verklaard* (Kampen, 1968).
[4] Mt. 8:28–34; 21:18–22; Mk. 5:1–20; 11:12–25; Lk. 8:26–39. Equally God saw fit to use animal sacrifice as his principal means of teaching the significance of atonement.

8 THE ABOMINATIONS
OF THE HEATHEN

The examination of this subject will occupy a long chapter. It will be necessary to cover a good deal of preliminary ground before getting to grips with it. We must first examine the command to dispossess the Canaanites in the broader context of the whole struggle with heathenism. We must then gain an adequate idea of the weakness and perversity of the Israelite people. Only after that shall we be able to see the matter in perspective and face the difficulties at all satisfactorily.

THE STRUGGLE WITH HEATHENISM

If the Old Testament narratives are to be taken as a straightforward record of history, there is no room for doubt that God intended to 'clear away' the Canaanite peoples, and that he ordered their utter destruction when defeated in battle by Israel. Here are the crucial passages:

> 'When the Lord your God brings you into the land which you are entering to take possession of it, and clears away many nations before you, the Hittites, the Girgashites, the Amorites, the Canaanites, the Perizzites, the Hivites, and the Jebusites, seven nations greater and mightier than yourselves, and when the Lord your God gives them over to you, and you defeat them; then you must utterly destroy them; you shall make no covenant with them, and show no mercy to them. You shall not make marriages with them, giving your daughters to their sons or taking their daughters for your sons.

'For they would turn away your sons from following me, to serve other gods; then the anger of the Lord would be kindled against you, and he would destroy you quickly. But thus shall you deal with them: you shall break down their altars, and dash in pieces their pillars, and hew down their Asherim, and burn their graven images with fire.'

'In the cities of these peoples that the Lord your God gives you for an inheritance, you shall save alive nothing that breathes, but you shall utterly destroy them, the Hittites and the Amorites, the Canaanites and the Perizzites, the Hivites and the Jebusites, as the Lord your God has commanded; that they may not teach you to do according to all their abominable practices which they have done in the service of their gods, and so to sin against the Lord your God.'[1]

These directions are represented as the most solemn commands of God. If they are in fact so, we have a deep problem to grapple with. If on the other hand they are merely directions which Moses wrongly attributed to God, or if they are directions such as a later generation thought God ought to have given to Moses, there is no problem at all. It is simply a case of fallible man misrepresenting God – one more example of a religious man sincerely believing that by an evil act he was doing God a service.

If it is argued that we are not meant to take passages like this literally, but that we are to extract some word of God from them – say, the need for complete dedication to good and for implacable opposition to evil – then an end is put to all sane exegesis. The passage purports to be literal; to take it in any other way is to throw oneself into a bottomless pit of subjectivism. It is a species of allegorizing, which relieves the Bible of all offence while depriving it of all relevance. If the supposed commands are not history, then there is no problem. But neither is there hope of the Bible giving answers to the problems of history.

It is true that our Lord did not directly endorse this particular act of judgment, as he did the annihilation of Sodom and Gomorrah and the drowning of Noah's contemporaries, yet he

[1] Dt. 7:1–5; cf. Ex. 23:23 ff.; Dt. 20:16–18.

sets his seal on the book of Deuteronomy in a peculiarly clear way. Judging by the number of his quotations from it, it might be regarded as his favourite book.[2]

As C. H. Dodd has shown,[3] our Lord does not quote proof texts without regard for their context. He is conscious of the context within which a saying is set, having steeped his mind in whole passages of Scripture. When he has to face the great crisis of his temptation, he answers the Devil three times by quotations from Scripture. The verses quoted are Deuteronomy 6 : 13 and 16, and 8 : 3. *The first and fullest command to slaughter the Canaanites comes in chapter 7.* There is no room for doubt that our Lord regarded all three chapters as equally authoritative.

Endorsement of a more specific kind is to be found at a number of places in the New Testament, and it will be noted that, when the occupation of Canaan is referred to, it is thought of as a work of God, not as a product of the excessive zeal of man. Stephen speaks of 'the nations which God thrust out before our fathers'. Paul says, 'The God of this people Israel . . . when he had destroyed seven nations in the land of Canaan, he gave them their land as an inheritance.' The writer of the Epistle to the Hebrews speaks of the inhabitants of Canaan who perished as 'those who were disobedient'. Then

---

[2] It is notoriously difficult to produce simple statistics, because some quotations are found in more than one book (*e.g.*, several are in Exodus as well as Deuteronomy) and because opinions differ as to which constitutes a quotation. However, the following list of passages, which are regarded as quotations from Deuteronomy by D. A. Huck (*Synopse der Drei Ersten Evangelien*, 8th ed., Tübingen, 1931), gives a rough idea of the extent of its use by Christ.

Mt. 4:4		Lk. 4:4	Dt. 8:3
Mt. 4:7		Lk. 4:12	Dt. 6:16
Mt. 4:10		Lk. 4:8	Dt. 6:13
Mt. 5:31			Dt. 24:1
Mt. 5:33			Dt. 5:11; 23:22
Mt. 5:38			Dt. 19:21
Mt. 15:4			Dt. 5:16
Mt. 18:16		*cf.* Jn. 8:17	Dt. 19:15
Mt. 19:7	Mk. 10:4		Dt. 24:1, 3
Mt. 19:18, 19a	Mk. 10:19		Dt. 5:16–20; 24:14
Mt. 22:24	Mk. 12:19	Lk. 20:28	Dt. 25:5, 6
	Mk. 12:29		Dt. 6:4
Mt. 22:37	Mk. 12:30	Lk. 10:27	Dt. 6:5

[3] C. H. Dodd, *According to the Scriptures* (London, 1952).

by way of solemn warning he takes up the description of God as 'a consuming fire' which was used by Moses, first in warning to the Israelites as they prepared to enter the Promised Land, and then with specific reference to God's destruction of the Canaanites.[4] Unquestionably the New Testament view is to take the Old Testament at its face value. It accepts the view that the whole world was lost in sin, without God and without hope. Not only was there no true knowledge of God, but the most debasing features of society found their focus in false religion. Idolatry went hand in hand with the blunting or perverting of all the highest human instincts, and became synonymous with lust and cruelty and the withering even of the natural affections. God's purpose was to establish again a knowledge of himself in the earth. This involved the most relentless warfare with heathenism.

God's plan was to select a man, and train him to live a life of faith in a heathen world. Then from his descendants to make a nation, whose whole people he might train in the knowledge of himself. At the heart of this purpose was not only the chosen people, but the promised land. The Lord promised to his people a land that was inhabited by heathen nations. *He* gave it to them. That this was a fact of history was the most deeply rooted conviction of Old Testament religion, and it is embraced without question in the New.

The entry into Canaan was only one phase of a long story. As we trace the varying fortunes of the struggle with heathenism, we shall see that many of the well-known problems of the Old Testament fit into place as parts of a coherent whole. The training of the nation began in the bitter bondage of Egypt, which prepared the desperate Israelite people to listen to Moses as a leader. Egypt was itself permeated with heathen superstitions and dominated by powerful religious cults. The Exodus deliverance was rightly seen in the Old Testament as the overthrow of the gods of Egypt by the God of Israel. The New Testament similarly sees the destruction of the first-born and the drowning of the Egyptians as acts of God wrought for men of faith.[5] In his contest with Moses, Pharaoh was to be-

---

[4] Acts 7:45; 13:17 ff.; Heb. 11:31; 12:29; Dt. 4:24; 9:3.
[5] Ex. 12:12; Heb. 11:28, 29.

come the type of all those who persistently harden their hearts against the true God. In the early stages, he is said either to have had a hard heart, or to have made his heart hard; but there came a time (it would seem) when he had passed a point of no return. Those who continually harden their hearts reach a point when they become impervious to God's Word. God hardens their hearts, and punishments of warning give way to punishments of destruction.[6]

There may be remorse, as with Esau; there may be regret, as with Pharaoh; there may be pity for others, as with the rich man in the parable of Dives and Lazarus; but one of the results of the refusal to repent is a deepening disinclination to repent. It is in the same light that we should regard the reference to evil spirits and to lying spirits sent by God. Those who persistently wish to believe lies will be allowed to hear them and will in the end actually believe them to their own destruction. The penalty for love of error is belief of error. Those who suppress the truth will eventually be given up by God to the hideous results of their own sin.[7] It was part of God's far-reaching plan for mankind to use this stubborn Egyptian king as a demonstration of the impotence of idols and of his own saving might.

The remarkable deliverance of Israel was widely recognized among the heathen peoples as having been given by the Lord their God. But no sooner had the chosen nation left Egypt than its very existence was threatened by a dangerous enemy, the Amalekites. They were not a Canaanite people, but were of Edomite stock. They are described in one place as 'the first of the nations' and in another place as 'the sinners'. Amalek 'did not fear God', and attacked Israel at a time when they were nearly exhausted by the rigours of the journey.[8] The conduct

[6] Ex. 7:13, 14, 22; 8:15, 19, 32; 9:7, 12; 10:1, 20, 27; 11:10; 14:8. See also Is. 6:10–12; Mt. 13:14, 15; Jn. 12:37–40; Acts 28:25–28; Rom. 9:17, 18. In view of the change of language between Ex. 9:7 and 9:12 it seems reasonable to infer a change from voluntary to involuntary hardening at this stage. The promise that God would harden Pharaoh's heart, however, dates from before the time of Moses' encounter with Pharaoh (Ex. 4:21; 7:3). In any case the eventual divine hardening was envisaged from the beginning.

[7] Rom. 1:18–32.

[8] Jos. 2:9–11; Nu. 24:20; 1 Sa. 15:18; Ex. 17:8–15; Dt. 25:17–19.

of war in the Near East throughout most of the Old Testament
period was usually completely without mercy. 'The Annals of
the kings of Assyria have a constant refrain of towns destroyed,
dismantled or burnt, levelled as if by a hurricane, or reduced
to a heap of rubble. It was the usual custom also in biblical
wars, from a period of the Judges to the time of the Macca-
bees.'[9] There was seldom any idea of humanity towards a
defeated foe. The hope of the attacker was usually booty or
slaves, and it was considered natural to dispose of an enemy in
such a way that there could be no fear of reprisals.

An attack by the Amalekites, therefore, threatened the
extinction of Israel. If Amalek were defeated, the survivors
would be able to scatter to their well-known haunts and
strongholds in the Negeb. But if Israel were defeated, they
would have no homeland to retreat to. The escaping remnant,
robbed of their flocks and herds, could scarcely have survived
in that inhospitable wilderness. The battle swayed back and
forth while Moses held up his hands in earnest supplication for
the preservation of the people of God. In the end, Israel survived.

But God solemnly warned his people of the danger of this
godless nation and gave instructions that they should be treated
like the Canaanites. They were to be placed under a *ḥērem*, a
solemn ban. This meant that there were to be no slaves. All
human beings were to be killed and all objects of heathen
worship were to be utterly destroyed. In some cases, as with
Jericho or with Achan or with an apostate Israelite city, it
included also the destruction of their possessions, which meant
that there was to be no booty.[1] On several occasions in the
later history Israel did in fact suffer at the hands of the
Amalekites.[2] In the early days of the monarchy it was for disobedience in not fully applying the *ḥērem* that Saul was rejected
from kingship.

[9] R. de Vaux, *Ancient Israel* (London, 1961), p. 255. But, as we have seen,
Israel did not altogether follow this custom. At a later date Christianity,
though totally unsuccessful in abolishing war, also succeeded in introduc-
ing into it elements of chivalry and codes of humane conduct.
[1] Jos. 6:18–24; 7:24, 25; Dt. 13:12–18.
[2] Nu. 14:45; Jdg. 3:13; 6:3; 7:12; 1 Sa. 15. There is also perhaps a hint
that the Amalekites were unusually cruel (1 Sa. 15:33).

It is thus in the context of the whole struggle with heathenism that we are to see this terrible call to drive out the heathen nations. It is the story of a group of people, few in number[3] and almost unbelievably weak and fickle in their spiritual loyalties, battling against mighty forces which were degrading, seductive and ruthless. For centuries on end the very survival of the cause of true religion seemed to hang on a thread. Heathenism is degrading at the best of times, but there is reason to think that the spiritual condition of the peoples in and around Canaan at the time of the Israelite occupation was one of particular filth. Some generations earlier Abraham had been told that his descendants, after a period of slavery, would come back to Canaan 'in the fourth generation; for the iniquity of the Amorites is not yet complete'.[4] It is the normal pattern of cultures that they grow strong in the early days of vigour and self-discipline, they hold their own with varying fortune for a time, and then they decline as a result of their own inner corruption. Or, to put it more biblically, when iniquity reaches a certain point, judgment begins. 'The Amorites' here seems to be used loosely for the Canaanite peoples as a whole, and the implication is that at the time of the Israelite return to the country, the state of these peoples would be ripe for judgment.

It is difficult from the dry reports of the archaeologists to form any adequate human picture of the nature of the heathen cults. In view of the fact that the Israelite invasion did not lead to their eradication, much useful information as to their nature can be gleaned from the later periods of the history. The Old Testament directs its bitterest venom against Baalism and the cult of Molech. Baalism was a fertility cult, in which sexual licence was glorified as something religious and meritorious. There were 'holy' prostitutes, male and female, for the gratification of the worshippers. Bright describes it in these terms: 'Canaanite religion presents us with no pretty picture . . . numerous debasing practices, including sacred prostitution, homosexuality, and various orgiastic rites, were prevalent.'[5]

[3] Reasons for estimating the fighting force at about 18,000 men may be seen in the author's 'Large Numbers in the Old Testament', *Tyndale Bulletin* 18 (1967), pp. 19 ff. This article has been separately reprinted.
[4] Gn. 15:16.
[5] J. Bright, *A History of Israel* (London, 1960), pp. 108 f.

G. E. Wright notes the element of cruelty in Canaanite mythology. Anath, wife of Baal, loved war, and one of her adventures is described in a poem.

> Deciding on a massacre, she smote and slew from seacoast (west) to sunrise. Filling her temple with men she barred the doors and hurled at them chairs, tables and footstools. Soon she waded in blood up to her knees – nay, up to her neck. 'Her liver swelled with laughter; her heart was full of joy.' She then washed her hands in gore and proceeded to other occupations.

Wright then goes on to remark:

> The amazing thing about the gods, as they were conceived in Canaan, is that they had no moral character whatsoever. In fact, their conduct was on a much lower level than that of society as a whole, if we can judge from ancient codes of law. Certainly the brutality of the mythology is far worse than anything else in the Near East at that time. Worship of these gods carried with it some of the most demoralizing practices then in existence. Among them were child sacrifice, a practice long since discarded in Egypt and Babylonia, sacred prostitution, and snake-worship on a scale unknown among other peoples.

Looking at another aspect of contemporary life he says:

> When we examine the world of polytheism more closely, we find beneath the surface a vast, dark uncomfortable world, comparable in its complexity to those depths of unconscious life laid bare by modern psychoanalysis. That is the world of demons, magic, and divination. [6]

It requires the disciplined skill of a historical novelist to convey to the imagination what such practices involve. Sholem Asch has used his skill to portray a Molech sacrifice in an imagined visit of our Lord to Tyre before the beginning of his ministry.[7] Molech sacrifices were offered especially in connection with vows and solemn promises, and children were sacrificed as the harshest and most binding pledge of the sanctity of a promise. Even Greek writers were disgusted with this Phoenician practice, which became a prominent part of

---

[6] G. E. Wright and F. V. Filson, *The Westminster Historical Atlas to the Bible* (London, 1945), p. 36. G. E. Wright, *The Old Testament against its Environment* (London, 1950), p. 78.
[7] Sholem Asch, *The Nazarene* (London, 1939), pp. 347 ff. See also C. F. Pfeiffer, *The Patriarchal Age* (Michigan, 1961), chapter 9.

the religion of Carthage, and might well have overspread the world had Hannibal won the day in Italy. Sholem Asch portrays the hideous fascination of the rite, with its combination of solemnity and spectacle, of excitement and horror, or merry-making and obscenity, in which, as its central act, a young lad (no baby) is thrown into the red-hot arms of the god.[8] Such practices could only prove a cancer in the life of any society, bringing a legacy of callousness and viciousness and fear, yet exercising a fascination which such a people's debased moral sense could not resist. A society nurtured in unwholesome excitement does not know how to live without it. It is not surprising that the Valley of Hinnom (Ge-henna), where Molech worship was practised in the days of Manasseh, should have provided the Jewish image of hell.[9]

These heathen practices were not only degrading and seductive, they were often backed by ruthless power. The popular picture of the priests of Baal as ignorant dervishes serving some primitive and insignificant cult can be shattered by the sight of a single photograph. The archaeologist normally has to be content with buried ruins, from which an idea of the original buildings can be reconstructed only by laborious processes of deduction. But at Palmyra it is possible to this day to see the remains of a Baal temple, its glorious columns rising 68 feet in the air, beautiful in proportions and beautiful in design. Although, of course, its relation to the Baalim of Canaan cannot be determined with great precision, yet merely to see this temple is to open the imagination to the sort of thing that Elijah was up against. Here was a religion exceedingly

[8] A late Bronze Age temple at Amman of 1400–1250 BC provides the best proof to date of child sacrifices in this area. J. B. Hennessey ('Excavation of a Late Bronze Age Temple at Amman' (*Palestine Exploration Quarterly* (1966), p. 162) writes: 'Two outstanding features associated with the use of the temple were the enormous quantities of animal, bird and human bones and the abundant evidence of fire . . . There can be little doubt that the temple was associated with a fire cult. It had a comparatively short life. The initial foundation probably dates just before 1400 BC. The latest material would suggest that the building went out of use sometime during the thirteenth century BC.' In a private communication to G. J. Wenham he wrote: 'At least 75% of them (the bones) belong to children between the ages of 3 and 14, or thereabouts.'

[9] 2 Ch. 33:6; *cf*. Lk. 12:5, *etc*.

attractive to the sensual nature of fallen man, unlike the austere simplicity and severe morality of the Mosaic religion. Here was a religion which won the devotion of the mightiest in the land, and was popular with the common people. Ahab, with his ivory palace and his 2,000 chariots, and Jezebel, daughter of the priest-king of Tyre and Sidon, were immensely wealthy, and she at least was utterly ruthless, thinking nothing of compelling the people of Jezreel to commit perjury to effect the murder of Naboth. She introduced 850 prophets. The true prophets were slain, the altars of the Lord were broken down, a remnant of faithful prophets were driven into hiding and Elijah had to flee for his life. When Elijah lay down and asked that he might die, he felt that even the revelation of divine power on Mount Carmel had not only failed to check Jezebel's schemes, but had goaded her into fresh zeal. He felt helpless against the might of a pitiless totalitarian regime. The struggle went on in the reign of Ahab's successor, Ahaziah. Elijah boldly rebuked him for turning to a Philistine Baal. The king sent soldiers to capture Elijah, but on two successive occasions 'the fire of God came down from heaven and consumed them', and Elijah escaped with his life.[1] It was at a moment when the cause of true religion was in dire peril that God repeatedly and dramatically intervened to vindicate his prophet.

The famous tale of Elisha and the she-bears is a sequel to the same story. Elisha has sometimes been pictured as a savage old man, who, because he could not take an innocent joke about his baldness, roundly cursed a number of little children, in response to which God sent two she-bears who killed no fewer than forty-two of them. On almost every count this is a misrepresentation. Elisha was not old; he was in fact a very young man just starting out on his ministry which was to last nearly sixty years. He certainly was not savage, as may be seen from the way in which he intervened to spare the Syrian army.[2] 'Go up' was presumably said in mockery of the reported ascension of Elijah – a sneering request for a repeat performance. The precise connotation of 'baldhead' is not clear,

---

[1] 2 Ki. 1 and see D. J. Wiseman, 'Ahab', *The New Bible Dictionary* (London, 1962), p. 20.
[2] 2 Ki. 2:23 f.; 6:1–23.

ɔyish rudeness. Some take it to
which case it was direct ridicule
ule not merely of Elijah and
mouthpiece they claimed to be.
g to do with physical baldness
usually cover their heads), but
that it was a highly offensive current epithet. 'Little children'
(AV) is certainly misleading. The Hebrew $n^{e'}ārîm\ q^{e}tannîm$
could be 'small boys' (RSV, NEB), though the Revised Version
marginal translation 'young lads' seems to fit the context
better.[3] Seeing there were forty-two of them hurt by the bears
(and one would imagine that many more got away unharmed
than were hurt), it was evidently a great mob of young roughs
deliberately organized for the occasion. To muster so many
from a small town they would presumably have ranged from
grown-up lads to small boys, with the lads in the lead and the
small boys gleefully chanting after them. The text does not say
that any of them were killed. 'Tearing' implies severe wounds.
Whether any of them were fatal or not, we do not know.

In truth Elisha was somewhat like a diffident ministerial
student straight from college, newly ordained and quite un-
tried, left alone in a hostile world. Elijah was gone, but Jezebel
was still very much present. Elisha was called to put his
vocation to the test. He set out from the Jordan Valley for the
Northern Kingdom, where his master's enemy still held sway,

---

[3] In this passage they are in fact called $n^{e'}ārîm\ q^{e}tannîm$ and also $y^{e}lādîm$. The
(singular) words $na'ar$ and $yeled$ both have a wide range of meanings. Both
are used of Moses aged three months (Ex. 2:6).

$na'ar$ is used most often for 'youths', sometimes for professional soldiers
(R. de Vaux, *Ancient Israel*, pp. 220 f.). $na'ar$ is used of Ishmael at the age
of 14 and of Joseph at 17 (Gn. 21:12; 37:2). The addition of $qāṭōn$ ('small'
or 'young') does not seem to make for much greater precision. When
Samuel went to anoint David, he and his older brothers are all $n^{e'}ārîm$ and
David is the 'young' $na'ar$ (1 Sa. 16:11), although he had already served for
a time as an armour-bearer. (It is hoped to discuss 1 Samuel 15-18, which
includes Saul's supposed failure to recognize his former armour-bearer, in a
later publication.) Solomon in the humility of prayer speaks of himself as a
'young' $na'ar$ (1 Ki. 3:7). Naaman's flesh after washing was like the flesh of a
'young' $na'ar$ (2 Ki. 5:14).

$yeled$ ranges from baby Moses to the contemporaries of Rehoboam at the
time of his accession when he was 41 years old (1 Ki. 12:8; 14:21). The
meaning of both expressions must therefore be determined by the demands
of the context.

doubtless with fear and foreboding in his heart, yet determined openly to maintain a witness for the Lord. A prospect which daunted the old warrior Elijah would certainly daunt this young and gentle man. He chose Bethel as his starting-point, the town which was notorious as the centre where Jeroboam had set up the idolatrous calf at the time when Israel in the North broke away from Judah in the South. When he arrived, weary in body as well as in heart, after the long 3,000-ft ascent out of the Rift Valley up to the mountain ridge, he had an unpleasant surprise. His coming had been reported, and a hot reception had been arranged. The lads, prompted no doubt by their elders, who had no use for Elijah, Elisha or anything they stood for, sallied forth in truculent mood to let him know the kind of welcome that Bethel was preparing for him. In those days life was cheap, and Elisha's life was in grave danger; and, with the possibility of Elisha's elimination from the struggle, it was a critical point in the history of mankind – for it meant that *the whole cause of true religion was threatened with extinction.* What was Elisha to do? Just as the apostle Paul pronounced a curse on those who preached a false gospel, just as our Lord bade his disciples solemnly to shake off the dust from their feet against those who would not receive his teaching, so Elisha solemnly cursed these boys. He did not pray for angry she-bears, but God saw fit to respond in this particular way in order that they should learn, even by painful means, that it is dangerous folly to defy God and his Word.

The difference between the curse of Elisha and that of the apostles is that in his case retribution came immediately, whereas in theirs retribution was promised for the day of judgment. 'If any one will not receive you or listen to your words, shake off the dust from your feet as you leave that house or town. Truly, I say to you, it shall be more tolerable on the day of judgment for the land of Sodom and Gomorrah than for that town.' Our Lord said that on the day of judgment it would be himself who would address those on his left hand as 'You cursed'. But in the case of Elisha, as in the case of Elymas the magician who was struck with blindness, the need was for an immediate lesson.[4]

[4] Mt. 10: 14, 15; *cf.* Mk. 6:11; Lk. 9:5; 10:11; Acts 13:51; Mt. 25:41; Acts 13:11.

No doubt the story of the she-bears was rapidly passed from mouth to mouth throughout the Northern Kingdom, for Elisha proceeded with his long ministry unmolested, never again (as far as we know) having to be the agent of an act of judgment. As far as Jezebel was concerned, the lesson was pressed home still further, for she met her deserved end at the hands of the evil man Jehu, in literal fulfilment of the grim prophecy of Elijah, who had foretold that as a reward for the murder of Naboth: 'The dogs shall eat Jezebel within the bounds of Jezreel.'[5]

It was in such times and in such ways that God raised up and preserved the line of prophets, who were to lead the battle against heathenism. The struggle was to be continued by Amos, Hosea, Isaiah, Jeremiah and others right into the days of the Babylonian captivity and beyond. But for the initial establishment of this 'goodly fellowship of the prophets' God saw fit to show his hand in special ways.

THE SPIRITUAL WEAKNESS OF ISRAEL

The heathenism from which Israel emerged and against which it had to struggle bore all the characteristics of its author. Just as Satan may at one time appear as a roaring lion to terrify the saints, and at another as an angel of light to deceive them, so his false religions possessed the same qualities – now towering above them in pitiless might, now enticing them with entrancing seductiveness. Over against the might of heathen idolatry the Bible is at pains to set with chilling candour the starkness of Israel's physical and moral weakness. The patriarchs learn the life of faith only because they are taken bodily out of the city life of Ur and Haran, and are made to live a self-contained nomadic existence, separated from their heathen neighbours. Lot, when he gets involved in city life, is soon in trouble.

The Israelites in Egypt evidently quickly lost the sense of divine call which had so powerfully moved Abraham, Isaac and Jacob. It required the agonies of slavery to bring them to the point where they would follow Moses. In spite of the spectacular deliverance which brought them out of Egypt, the

[5] I Ki. 21:23; 2 Ki. 9:30–37.

people as a whole seem never truly to have embraced his teachings in their hearts or in their minds. Throughout they were a 'stiff-necked people', stubborn and rebellious. It is one long story of trouble. Though Moses himself had a penetrating understanding of the truths he taught, the people seem to have understood little. They grumbled at the hardships and hankered for Egypt again. When Moses' back was turned, even Aaron was prevailed upon to make them a golden calf to worship. Under Korah, Dathan and Abiram, Moses had to face a dangerous rebellion.

There is a strange silence concerning the period of some thirty-eight years when apparently the Israelite headquarters was established at Kadesh Barnea.[6] Of the period between the return of the spies with their discouraging reports of the land and the final departure from Kadesh, we know very little. It seems as though it was necessary for a whole generation to die off before Moses could start again in earnest in an attempt to weld the people into a God-fearing nation. He appears to have had little hold over them. The law was more honoured in the breach than in the observance. Circumcision was not practised; not only were the sacrifices not faithfully observed, but heathen images were made for worship. It is likely enough that the tribes went their separate ways to forage for a subsistence in the inhospitable wilderness. When at last Moses led them forward once more, they quickly fell a prey to the attractions of Baal worship on Mount Peor. Moses, acting under God's orders, exercised the full rigour of his authority and dictated that all who had 'yoked themselves to Baal' be forthwith publicly hanged. At the same time a devastating plague, which was recognized as a token of divine wrath, struck the camp.[7]

Such was the background of human frailty against which the uncompromising commands of Deuteronomy were delivered not long after in the plains of Moab. It was clear beyond all

[6] Nu. 20:1; 33:36.
[7] Jos. 5:5; Am. 5:25 f.; Acts 7:42 f.; Nu. 25. It has been conjectured that part of the reason for the severity of the treatment of the Canaanites may have been physical. A society riddled with disease, having itself built up a strong resistance, may be catastrophically dangerous to an immigrant population. H. Zinsser, *Rats, Lice and History* (New York, 1960), gives numerous startling examples of this. Be this as it may, the primary reason or avoiding contamination is clearly spiritual.

possibility of doubt to one who knew the spiritual state of the people of Israel, that, if they were to live cheek by jowl with the heathen, they would be incapable of maintaining their beliefs and standards. And so it proved. There was an outward allegiance to the Lord under Joshua's leadership, and Joshua himself faithfully carried out the command to destroy the inhabitants of the captured cities, but Joshua was well aware of the shallowness of his people's loyalty. There were those who still served Akkadian gods, and there were those who were inclining towards Canaanite deities,[8] and it was necessary for Joshua to issue a direct challenge before he died, as to whether they would serve the Lord or not. When Joshua's generation had died, the rot set in. The period of the judges was a time of idolatry, anarchy and disintegration; it was a time of spiritual darkness relieved only for brief periods when some leader, often with only the crudest faith, rose to challenge Israel's oppressors in the name of Israel's God.

It was not till the days of Samuel that there appeared some hope of a turn for the better. There was a revival of national consciousness and a desire for national unity, which led to the establishment of the monarchy. *With this revival there came reminders of the uncompromising nature of the Lord's demands.* Thus Saul was rejected for ignoring Samuel's call for a complete break with Baalism and for failing to 'blot out the remembrance of Amalek from under heaven'.[9] There were instances of dis-

---

[8] Jos. 24:14, 15.

[9] 1 Sa. 7:3; Dt. 25:19; 1 Sa. 15:23; 28:18. The grisly account tells us that 'Samuel hewed Agag in pieces before the Lord' (1 Sa. 15:33). The word translated 'hewed in pieces' is obscure. There is certainly no need to suppose that he was tortured before being killed. Nonetheless it seems at first sight a very unpleasant incident. It comes as a salutary shock, therefore, to find at the central point of the narrative the substance of an Old Testament quotation which our Lord used more than once. The whole passage is concerned with Saul's attitude of heart towards God, and is summarized in the saying: 'To obey is better than sacrifice' (1 Sa. 15:22). This in turn is taken up by Hosea (6:6) and reproduced in the form: 'I desire mercy, and not sacrifice' (RV). The Hebrew word *hesed*, translated 'mercy', is a rich Old Testament term with a range of meanings including 'solidarity', 'devotion', 'loyalty', 'steadfast love', 'kindness', 'grace'. In the context it is clear that by 'mercy' Hosea meant 'loyal devotion', which manifests itself in separation from false gods and obedience to the Lord from the heart. Our Lord takes up the quotation of Hosea and applies it to situations where a right attitude of heart is contrasted with merely formal correctness (Mt. 9:13;

obedience being met by sudden death. With the recovery of the ark from the Philistines, some of the inhabitants of Beth-shemesh presumed to look inside the ark, and seventy of them died at God's hand. An Israelite, named Uzzah, presumably intending to be helpful, put out his hand to steady the ark and was struck dead – for disobeying God-given regulations. David, who witnessed the event, was first angry and then afraid.[1]

It is clear from the account in 1 Chronicles that the whole incident deeply impressed David with the need for obedience to God's commands. We are not told the full circumstances, but we know enough to get a good idea of the real significance of the event. It was a critical moment in the training of the Israelite nation. National observance of the law of Moses had been virtually impossible and had almost disappeared during the time of the judges. Now, under David, was the chance to begin again. As so often in the formative stages of the history of the chosen people, God accompanied the new beginning with a sharp warning. The Mosaic regulations were elaborately framed to emphasize the yawning gulf between a holy God and an unholy people. The ark was to stand in the holy of holies, where God's presence was manifested. The holy of holies was to be entered only once a year, by a high priest specially set apart, after special sacrifices and purifications. If ever the ark had to be moved, it was never to be touched or looked upon by any but the priests on pain of death, but was to be fitted with shafts and carefully covered over. Then it was to be carried on the shoulders, not of ordinary Israelites, but of Levites.[2]

Now David knew much of the joy of communion with God, but he evidently had a very imperfect realization of his holiness, and when it came to the re-establishment of the Mosaic order he ignored the God-given way. Not long before Israel had tried to use the ark in a magical way. Magic tries to manipulate supernatural powers, whereas true piety puts itself

---

12:7). This is not of course a direct endorsement of 1 Sa. 15 by our Lord, but he must have been fully aware of this memorable passage when he adopted the saying for his own use.

[1] 1 Sa. 6:19; 2 Sa. 6:6–9; 1 Ch. 13:5–14.

[2] Nu. 4:5, 15, 19, 20.

into the hands of God to be used according to his will. The Israelites had brought the ark into the battle in order to make use of God for their own ends. God's response was to allow them to be defeated by the heathen Philistines and the ark to be captured. But the lesson of obedience had not been learnt. Uzzah was presumably a Levite, but neither he nor David had given serious attention to the injunctions of the divine law. Instead they copied the example of the Philistines and put the ark upon a new cart. Not unjustly (since Uzzah had infringed a divine regulation, and since, in any case, all men, being transgressors of God's law, deserve to die and are heading for death), yet unexpectedly, God strikes Uzzah down. There is no suggestion that this meant eternal death and Uzzah himself had no suffering, yet it was a shocking thing to those who saw it or heard about it and a terrible thing for his family. David and the whole nation spent three months in digesting the lesson. When the ark was finally brought to Jerusalem, it was carried on the shoulders of the Levites, and sacrifices were offered.[3] At least some dent had been made in Israel's perennial disregard for God's law.

The intensity of David's devotion to the Lord had raised the spiritual life of the people to a new high-water mark, but, in spite of a promising start, Solomon threw away all that had been gained. 'He loved many foreign women', and 'his wives turned away his heart after other gods'.[4] The heathen abominations came back in a flood. After his death the kingdom was divided, and Jeroboam established the idolatrous centres of worship at Dan and Bethel, to keep his people from visiting Jerusalem.

Century after century the struggle went on, with a persecuted minority battling against the incorrigible perversity of the mass of the people. It required the Babylonian captivity to work a decisive and lasting change of outlook. But even when they had returned from captivity the struggle was by no means over, though they had at least come to a national recognition of the Lord as the one true God and to a national repudiation of idolatry. No-one can pretend that the spiritual life of Jewry

[3] 1 Sa. 4; 6:7 f.; 1 Ch. 15:11–28.
[4] 1 Ki. 11:1–8.

was even then at a very high level. It had taken the best part
of a thousand years of failure and suffering to teach the people
of Moses to heed the *Shema*; 'Hear, O Israel, the Lord your
God is one Lord.' Such was the rate of learning of those who
thought that they could safely fraternize with their Canaanite
neighbours.

THE REALITY OF TEMPORAL JUDGMENT

It is worth looking again at the precise terms of the commands
given regarding the Canaanites. The primary concern
throughout is the total ejection of their evil religions from the
land. God is going to clear away the seven nations. Israel must
make no covenant with them and show no mercy to them. In
particular, they are not to marry with them, for this will turn
them away to serve other gods. The Baal altars and pillars and
the Asherim are to be totally destroyed. God keeps covenant
with those who love him, and requites to their face those who
hate him, by destroying them. 'Not because of your righteousness or the uprightness of your heart are you going in to possess
their land; but because of the wickedness of these nations the
Lord your God is driving them out.'[5] It is to be noted that
these commands are to be thought of, not primarily in terms of
one nation against another, but in terms of those who love
God against those who hate him. As in the days before the
Flood and before the destruction of Sodom there was a way of
escape for those who sought the true God, so now there is room
within the company of Israel for those who are not Israelites by
race. There are the noteworthy examples of Rahab (who by
faith gave friendly welcome to the spies) and Ruth the
Moabitess, who were both ancestresses of Jesus. There was the
'mixed multitude' who came out of Egypt with the Israelites.
There was Hobab, the son of the priest of Midian, who was
invited to join the Israelites.[6] Job, who dwelt in the land of
Uz, was regarded as an example of blameless piety. In the very
context which we are discussing, special injunctions are given
for the care of the sojourner. He is to observe the same laws,
and he is to be received in love as one of themselves: 'The

[5] Dt. 7:1–11; 9:5.
[6] Heb. 11:31; Ex. 12:38; Nu. 11:4; 10:29–33.

stranger who sojourns with you shall be to you as the native among you, and you shall love him as yourself.'[7] There is certainly no obstacle to the individual repentance of a Canaanite, nor even presumably to migration, since the conquest was to be little by little. The one indispensable requisite is that the centres of idolatry must be eradicated from the Promised Land, and the people are to be taught to 'utterly detest and abhor' their abominations. Against the Edomites, Moabites, Ammonites and other more distant nations there was to be no such policy of extermination.[8]

Christians would find no great difficulty with the overthrow of the Canaanites had it taken place at the hands of their heathen neighbours. It is a commonplace of history that civilizations grow weak through their inner corruptions, and it is part of the continuing providence of God that such should be swept away. It is a judgment of God which is readily understood and accepted. It is no more than the desert of those who have become slaves of evil practices. There is possibly a hint that this process was at work in Canaan. The Israelites were told concerning the Canaanites, 'The Lord your God will send hornets among them . . . and throw them into great confusion, until they are destroyed.' J. Garstang believed that 'the hornet' was the Egyptian Empire, which first of all dominated and disarmed the area, and then left the nations unprotected.[9] Be that as it may, part of the judgment at least was in this case put into the hands of God's people. It was not left to godless nations to destroy each other under the silent, over-ruling permission of God. It was a direct injunction of God to one relatively God-fearing nation to drive out seven particularly evil nations.

The distinction between the permissive will of God and the expressed will of God is important, but it cannot rightly be used to cut all the knots in the mysteries of providence. Israel suffered what she deserved when the Lord permitted the haughty Assyrians to act unwittingly as 'the rod of my anger'

[7] Dt. 10:18, 19; Ex. 20:10; Lv. 24:16, 22; 19:34.
[8] Ex. 23:30; Dt. 7:26; 2:5, 9, 19; 20:10.
[9] Dt. 7:20–23; *cf.* Ex. 23:28; Jos. 24:12. J. Garstang, *Joshua-Judges* (London, 1931), pp. 112 ff., 258 ff.

against her.[1] It would have been perfectly just if God had expressly directed some nation wittingly to wield the rod of chastisement against her. Just as it is a moral, if singularly unpleasant, calling to be a state executioner, so it could be a moral, though very unpleasant, duty for one nation to inflict God's chastisement upon another. Everything turns upon the reality and certainty of the divine calling to do the deed. If we are to believe the records of the Pentateuch, the command given through Moses was inescapably clear in itself, and the credentials of Moses were demonstrated repeatedly and with immense force. The only question which remains is the probable effect on Israel of carrying out such a command. The hangman's job might have a most undesirable effect on a morbid or sadistic nature. Would Israel suffer morally, in the execution of such a duty? The answer must surely depend on the spirit in which it was carried out. If it was done for material gain or in love of cruelty, the results would be appalling. If it was done with an intense realization of the holiness of God, and of the horror both of their own sins and of those of their enemies, it could serve as an indelible lesson.

That this was the spirit enjoined by God is emphasized again and again. The judgment was upon sin, not upon enemy nations as such. If one is tempted to suspect that the Old Testament merely rationalized Israel's need for living space, it is well to remember that in fact God kept his people waiting for 400 years till the time for judgment on Canaan was ripe and that (when completely helpless) he rescued them from slavery. Their occupation of the land was no matter for nationalistic pride, it was the Lord's doing. And the Lord's commands were every bit as severe with regard to erring Israelites as they were to the Canaanites. When Achan sought material profit from the conquest of Jericho, he and his family and his animals and his tent and his ill-gotten gains were all stoned and burnt.[2] The inclusion of women and children in such judgments is sometimes regarded as the refinement of cruelty. Yet, not only is the family principle itself biblical, but in this case it might also have proved practical and humane. As far as the heathen were concerned, the danger from female devotees of Baal (as was

[1] Is. 10:5.   [2] Jos. 7.

evidenced by the daughters of Moab on the threshold of the Promised Land[3] and later by Jezebel) was quite as great as that from the men; and what sort of society would it be for either the women or the children, if (as would have been almost inevitable) they were reduced to the status of foreign slaves and were left with no menfolk of their own nationality to give them support?

The stoning of Achan was no isolated case. The death penalty, as we have seen, was prescribed for a whole series of sins: Molech worship, spiritualism, adultery, sex relations within the prohibited degrees, homosexual acts. Anyone who tried to entice Israel to follow other gods was to be stoned; any city that was drawn away by such teaching was to be utterly destroyed, with all its inhabitants and all its spoil. It was to be offered as a whole burnt-offering to the Lord, and never to be rebuilt. A man found gathering sticks on the sabbath was stoned, as was also one who blasphemed the name of the Lord. Not only were the laws severe, but God's own treatment of his people when they disobeyed was relentless in its severity, as the whole book of Judges bears witness. 'They forsook the Lord, and served the Baals and the Ashtaroth. So the anger of the Lord was kindled against Israel, and he gave them over to plunderers, who plundered them; and he sold them into the power of their enemies round about, so that they could no longer withstand their enemies. Whenever they marched out, the hand of the Lord was against them for evil, as the Lord had warned, and as the Lord had sworn to them; and they were in sore straits.'[4]

It would be hard to conceive of any system better calculated to bring home the limitless chasm which separates the worship of the true God and the worship of an evil being excogitated from the minds of sinful men. Israel was taught that it is the difference between life and death – between finding one's true end and missing it, the difference (as we should say) between heaven and hell. Such gods are no gods, but deluders and debasers of their worshippers. A lost world, without God and without hope, desperately needed the true God. But how could the world learn till Israel had first learnt? God's dealings are

[3] Nu. 25.   [4] Dt. 13; Nu. 15:36; Lv. 24:10–23; Jdg. 2:13–15.

terrible. But is there any reason to think that Israel could have
learnt her lessons with *less* severe treatment? Indeed, when we
view God's providential treatment of the world as a whole, is
there any reason to think that mankind generally could have
learnt its lessons better with less severe judgments?

Put this way, the credibility of the whole Old Testament
scheme of things takes on a different light.

Yet the nagging doubt keeps returning. Can so dreadful a
plan really be right? Is there a flaw in the reasoning some-
where?

When analysed, this doubt seems to resolve itself into four
questions. 1. Can we really square this teaching with that of
Christ? 2. Can we really be sure that it was a command of
God and not simply a shrewdly calculated policy of Moses?
3. Could not such teaching be used as an argument for the
propagation of the faith today by means of the sword? 4. Could
it not be used as an argument for harshness in society and ruthlessness in war-making by the modern state?

But to bring these doubts out into the open is largely to
answer them. As we have already seen, our Lord does not
minimize the severity of God's judgment; he underlines it. He
does not repudiate the idea of material force, saying of the
Flood in Noah's day which 'swept them all away', 'So will be
the coming of the Son of man'; and of those who are not ready
at his coming that they will be sent where men 'weep and
gnash their teeth'. He does not question the judgment on the
people of Sodom, when 'fire and sulphur rained from heaven
and destroyed them all'; to him it is a warning which we are to
remember.[5] There may be difficulty in squaring the teaching
of Deuteronomy with that of some Jesus of modern invention.
But as far as the Jesus of the Gospels is concerned, there is an
inescapable and indeed a fearful consistency between them, for
(as we have seen) the judgments of hell as portrayed by Jesus
are more terrible even than the judgments of Deuteronomy.

Nagging doubts about the historicity of the records can be
laid to rest only by much careful, prayerful and honest thought,
culminating in a decision. Careful thought must be given to the
question, 'Has the history of the Old Testament been proved

[5] Mt. 24:37–51; Lk. 17:26–32.

to be inaccurate?' It is not of course possible to prove the Old Testament to be historically accurate throughout (only a small proportion of generally accepted conclusions concerning ancient history are demonstratively proved). Belief in the entire truth of the Old Testament can be derived only from a belief in revelation and inspiration. The student who wishes honestly to face the challenge of modern biblical criticism must ask the negative question, 'Is the Bible's *in*accuracy proved beyond reasonable doubt?' *When anti-supernatural presuppositions are laid aside*, it is our conviction that close examination of the facts does not create even a presumptive case against the Bible, certainly not a demonstrative one. There is no *proof* either way.[6] When this is realized, a stage has been reached where the decision has to be made whether or not to trust Christ as a teacher. When the die is cast the results are inevitable. Christ accepted the history of the Old Testament and Christ loved the book of Deuteronomy. Doubts will be laid to rest in proportion to our ability to trust him.

Perhaps the horror of the misuse of these scriptures causes the most persistent uneasiness. They have been misused in the past, and they may be misused again. But this objection, though very searching, is not really valid. Of course the Devil can cite Scripture for his purpose. He did so during our Lord's temptation,[7] and he has done so all down the history of the church. 'Cursed be every one who hangs on a tree' must have been a goad in the mind of Saul the persecutor, as he thought of the Christian's belief in a crucified Messiah. Thinking to make himself a eunuch for the kingdom of God's sake, Origen is said to have castrated himself. Christians have persecuted unbelievers into the church, because our Lord said 'Compel them to come in'. The great churches and the little sects have all erred. Every heresy and every malpractice have their text. People will sit in filth for a lifetime on the tops of poles, they will climb mountains to await the Second Coming, they will indulge in wild orgies, they will set up fanatical common-wealths, they will smell out innocent people and burn them as

[6] The author has a book in preparation on the historicity of the Old Testament.

[7] Ps. 91:11, 12; Mt. 4:6; Lk. 4:10, 11.

witches or heretics, they will argue the flatness of the earth – every kind of wickedness and folly will seek to justify itself from Scripture. Yet this is no argument against the truth of Scripture, nor against its entire wholesomeness when rightly understood.

It is part of God's training for his church that she should learn in love and humility to know his mind from the Scriptures. It is part of his training also that she should at times be allowed, through pride and malice, to taste the bitterness of the misinterpretation of her holy book. It is clear enough that the training of Israel in the Old Testament and the evangelization of the world in the New are two totally different things. Israel was to be established as a self-contained nation in a single country. The church was to be drawn out of every nation to act as a centre of witness in every country. Her weapons were not to be carnal. She was to preach the Word, and to bear her witness by patient suffering. It is unthinkable that any Christian group could rightly claim to have received a direct, specific command to slaughter their enemies without mercy; this alone justified the Israelites in their actions.

Misuse of the Bible has not, of course, been the prerogative of the lunatic fringe of the Christian church. Living Christianity is a force of truth and love which influences the whole of a man's life and all his relationships. Inevitably and inescapably a Christian group has a social (and eventually a political) power directly proportional to its spiritual power. No matter how other-worldly the emphasis of the movement and how averse in theory to any partnership between church and state, it cannot (if genuine) remain passive in face of social injustice, when it alone has the power effectively to challenge it. So the Quakers worked to reform the prisons, the Methodists built up the trades unions, the Clapham sect fought slavery, Shaftesbury battled against the horrors of the Industrial Revolution, the Salvation Army worked among the drop-outs and the Pentecostalists among the drug addicts. But involvement in the real world means a partial Christianizing of society, bringing with it an outward approval of Christian ideals. At this stage selfishness and avarice are still the primary motives in society, but selfishness and avarice will seek every possible means to disguise themselves in respectable Christian clothing. If the Bible is regarded as authoritative it will be ransacked to produce evidence for evil practices. It will not be a balanced statement of the whole teaching of the Bible on a topic, but it will consist of one-sided (and often misinterpreted) extracts. It will be cynical rationalization.

In this way, because of the hardness of men's hearts, the toleration of a very humane form of slavery in the Old Testament was used to justify the barbarities of the West Indian slave traffic. The biblical emphasis on the freedom and responsibility of the individual was used to justify the callousness of unbridled capitalism. Little attention was paid to the denunciation of prophets such as Isaiah, who said:

> 'Woe to those who join house to house,
> who add field to field
> until there is no more room.'

Nor to the law which required that every fifty years lands acquired by the richer families were to be returned to their original owners.[8] The Bible's recognition of governmental authority was used to justify uncritical acceptance of gross inequalities of privilege and wealth – little heed was paid either to the egalitarian ideals of the holy nation redeemed from a common slavery, or to the denunciations of the rich in both Testaments. The recognition of the significance of race and nationhood in a fallen world has been used to justify the domination of tiny white minorities over their black neighbours.[9] Selected texts have been used to exaggerate and

[8] Is. 5:8; Lv. 25.
[9] The Tower of Babel story in Genesis 11, which follows immediately on the catalogue of nations in the previous chapter, seems to show that the differentiation of language (which may not have been instantaneous) and the rise of separated tribes and nations is part of God's plan for the preservation of the human race. The barriers between peoples are like the groynes on the sea-shore which prevent the tides sweeping the beach away and eating into the land. The Nimrods (Gn. 10:8–10) of this world who would set up world-wide tyrannies are continually thwarted by human abhorrence of domination by a foreigner.

Special laws governing foreigners in the land of Israel (Dt. 15:3; 23:20) have been seen by some as justifying racial discrimination. But the distinction in this case is not between those of different race, but between those who belong permanently to the community and those who do not. As we

polarize differences of belief between Catholics and Protestants, so promoting fear and hatred between communities, in disregard of the profound truths which they have in common and of our Lord's exhortations to his followers to love one another. The quite special case of Israel's dispossession of the Canaanites has been used to justify lack of love towards the heathen, resulting in missionary torpor and military rigour by so-called Christian nations, in defiance of the whole New Testament and in disregard even of the Old Testament's concern for other nations. This is the supreme example of the Devil citing Scripture for his own purposes.

It would be idle to pretend that it is easy for the Christian always to know what is the right course. The church *qua* church can certainly never rightly take up arms for the propagation of the gospel. The state on the other hand has a duty to protect its citizens from both internal and external dangers, and may become involved in revolution or war. The church's weapon is the cross, but the state's weapon is the sword – and the Christian, with duties to both, will find inescapable tensions and difficulties of conscience. Problems of political and international action are immensely complicated and it would be unreasonable to expect often to find neat Christian answers. Where Christianity is strong, it is particularly difficult to disentangle religion and politics. In the Middle Ages when the Muslim pincers began to close on Europe, resistance was a matter of political survival, but inevitably the ensuing conflicts with the Turks were seen as wars of religion. The survival of Christianity was secured in Europe, but at the expense of great damage to the Christian image. Similar problems face the modern world as militant atheist states face countries which have not yet formally discarded their Christian tradition. The Christian's duty to the state is perplexing, involving judgments precariously based on fragmentary knowledge; it means that his loyalty to his country can never be uncritical or absolute. But his duty to the gospel is clear: his best energies

---

have seen, a foreign slave may become part of the community and share its covenant privileges. But a foreign trader who is temporarily resident and who has no permanent stake in the welfare of the community obviously cannot claim all the privileges of the covenant people.

must be thrown into uplifting the cross of Christ on both sides of every political divide.

Some perhaps will still want to argue that a return to a belief in the severity of God must tend towards a harsh and cruel society. It is indeed sadly true that nations and groups, loudly vocal in their profession of Christian orthodoxy, have often been guilty in the past and are still guilty today of ruthlessness and oppression. Two things need to be said about this. The first – not by way of exoneration, but in the interests of fairness and realism – is to note the difficulty of the position of the well-intentioned statesman or politician. A national leader, be he Protestant (as in, say, South Africa), Catholic (as in Spain) or Orthodox (as in Greece), Muslim (as in Pakistan), Hindu (as in India) or Marxist (as in the USSR), will from time to time be faced (particularly if his regime is precariously based) with grim options, all of which are undesirable. He may see that the use of force is necessary if the society is to be held together and decide to use it, knowing that relatively innocent people will get hurt. Or he may have on his hands seemingly insoluble problems of race, in which the ideal of a harmonious multi-cultural society or of a single and more or less homogeneous community seems equally unobtainable. The politician is caught up in the corporate sin of humanity, and in practice the highest criterion he can invoke in matters of public concern is enlightened self-interest. The spectator who does not carry the burden of direct responsibility needs to be charitable in his judgments and to accept his share of blame for the evils of political decisions. It seems unrealistic to imagine that the presence of a minority of (very sinful) Christians in a less-than-semi-Christian society should be expected to produce a situation where strife and violence cease. Nevertheless a leaven of people with a high sense of justice and a genuine love for God may exert an influence out of all proportion to their numbers, occasionally preventing strife and often mitigating its miseries.

Secondly, it is erroneous to think that a truly godly severity, which comes from a recognition of the exceeding sinfulness of sin, especially one's own, can ever be divorced from love, which comes from a knowledge of that sin's forgiveness. Sadism can rationalize itself as exemplifying biblical severity, but in fact cruelty and love are mutually exclusive, whereas godly severity and godly love are complementary. The just exercise of authority does not make for a harsh society. It makes for a stable society, where there is little incentive to crime. It is injustice and laxness of authority which breed first violence and then callousness. Severity proceeding from love is neither excessive nor is it usually resented. It provides the framework for a caring society. It has yet to be proved that a society can work without an element of severity. Authority, backed ultimately by sanctions, is necessary for any society. Permissiveness, or the removal of sanctions, is a short-term luxury which lives on the capital built up in times of discipline. It ill-behoves a society which is in danger of disintegrating to decry authority and its sanctions simply because authority is capable of abuse. A severity which gains its inspiration from the severity of Christ's teaching is wholesome and neither harsh nor cruel.

The danger of the misuse of the Bible to justify cruelty or to promote evil for political ends is real, but it does not in fact make the severity of God's dealings with the Canaanites incredible. The severity of God's dealings as he trained his people in the principles of holiness becomes intelligible when we see what was at stake. It was nothing less than the salvation of the world. The Chosen People was the precious casket in which was to be placed a priceless jewel: the Messiah of Israel and the Saviour of men. Against this people Satan directed his fiercest attacks, and to the preservation of this people in righteousness God directed his fiercest defence. The battle was real and bloody. Humanly speaking their very survival seemed in doubt. Yet God kept them and prepared them for the coming of Christ. Since his coming the task has been a different one, calling for different methods, but the battle is as real and as bloody as ever before. The battle for souls is relentless and, for many, entry into the kingdom is through great tribulation. For many, quite literally the martyr spirit is still needed. There are many tightly knit, fanatical communities in which to become a Christian may still be to take one's life in one's hands. For many others, in a society conditioned by materialist vices and materialist values, to become a Christian means a costly surrender. It is only through suffering that the kingdom of God goes forward. It is still only the few who find the narrow way of life, while the many take the broad road to destruction. It is those who know most of the fierceness of the struggle who best understand the fierceness of God's commands. Christ fed his soul upon the book of Deuteronomy; we need not fear to do the same.

9 CURSINGS

If it is true that the book of Deuteronomy was much in our Lord's mind, it is equally true that he meditated deeply upon the psalms. The Psalter was meat and drink to Christ, and it has been meat and drink to Christians ever since. Yet there are passages in the Psalter which are a stumbling-block to many. Sentences such as these haunt the memory:

'The righteous will rejoice when he sees the vengeance;
   he will bathe his feet in the blood of the wicked.'

'God will shatter the heads of his enemies.'

'Add to them punishment upon punishment;
   may they have no acquittal from thee.'

'Return sevenfold into the bosom of our neighbours
   the taunts with which they have taunted thee, O Lord!'

'Let there be none to extend kindness to him,
   nor any to pity his fatherless children!'

'Happy shall he be who takes your little ones
   and dashes them against the rock!'

'Do not I hate them that hate thee, O Lord?
   And do I not loathe them that rise up against thee?
I hate them with perfect hatred;
   I count them my enemies.'

C. S. Lewis, who was by no means prone lightly to discard the unpopular features of traditional Christianity, finds him-

self commenting thus: 'In some of the psalms the spirit of
hatred which strikes us in the face is like the heat from a furnace
mouth'; he speaks of 'the refinement of malice', 'the pettiness
and vulgarity of it'; he regards it as 'diabolical', 'contemptible'.
'We must not either try to explain them away or to yield for
one moment to the idea that, because it comes in the Bible, all
this vindictive hatred must somehow be good and pious. We
must face both facts squarely. The hatred is there – festering,
gloating, undisguised – and also we should be wicked if we in
any way condoned or approved it.'[1]

Before attempting to evaluate this judgment, it will be well
to look at these passages in a broader context. It is interesting
to ask the question, How many imprecatory psalms are there?
It will be found that different writers give different answers.
The seven passages from which we have quoted are perhaps
the most striking. But R. M. Benson[2] discusses no fewer than
thirty-nine psalms in which there are 'comminatory' passages.
This quotation from *The Times* (23.8.62) rates the number of
unchristian psalms far higher: 'Earlier this year 14 church
study groups in Woodford looked at the Old Testament psalms
and concluded that 84 of them were "not fit for Christians to
sing" '; and J. C. Wansey, compiler of the useful collection of
New Testament passages which have been printed for con-
gregational chanting under the title *A New Testament Psalter*,
commented: 'These psalms and parts of many others are full
of tribal jealousies, bloodthirsty threats and curses, whinings
and moanings, which are shocking in themselves and time-
wasting to God and man. The New Testament psalms are
Christian through and through.' But to jettison half the Psalter
is a dubious expedient, for, as C. S. Lewis realizes, the harsh
passages and the tender passages are hopelessly mixed up, and
it is not possible just to ignore the unpleasant sections.

[1] *Reflections on the Psalms* (London, 1958), chapter 3. Though we shall take
issue with C. S. Lewis over this evaluation, it is only fair to add that his
conclusions are very much more discerning than those of the many writers
who reject these psalms out of hand.
[2] *War Songs of the Prince of Peace* (London, 1901) I, pp. 276 ff. His full list is:
5, 7, 9, 10, 16, 17, 28, 35, 36, 40, 41, 44, 49, 52, 54, 55, 57, *58*, 59, 62, 63,
64, *68*, *69*, 70, 71, 74, 75, *79*, 83, 87, 92, 94, 108, *109*, *137*, *139*, 140, 143.
The psalms quoted are those in italics.

'Unfortunately,' he says, 'the bad parts will not "come away clean"; they may be . . . intertwined with the most exquisite things.'[3] Side by side with the imprecations there are evidences of the highest and most enviable spirituality.

THE PROPHETS

Again, these sentiments are not peculiar to the Psalter in the Old Testament. We find them also in the prophets. For instance, in the writings of Jeremiah, who is regarded as one of the most sensitive of the prophets, we find the same sort of language. When God reveals to Jeremiah that some are plotting his death, he prays:

> 'O Lord of hosts, who judgest righteously,
>   who triest the heart and the mind,
> let me see thy vengeance upon them,
>   for to thee have I committed my cause.'

And God replies:

> 'Behold, I will punish them; the young men shall die by the sword; their sons and their daughters shall die by famine; and none of them shall be left.'

Later we find an even more terrible prayer:

> 'Give heed to me, O Lord,
>   and hearken to my plea.
> Is evil a recompense for good?
>   Yet they have dug a pit for my life.
> Remember how I stood before thee
>   to speak good for them,
>   to turn away thy wrath from them.

---

[3] *Reflections*, p. 22. The question of the use of cursing psalms in public worship is a delicate matter. By the time we have finished this chapter I hope that it will be clear that there is every reason why a congregation well taught in biblical doctrine should use the whole Psalter. These shocking imprecations are like so many burrs which stick in the mind and force the reader to think. A wise pastor will find that they provide a direct road to deep instruction. But for a congregation with no such foundation and with no deeply taught leader, there is clearly a case for not inviting them to take on their lips even inspired words which they will totally misunderstand.

> Therefore deliver up their children to famine;
>   give them over to the power of the sword,
> let their wives become childless and widowed.
>   May their men meet death by pestilence,
>   and their youths be slain by the sword in battle . . .'
>   'Forgive not their iniquity,
>   nor blot out their sin from thy sight.'

God answers the prayer with a promise of horrifying judgments:

> 'Behold, I am bringing such evil upon this place that the
> ears of every one who hears of it will tingle . . . because they
> have filled this place with the blood of innocents, and have
> built the high places of Baal to burn their sons in the fire as
> burnt offerings to Baal . . . therefore, behold, days are
> coming, says the Lord, when this place shall be no more
> called Topheth, or the Valley of Ben-hinnom, but the
> Valley of Slaughter . . . I will give their dead bodies for
> food to the birds of the air and to the beasts of the earth.
> And I will make this city a horror, a thing to be hissed at;
> everyone who passes by it will be horrified and will hiss be-
> cause of all its disasters. And I will make them eat the flesh
> of their sons and their daughters . . .'[4]

The immediate juxtaposition of a prayer for judgment and
a promise of its answer is, in this precise form, comparatively
uncommon in the Bible. But such promises of judgment (without any specific prayer) are very common, especially in the
prophets. And without question they are regarded as completely deserved and just. God gives his warning, making it
clear that he has willed that such penalties shall be meted out
for such sins. For example, Nahum utters this terrible oracle
which God has given him against Nineveh:

> 'The Lord is a jealous God and avenging,
>   the Lord is avenging and wrathful;
> the Lord takes vengeance on his adversaries
>   and keeps wrath for his enemies.
> The Lord is slow to anger and of great might,
>   and the Lord will by no means clear the guilty . . .'

[4] Je. 11:18–23; 18:19 – 19:9. For examples of curses pronounced (or judgments promised) on individuals, see Je. 20:6; 28:16; 29:30–32; 36:30 f.;
cf. Am. 7:16 f.

'Who can stand before his indignation?
    Who can endure the heat of his anger?
His wrath is poured out like fire,
    and the rocks are broken asunder by him.
The Lord is good,
    a stronghold in the day of trouble;
    he knows those who take refuge in him.
But with an overflowing flood
    he will make a full end of his adversaries,
    and will pursue his enemies into darkness.'

'Woe to the bloody city . . .'

'Yet she was carried away,
    she went into captivity;
her little ones were dashed in pieces
    at the head of every street.'[5]

Similarly, Isaiah utters his oracle against Babylon:

'Behold, the day of the Lord comes,
    cruel, with wrath and fierce anger,
to make the earth a desolation
    and to destroy its sinners from it . . .'

'Their infants will be dashed in pieces
    before their eyes;
their houses will be plundered
    and their wives ravished.'

Nineveh and Babylon were in turn capital cities of cruel and ruthless empires, that had brought untold misery to their subject peoples. It so happens that, in the case of Babylon, there is a psalm in which her devastations are recalled, and in which God's judgment is invoked, leading finally to:

'Happy shall he be who takes your little ones
    and dashes them against the rock!'[6]

Such a sentiment may indeed seem appalling, but it is on all fours with the judgments which are uttered against both cities,

<hr>

[5] Na. 1:2–8; 3:1–10.   [6] Is. 13:9, 16; Ps. 137:9.

and which are regarded as the righteous response of a good God to great human wickedness. Other judgments, scarcely less severe, are to be found in many places throughout the prophets.

DEUTERONOMY

Such invocations and promises of judgment in the Psalms and in the Prophets have their basis in the Pentateuch. Moses gave directions that upon entry into the Promised Land they were to have a solemn ceremony of blessing and cursing in the valley which separated Mount Ebal and Mount Gerizim. Twelve solemn curses were to be read out by the Levites, to each of which all the people were required to say 'Amen'. They were to invoke God's curse upon such of their number as did not obey God's commandments. Then there follow more than fifty verses in which the judgments are detailed – surely one of the most appalling passages in literature concerning the sufferings of any people. Here are some extracts:

'The Lord will send upon you curses, confusion, and frustration, in all that you undertake to do, until you are destroyed and perish quickly, on account of the evil of your doings, because you have forsaken me . . . The Lord will smite you with consumption, and with fever, inflammation, and fiery heat, and with drought, and with blasting, and with mildew . . .

'The Lord will cause you to be defeated before your enemies; you shall go out one way against them, and flee seven ways before them; and you shall be a horror to all the kingdoms of the earth. And your dead body shall be food for all birds of the air, and for the beasts of the earth; and there shall be no one to frighten them away . . . The Lord will smite you with madness and blindness and confusion of mind; and you shall grope at noonday, as the blind grope in darkness . . . You shall betroth a wife, and another man shall lie with her . . . Your sons and your daughters shall be given to another people . . . and it shall not be in the power of your hand to prevent it . . . so that you shall be driven mad by the sight which your eyes shall see . . . And you shall become a horror, a proverb, and a byword, among all the peoples where the Lord will lead you away . . . All these curses shall come upon you and pursue you and overtake you . . . and upon your descendants for ever.

'Because you did not serve the Lord your God with joyfulness and gladness of heart, by reason of the abundance of all things, therefore you shall serve your enemies whom the Lord will send against you, in hunger and thirst, in nakedness, and in want of all things . . . And you shall eat the offspring of your own body, the flesh of your sons and daughters, whom the Lord your God has given you, in the siege and in the distress with which your enemies shall distress you . . . The most tender and delicately bred woman among you, who would not venture to set the sole of her foot upon the ground because she is so delicate and tender, will grudge to the husband of her bosom, to her son and to her daughter, her afterbirth that comes out from between her feet and her children whom she bears, because she will eat them secretly, for want of all things, in the siege and in the distress with which your enemies shall distress you in your towns.

'If you are not careful to do all the words of this law which are written in this book, that you may fear this glorious and awful name, the Lord your God, then the Lord will bring on you and your offspring extraordinary afflictions, afflictions severe and lasting, and sicknesses grievous and lasting. And he will bring upon you again all the diseases of Egypt, which you were afraid of; and they shall cleave to you. Every sickness also, and every affliction which is not recorded in the book of this law, the Lord will bring upon you, until you are destroyed . . .

'And the Lord will scatter you among all peoples, from one end of the earth to the other; and there you shall serve other gods, of wood and stone, which neither you nor your fathers have known. And among these nations you shall find no ease . . . In the morning you shall say, "Would it were evening!" and at evening you shall say, "Would it were morning!" because of the dread which your heart shall fear, and the sights which your eyes shall see . . . you shall offer yourselves for sale to your enemies as male and female slaves, but no man will buy you.'[7]

Such a passage can be matched by only one thing: that is, by a historical recital of the actual sufferings of the Jewish people. It takes an Eichmann trial to equal the horror of the divine warnings in Deuteronomy. Yet God's people were bidden to pray for such curses of God upon themselves, if they forsook him. The 'jealous' God of the Old Testament is every bit as severe on his own covenant people when they are unfaithful to him, as he is on the nations who have always served other gods.

THE NEW TESTAMENT

The divine curse is not only an Old Testament theme, but is also to be found in the New. Paul invokes an anathema on preachers of a false gospel, and on those who do not love the Lord. He declares of Alexander the coppersmith, who had done him great harm, 'The Lord will requite him for his deeds'. In this life no higher penalty can be exacted from a human being than exclusion from the church of God, yet excommunication and the forbidding of table fellowship, which are outward tokens of the withdrawal of God's blessing and of exposure to the malice of Satan, were New Testament commands. In the book of Revelation there are both prayers and praises for the judgment of God. The martyrs cried out with a loud voice,

'O Sovereign Lord, holy and true, how long before thou wilt judge and avenge our blood on those who dwell upon the earth?'

Again:

'I heard the angel of water say,
    "Just art thou in these thy judgments,
    thou who art and wast, O Holy One.
    For men have shed the blood of saints and prophets,
    and thou hast given them blood to drink.
    It is their due!"

[7] Dt. 27:11–26; chapter 28.

And I heard the altar cry,
   "Yea, Lord God the Almighty,
     true and just are thy judgments!" '

The heavens are called to rejoice over the fall of Babylon. Again and again the hallelujahs roll forth 'like the sound of mighty thunderpeals'.[8]

THE TEACHING OF CHRIST

The divine curse is not only a theme of the New Testament writers, it is also a theme of our Lord's. When he describes his own part on the Judgment Day, it includes his giving of sentence: 'Depart from me, you cursed, into the eternal fire.' And this is only the culmination of the severe warnings which he gave throughout his ministry. In Luke's account of the Sermon on the Mount the blessings and woes[9] are recounted in a way that is reminiscent of the scene at Mount Ebal and Mount Gerizim, and our Lord finishes the sermon with a warning of great ruin to the disobedient.

Other examples of his 'Woes' are:

'Woe to you, Chorazin! woe to you, Bethsaida! for if the mighty works done in you had been done in Tyre and Sidon, they would have repented long ago, sitting in sackcloth and ashes. But it shall be more tolerable in the judgment for Tyre and Sidon than for you.'

'But woe to you Pharisees! for you tithe mint and rue and every herb, and neglect justice and the love of God . . .

'Woe to you lawyers also! for you load men with burdens hard to bear, and you yourselves do not touch the burdens with one of your fingers. Woe to you! for you build the tombs of the prophets whom your fathers killed . . . that the blood of all the prophets, shed from the foundation of the

[8] Gal. 1:8, 9; 1 Cor. 16:22; 2 Tim. 4:14. 1 Cor. 5:3–5; 2 Cor. 2:5–11; Tit. 3:10; 2 Jn. 10. Rev. 6:10; 16:5–7; 18:20; 19:1–16.
[9] Mt. 25:41; Lk. 6:20–49. The word translated 'woe' can also be translated 'alas', the rendering preferred by NEB. The two ideas, of warning or denunciation on the one hand, and of sorrow on the other, are not of course mutually exclusive. But in the majority of the instances of its use in our Lord's teaching, the former meaning appears to be in his mind. It is a warning or denunciation of great severity.

world, may be required of this generation, from the blood of Abel to the blood of Zechariah, who perished between the altar and the sanctuary. Yes, I tell you, it shall be required of this generation. Woe to you lawyers! for you have taken away the key of knowledge; you did not enter yourselves, and you hindered those who were entering.'

'Temptations to sin are sure to come; but woe to him by whom they come! It would be better for him if a millstone were hung round his neck and he were cast into the sea, than that he should cause one of these little ones to sin.'

'The Son of man goes as it has been determined; but woe to that man by whom he is betrayed!'[1]

His command to his disciples, to shake off the dust from their feet as a testimony to those who would not receive their message, is a symbolic act of solemn cursing.[2] The solemnity is emphasized in Matthew's account, where he continues: 'Truly, I say to you, it shall be more tolerable on the day of judgment for the land of Sodom and Gomorrah than for that town.'

NEW TESTAMENT QUOTATION OF CURSING PSALMS

Such is the broader background against which the imprecatory psalms are to be read. The sentiments in these psalms are by no means unique. In the biblical context they do not stand out, like so many erratic boulders, as though belonging to a different environment. They take their place with many other passages written in similar vein. Had they been alien to the spirit of the New Testament, one might have expected to have found them tacitly shunned by its writers. But in fact this is not the case at all. If the seven psalms discussed at the beginning of this chapter are regarded as a group, they are, on average, actually quoted in the New Testament more frequently than

[1] Lk. 10:13, 14; 11:39–52; 17:1, 2; 22:22.
[2] Mt. 10:14; Mk. 6:11; Lk. 9:5. See A. Edersheim, *The Life and Times of Jesus the Messiah* (London, 1901), I, p. 644. Vincent Taylor (*The Gospel according to St. Mark*, London, 1952) on Mk. 6:11 denies that it is an acted curse, saying that the testimony was intended to provoke thought and to lead men to repentance. But these two things, surely, are not mutually exclusive. The disciples' curse is a most solemn warning of the day of judgment, but it is not the day of judgment itself. It is the sharpest possible call to think again.

the rest of the psalms. As we have already seen, statistics must necessarily be approximations only, since it is not possible to give an exact definition of what is meant by a quotation. But these are the rough figures: the 150 psalms are quoted about 125 times in the New Testament, that is, considerably less than once each on average; whereas there are, according to Kirkpatrick,[3] thirteen quotations from the imprecatory group. This would give a rate of quotation more than twice the average for the Psalter as a whole. Kirkpatrick's list includes five references to Psalm 69:21, all of which are rather slender to be dignified by the term 'quotation', though they are almost certainly conscious allusions. But even if these quotations are omitted altogether, and all the border-line cases in other psalms are retained, the average for these psalms remains distinctly greater than that for the rest of the Psalter. It is Psalm 69 which seems particularly to have entrenched itself in the mind of the apostolic church. Is this because our Lord himself directed their attention to it? His quotation, 'They hated me without a cause' (Jn. 15:25), comes from this psalm, or from Psalm 35 (verse 19), which is also full of prayers for the overthrow of David's enemies. Though not included in Kirkpatrick's list, our Lord's words in Luke 19:44, concerning the enemies who will 'dash you to the ground, you and your children', seem to be a deliberate echo of the supposedly most notorious imprecation in the Psalter.

OLD TESTAMENT ETHICS

Are we right to regard these passages as expressions of vindictive hatred, 'festering, gloating, undisguised'? There are two considerations which tell against its intrinsic probability. In the first place, the Old Testament itself is perfectly clear that this is not the right attitude to one's enemies. 'If you meet your enemy's ox or his ass going astray, you shall bring it back

[3] These statistics are based on the list in A. F. Kirkpatrick, *Psalms* (London, 1903), III, pp. 838 ff. The relevant references are: Ps. 68:18 = Eph. 4:8; Ps. 69:4 = Jn. 15:25; Ps. 69:9a = Jn. 2:17; Ps. 69:9b = Rom. 15:3; Ps. 69:21 = Mt. 27:34, 48; Mk. 15:36; Lk. 23:36; Jn. 19:28, 29; Ps. 69:22, 23 = Rom. 11:9, 10; Ps. 69:25 = Acts 1:20; Ps. 109:8 = Acts 1:20; Ps. 109:25 = Mt. 27:39. It will be seen that three out of the seven psalms in the group are quoted.

to him. If you see the ass of one who hates you lying under its burden, you shall refrain from leaving him with it, you shall help him to lift it up.' 'You shall not hate your brother in your heart, but you shall reason with your neighbour, lest you bear sin because of him. You shall not take vengeance or bear any grudge against the sons of your own people, but you shall love your neighbour as yourself.'[4] If given a universal reference, there is no higher ethic than this, and our Lord can do no other than quote it, when he wishes to set up an absolute standard. Paul also turns to an Old Testament verse to express the same thought. In the book of Proverbs we read, 'If your enemy is hungry, give him bread to eat; and if he is thirsty, give him water to drink; for you will heap coals of fire on his head,[5] and the Lord will reward you.' 'Do not rejoice when your enemy falls, and let not your heart be glad when he stumbles; lest the Lord see it, and be displeased, and turn away his anger from him.'[6]

Vengeance belongs to God. There is to be no jubilation, even in your inmost heart, that you have gained an advantage over your enemy. If God sees fit to punish, that is one thing. For you to crow over him, is to invite the transference of divine punishment to yourself. This teaching is perfectly well understood in the Old Testament. Job protests that he has not 'rejoiced at the ruin of him that hated me, or exulted when evil overtook him'; 'I have not let my mouth sin by asking for his life with a curse.' Jeremiah prefaces a prayer that God will destroy his persecutors 'with double destruction', by the plea, 'I have not pressed thee to send evil, nor have I desired the day of disaster, thou knowest.'[7]

There are passages in some of the psalms which are sometimes considered to be self-righteous in tone. But of course the psalm writers do not in fact regard themselves as righteous in an absolute sense. Quite the reverse. They all know that they

---

[4] Ex. 23:4, 5; Lv. 19:17, 18.
[5] That is, you will evoke pangs of contrition, which will make your enemy become your friend. Pr. 25:21, 22; cf. Rom. 12:20.
[6] Pr. 24:17, 18; i.e. 'your glee may well be a more punishable sin than all the guilt of your enemy' (F. D. Kidner, *Proverbs*, London, 1964). Cf. Pr. 20:22; 24:29.
[7] Jb. 31:29, 30; Je. 17:16–18.

are sinners, and the Psalter contains much sincere penitence.
But the psalmists know what it is earnestly to have searched
their hearts, and to have examined the sincerity of their
motives. They have honestly tried to do the right thing towards
their enemies. Yet in spite of this their enemies are bent on
their destruction. It is in such a situation that David can first
say, 'If there is wrong in my hands, if I have requited my friend
with evil or plundered my enemy without cause, let the enemy
pursue me and overtake me.' Then he goes on to pray: 'O let
the evil of the wicked come to an end, but establish thou the
righteous.' [8]

WAS DAVID VINDICTIVE?

The second reason for doubting that these passages are vindictive lies in the character of David himself. Five out of the
seven psalms are attributed to him. (Of the 39 psalms discussed
by Benson, 27 are attributed to him.) Nineteenth-century
criticism gave the psalms very late dates and consigned the
headings to the dustbin. The tendency nowadays is to return
to earlier dates. There is in any case no need for such great
scepticism with regard to the value of the headings. Acceptance
of the headings is at times a help in interpretation. There is,
moreover, an interesting piece of direct evidence that they are
ancient. When the Septuagint translators came to translate
them into Greek, the musical terms in particular frequently
eluded them. The best they could do was to transliterate them.
And it was still the best that the translators of the Revised
Standard Version could do. So the RSV is replete with its
Selahs, its *Sheminith, Shiggaion, Gittith, Muth-labben, Higgaion,
Miktam, Maskil, Alamoth, Mahalath, Shushan Eduth, Mahalath
Leannoth*! [9] It seems irrational to regard these as late editorial
additions; it is better to take them as evidence of their primitive
character. Possession is nine points of the law, and it is folly to
reject ancient testimony in favour of pure speculation, unless
there are compelling reasons. There is no good reason for
doubting that most of the psalms attributed to him were composed by David.

But David was not a vindictive person. Though, like all his

[8] Ps. 7:3–9.   [9] Psalms 6, 7, 8, 9, 16, 32, 46, 53, 60, 88.

contemporaries, he was ruthless enough to his country's enemies,[1] yet he showed extraordinary generosity to personal enemies who sought his death. Saul, without any justification, repeatedly tried to kill him, but David twice refrained from touching him when he had him at his mercy. He was culpably weak when his own son Absalom was plotting his overthrow and when he finally raised armed insurrection. On the death of Saul he composed an elegy which contained not a word of reproach; on the death of Absalom he was almost heart-broken. When Abigail intervened to prevent the death of her churlish husband at his hands, David was deeply grateful: 'Blessed be you, who have kept me this day from bloodguilt and from avenging myself with my own hand!' When David's fortunes were at their lowest ebb, and Shimei rained curses on him, he refused the request of Abishai to 'go over and take off his head'. This was doubtless against his better judgment, as may be seen from the sequel. On his death-bed he warned Solomon of the grave danger that Shimei's continued presence constituted to his kingdom, whereupon Solomon put him under house arrest. To his personal enemies David was not vindictive; he was generous to a fault.[2]

THE VINDICATION OF GOD'S NAME

In what light then are we to regard these psalms? In the first place, it is important to note that biblical cursings are not 'vulgar'. Cursing as we know it has become inextricably mixed up with idle swearing and blasphemy. The cursings of the psalmist, on the other hand, are serious, premeditated, religious. In the second place, they are not utterances to the people concerned. The psalmist is not answering back to his enemies, nor trying to pay them out. They are prayers – prayers made solemnly and urgently to the Sovereign Ruler of the world. He is bringing the matter to God. The imprecations are therefore fundamentally expressions of trust in God, rather than of hate for man. The motive lying behind these words of David (and the other writers) is a passionate longing that God

---

[1] 1 Sa. 27:9, 11; 30:17; 2 Sa. 8:2.
[2] 2 Sa. 1:19 ff.; 18:33 ff.; 1 Sa. 25:33; 2 Sa. 16:5 ff.; 19:16 ff.; 1 Ki. 2:8 ff., 36 ff.

will vindicate his own name. Their deepest desire is that God, and the servants of God, should triumph over the mighty powers of evil.

It needs to be noted, however, that this desire is not expressed in abstract terms. Hebrew modes of thought tend to be concrete, where ours are abstract. They express a principle by an example. They are praying that God will vindicate his cause in a manner appropriate to his holy nature, but they know that this is likely to mean in practice the judgment of war, which will bring suffering to men, women and children. And so they couch their prayers in these terms. It is not necessarily lack of realism and honesty on our part that we do not pray this way, nor is it evidence of gloating on their part that they do. They are two different ways of saying the same thing.

The psalmist knows that God has pronounced such judgments repeatedly through the mouths of his servants. As he turns to God in prayer, he recognizes the present time as one such moment of divine wrath. He knows that the day of grace is (at least for the time being) over. The soft answer, the returning of good for evil, has elicited no response. The enemies of God are implacable. It is necessary for the vindication of God's authority and God's goodness that just retribution should not be long delayed. He prays for it, not shutting his eyes to the horrors which it involves. There is no sadistic pleasure in seeing his enemy suffer, no sense of getting his own back, but simply a deep desire that the world might see that God is just.

It is not in God's nature to delight in punishment.[3] As Ezekiel was later to put it: 'As I live, says the Lord God, I have no pleasure in the death of the wicked, but that the wicked turn from his way and live; turn back, turn back from your evil ways; for why will you die, O house of Israel?' It is God's delight to show mercy and to shower upon man his grace, but this in no way alters the fact that he will allow the impenitent to suffer the consequences of their sins. God's attitude was perfectly expressed by our Lord:

'O Jerusalem, Jerusalem, killing the prophets and stoning those who are sent to you! How often would I have gathered

[3] Even though in terrible metaphor the opposite may occasionally be suggested, e.g. Dt. 28:63.

your children together as a hen gathers her brood under her wings, and you would not!'

'When he drew near and saw the city he wept over it, saying, "Would that even today you knew the things that make for peace! But now they are hid from your eyes. For the days shall come upon you, when your enemies will cast up a bank about you and surround you, and hem you in on every side, and dash you to the ground, you *and your children* within you, and they will not leave one stone upon another in you; because you did not know the time of your visitation." '[4]

In the heart of God there are tears, even when there is a rod in his hands. When looked at fairly in their context, the imprecatory psalms show the same paradoxical combination of love and severity. This explains why what C. S. Lewis calls 'the bad parts' are 'intertwined with the most exquisite things'. Both his acts of tenderness and his deeds of wrath show the world the authority and goodness of God.

That the writers have a consuming desire that God will vindicate his own name is clear when we look at the individual psalms. The whole point of the prayer of Psalm 58 comes in the last two verses. We have been told in the starkest figurative language that when God has answered this prayer, 'The righteous will rejoice when he sees the vengeance; he will bathe his feet in the blood of the wicked.'[5] But what is the reason for this public exhibition of divine vengeance? 'Men will say, "Surely there is a reward for the righteous; surely there is a God who judges on earth." ' Psalm 68 opens with the prayer: 'Let God arise, let his enemies be scattered; let those who hate him flee before him!' Then God is pictured both as 'Father of the fatherless and protector of widows', 'a God of salvation', and as the one who 'will shatter the heads of his enemies'.

[4] Ezk. 33:11; Mi. 7:18; Lk. 13:34; 19:41-44. There seems to be a direct line from Is. 13:16, in which is prophesied the Lord's wrath upon Babylon, whose infants are to be dashed in pieces, to Ps. 137 which yearns for its fulfilment, to Lk. 19:41-44 where a similar judgment is prophesied upon the city which rejects Messiah.

[5] Similar language is used in Rev. 19:11-16, where Christ is portrayed as judging in righteousness. 'He is clad in a robe dipped in blood . . . he will tread the wine press of the fury of the wrath of God the Almighty.'

Psalm 69 is written in deep humility by one who knows himself to be hated without cause, who is bearing reproach for God's sake. The answer to his prayer will bring gladness to the oppressed: 'You who seek God, let your hearts revive. For the Lord hears the needy, and does not despise his own that are in bonds.' Psalm 79 prays 'for the glory of thy name' against the heathen who have poured out the blood of the saints like water. 'Why should the nations say, "Where is their God?"' Let the avenging of the outpoured blood of thy servants be known among the nations before our eyes!'

In Psalm 109, David has been condemned to death, by wicked and deceitful men who have returned hatred for his love. His prayer for judgment is so that his people may 'know that this is thy hand' and that he may live to praise the Lord in their midst once more. Psalm 137 is inspired by a passionate love for Jerusalem (upon which all the hopes of Israel – and ultimately of mankind – were centred), and by the fearful recollection of what the heathen had done to the city of the Lord. The desire is at all costs to keep alive the memory and knowledge of the things of God in spite of the torments of exile. A reversal of fortunes in fulfilment of Isaiah 13:16 is necessary for the vindication of God's name. Psalm 139 is a lovely acknowledgment of the marvels of God's omniscience and omnipresence. Realizing something of this, David asks God to search his heart to see if there is any wicked way in him, and to lead him in the way everlasting. It is in this context that he prays for the overthrow of the wicked. He desires a perfect hatred of all that is evil. 'Do I not hate them that hate thee, O Lord? . . . I hate them with perfect hatred; I count them my enemies.' In these psalms there is severity indeed, but not personal vindictiveness. The supreme concern is for the glory of God.

REJOICING IN GOD'S SOVEREIGNTY

All this rings strangely in the ears of those who have been nurtured in an age of sentimental, unbiblical Christianity, which has forgotten that our *first* allegiance is to God, not to our fellow-man. The natural man in us does not at all like a doctrine so uncompromising and so painful. Gentle and peaceful persuasion is all right. But to think that God punishes, that God fulfils his purposes through pain, that God wills the destruction of sinners – No! But this is where we have got to make up our minds. Do we believe that God rules the world? If we do, then we must accept the fact that punishment, pain and destruction are part of his infinitely wise and loving order. Do we believe in the teaching of Christ? If we do, we must accept the fact that *he* taught us to believe that punishment, pain and destruction are part of his Father's wise and loving purpose. When, by the grace of God, we have made up our minds, it is our duty and wisdom (and it should become our joy) to embrace this belief with every particle of our being. Our whole soul should rejoice that God rules the world as he does. Like our Lord and like Stephen we should pray prayers of forgiveness for those who injure us or take our life. Like Paul we should have great sorrow and unceasing anguish in our hearts for those who will not turn from their sins. Yet if such, unwilling to yield to the loving invitations and loving chastisements of God, come under judgment, we must rejoice at the vindication of God's name.

It is contrary both to Scripture and to experience to believe that all will yield to gentle persuasion. It is not true even of those who are soundly converted. They learn many of life's deepest lessons (and they could probably learn them no other way) by prolonged suffering. And of the unconverted, it is sadly true that many go impenitent to the grave. For such the day of grace must one day pass, whether at death or before, and the day of judgment must begin. When we pray 'Thy kingdom come', we pray for the overthrow of evil. We know that the answer to that prayer will be partly by grace and partly by judgment. It is not for us to choose which it shall be. We shall rejoice with the angels over the sinner that repents. And when God himself makes plain that they will not yield to his love and that the day for anguished intercession is over, we shall rejoice with all the servants of God at the destruction of those who sought to destroy God's fair earth.[6]

We are strangely inconsistent in our attitude to prayers for judgment. When we pray for victory in war, even if it is a

[6] Mt. 7:13; Rev. 11:17, 18.

prayer with many qualifications in it, we are praying for the forcible and painful overthrow of the enemy. We are not usually so realistic (and perhaps not so honest) as the psalmists, and do not picture even to ourselves what we are actually praying for. We are praying that the whole pitiless machinery of war may go forward to bring, if possible, a speedy conclusion. It is mangled bodies, tortured minds, orphaned children that we are concerned with. There will be unstable children growing up to be parents of unstable homes, till the third and fourth generation, as the result of our war. Yet to most Christians it has seemed that, when the issue has had to be faced, the choice of war has often appeared to be the lesser of evils. The Old Testament contains many prayers for victory in war, but it has not generally been noticed that every one is necessarily an imprecatory prayer. As R. M. Benson says, 'Every Psalm of triumph involves a Psalm of vengeance, and *vice versa.*'[7] So these prayers for victory are matched with their hymns of thanksgiving.

The end of Psalm 137 is perhaps the most appalling thing in the whole Bible:

> 'O daughter of Babylon, you devastator!
>   Happy shall he be who requites you
>   with what you have done to us!
> Happy shall he be who takes your little ones
>   and dashes them against the rock!'

Is it possible to imagine any circumstance in which a godly man might rightly utter such words in the presence of God? I think it is. What would have been the thoughts of a devout old Jew, who had lived with the insults, humiliations and terrors of the Nazis and now found himself at Auschwitz standing naked in one of the endless queues which led to the gas-chamber? He might well have been beyond feelings of personal hatred against his captors, but his whole soul would cry out:

'O you Nazis, you tormentors, you destroyers,
God will terribly avenge you for this.
Lord, how can men believe in your name if such evil triumphs,
And if little children grow up into a world like this?

[7] R. M. Benson, *War Songs*, I, p. 291.

You cannot let them blot us out utterly.
Speed the bombers, blast their homes and families,
Beat them to their knees, stop this devilry.
Lord, blessed are those whom you call to this dread work of
    judgment.'

No-one thinks that it is a happy thing for the individual concerned that he has to be the instrument of such judgments. It
is no case of personal blessedness for the man who takes little
ones and dashes them against the rock. But it is a blessed thing
that cruel nations like Babylonia should not be allowed to
triumph for ever, and that they should in turn suffer at the
hands of ruthless enemies. No-one could envy the task of
bomber crews. But it was a blessed thing that Eichmann was
halted before he had completed the 'final solution' of the
Jewish question. There are times when kindness has to be in
abeyance and severity alone is called for. Members of a vice
gang, who for money and power murder and corrupt the
defenceless, need not be handled with kid gloves. They must be
brought to book, painfully if necessary, and be made to feel
something of the hell-deserving loathesomeness of their deeds.
They need to hear and heed our Lord's 'Woe to you!' before
they are ready for his gospel of forgiveness. God knows when to
conceal his heart of love behind a stern countenance.

Speaking of these same imprecatory psalms, J. A. Motyer[8]
emphasized that the psalmists based their prayers on a known
truth – the certainty of the judgment of the ungodly. He then
writes:

> But what of the actual forms of expression? It is all very well to
> attempt to justify the spirituality of the writer, to show the sound-
> ness of his theology, and to admire his moral passion, but how is it
> possible to come to any terms with the things he actually asked for?
> And at once the awful petitions of 109:9–15, and the children
> against the rock of 137:7—9 spring to mind!
>   In some answer to this question, let us first ask another: do
> we stop to consider what we are asking when we pray for the
> Return of the Lord Jesus? Probably we do not couch our prayer in
> the following terms: In flaming fire take vengeance on those who
> know not God and who obey not the gospel; give them their due

[8] In an article in *Church of England Newspaper*.

punishment, even eternal destruction from Thy face. But, according to 2 Thessalonians 1:8, these things are inseparable from the coming, and therefore by implication, if not explicitly, we are asking for them.

Or again, do we pray for the deliverance of God's persecuted children in China or elsewhere? How do we imagine that the Lord of history will in the long run rescue them? Will it not be either by the Return, or by some other act of justice and vengeance?

It seems to be exactly the element of realism, which is absent from our prayers, and which gives us such offence in the prayers of the psalms. We are prepared for the prayer (143:11): 'In thy righteousness bring my soul out of trouble.' We are upset by the biblical realism of 143:12: 'And in thy loving-kindness cut off my enemies, and destroy all them that afflict me.'

In Ephesians 4:26, Paul does not forbid the Christians to be angry; he commands a harder thing: that the Christian should be sinlessly angry. This is an emotion which is rarely felt – if ever – and it is for this reason that we fail to understand it when we find it in the psalms.

THE CURSE OF THE CROSS

But the supreme example of the biblical curse is the cross of Christ. The Old Testament had laid down clearly that, if a man is hanged, 'his body shall not remain all night upon the tree . . . for a hanged man is accursed by God'. To Paul as a young rabbi the fact that God allowed Jesus to hang on a tree was the decisive disproof of his Messiahship. He was plainly cursed by God. It was only later, after he had seen the risen Christ, that he could endorse the testimony of the other apostles: 'The God of our fathers raised Jesus whom you killed by hanging him on a tree.' Then he recognized the marvellous truth that Jesus was both cursed for us and raised for us. 'Christ redeemed us from the curse of the law, having become a curse for us.' And, as the ascended Lamb of God, he opened the way to the New Jerusalem, where the curse is no more.[9]

The Bible gives no more than glimpses into this great mystery, though it is in fact upon the death of Christ that the Gospels focus their fullest attention. For the Saviour himself the cost was immeasurable. We cannot begin to understand what pains of body and soul he suffered, but we know that his

[9] Dt. 21:23; Acts 5:30; Gal. 3:13; Rev. 22:3.

whole being shrank from what he had to go through. There was something so solemn about the way that he spoke of his death that the disciples were afraid to ask him what he meant. There was something so frightening about his demeanour as he strode ahead of them that they were 'filled with awe'. In the Garden of Gethsemane he was in an agony as he prayed that, if it were the Father's will, the cup might be removed from him. On the cross itself there came from his lips the fearful cry, 'My God, my God, why hast thou forsaken me?'[1] For the first and last time in his earthly ministry it is recorded of him that he did not address God as 'Father', but as 'My God'. The Evangelists do not explain why the perfect communion of Father and Son was cut off, why in the depths of his soul Jesus felt himself forsaken. They simply record the fact. Jesus, under the divine curse, was bearing away the sins of the world.

This act is the focal point in the history of the world. This act is the very heart of the gospel. Here 'once for all' (as the writer to the Hebrews delights to tell us) was sin dealt with. Its finality is brought out in John's account of the crucifixion. Sometime after the cry of dereliction there followed the cry of triumph: 'It is finished.' The work of atonement was finished. The ransom-price of our redemption was paid.[2] Now it was possible to proclaim to all men forgiveness of sins through Christ; the guilty one could go free, his punishment borne by another; the rebel could become a son through his union with the Son of God; the helpless could be recreated by the power of the divine Spirit in his heart. The church of the new covenant was bidden to keep this doctrine central to its life and worship by observance of the holy Supper. Again and again they were to remember the body broken and the blood poured out for the remission of sins. The church was thus to feed her faith and nurture her life on this foundation truth.

But this brings us to the last moral problem of the Bible which we have to consider. For to many the doctrine of atonement which this implies seems to be highly immoral. That God should curse the sinless Jesus, in order that sinners might escape the curse, seems unjust. That Jesus should be chastised

[1] Mk. 9:32; 10:32, NEB; Lk. 22:40–44; Mk. 15:34.
[2] Jn. 19:30; Mk. 10:45.

to make us whole[3] seems to invert the whole moral order. The wrong person was punished.

Or, is this doctrine of vicarious suffering the pinnacle of divine *morality*? Is this the doctrine which pre-eminently takes sin and retribution seriously?

There are two aspects of the doctrine: one concerned with the work of God as Judge, the other with the work of God as Saviour. Throughout the Bible, from beginning to end, runs the theme of retribution. God is the just Judge who will by no means clear the guilty. The remission of a just penalty is regarded as immoral. For God simply to let wrongdoers off would be injustice. Eternal death is the desert of every sinning human being.

But the triune God is also Saviour. Through the incarnation, God and Man together paid the penalty. The God of the Bible is a personal being – personal in a higher sense than that of any other person. In his complex personality are three persons, united yet distinct. The Holy Trinity was from all eternity a unity, yet community, of divine love, who, before the world began, planned man's salvation. The Father's love sent forth the Son, the Son's love drew him to earth to become Man, so that he might save man. God himself bears our sins. 'God was in Christ reconciling the world to himself.' Forgiveness does not evade the penalties of sin. The one who forgives bears the effects of the other's sin himself, and thus takes the sinner's place.[4] Christ was the sinner's Substitute, who bore the sinner's deserts. The price was fully paid.

But this was not only an act of God, it was also an act of Man. Not only was *God* in Christ; *redeemed humanity* was in Christ as well. Jesus, the Son of man, was the Representative Man, the Last Adam. It was by taking humanity into himself that he, the Sinless Man, was able to bear the penalty of our sins. 'God made him to be sin who knew no sin.' As Man he experienced the full impact of his Father's holy wrath. By his voluntary obedience to his Father's will, he satisfied the divine justice. In his person, as he hung on the cross, heaven's love

[3] Is. 53:5.
[4] 2 Cor. 5:19. This concept of substitution permeates the New Testament. See L. Morris, *The Apostolic Preaching of the Cross* (London, 1965).

and heaven's justice met. He was our Mediator. In the God-man were joined together the infinite wrath and infinite love of God whereby propitiation was made for our sins, and wherein God was himself both just and at the same time the justifier of all who believe in Jesus.[5] The biblical way of salvation is gloriously moral. Far from being a legal fiction, this act was a mighty, saving force. Those who are literally and in fact 'in Christ' were (in the mind and purpose of God) crucified with him when he died, and they were raised with him at his resurrection, and they live now with the Holy Spirit within them to mould them into his likeness. The church, the Body of Christ, was one with Christ, the Head of the church, when he died.

In this life, however, we Christians fall far short of the moral stature of Christ. The difference between Jesus Christ and ourselves is simply this: he desired the fulfilment of the righteous will of God with all his soul. On the one hand, in his work of grace he was prepared to fall under his Father's curse that he might bear the sins of men. On the other, he willingly accepted from his Father's hand the office of Judge on the last day. But we only partly care about the eradication of evil in ourselves and in others. We flinch at the thought of pain in ourselves; we feel inwardly that the judgments of God on others are too severe. We pray 'Thy kingdom come' half-heartedly. The fault is in ourselves. We should, like David, hate evil with a perfect hatred. This is not to plot with sly cunning against wicked people, nor to take delight in revenge. But it is to have one's whole soul opposed to evil, with no desire to compromise and with no desire secretly to enjoy the pleasures of sin. Yet, while

[5] 2 Cor. 5:21; Rom. 3:25, 26. It is unfortunate that both the Revised Standard Version and the New English Bible shy away from the translation 'propitiation' at Rom. 3:25 and 1 Jn. 2:2. 'Propitiation' means 'that which appeases anger'. While this concept is of course liable to misunderstanding, it is unquestionably what the word means. The wrath of God in Scripture is a real and terrible fact. It is the personal reaction of the divine Being to sin. For the debate concerning the word 'propitiation', see C. H. Dodd, *The Bible and the Greeks* (London, 1935), ch. 5; L. Morris, *The Apostolic Preaching of the Cross* (London, 1965), pp. 144–213; R. R. Nicole, 'C. H. Dodd and Propitiation', *Westminster Theological Journal*, 17 (1955), pp. 117–157; D. Hill, *Greek Words and Hebrew Meanings* (Cambridge, 1967), pp. 23 f.

hating with a perfect hatred, we should love with a perfect love, our souls filled with compassion and tenderness and unceasing prayer, especially towards those who have no knowledge of Christ. But two such apparently mutually contradictory ideals seem utterly beyond our grasp. We can only humble ourselves in the dust at our failure in both respects. It means that all our hopes must lie in Christ himself. Our hope must be to open our hearts to the fullness of his Spirit, that he may show the things of Christ to us – for from the one Christ there flowed forth both the consuming fire of God's holy vengeance against sin and his consuming love for those who had sinned against him.

When our inmost being has been laid hold of by the Holy Spirit, we are overwhelmed by a realization of our sin and weakness and of God's holy love. Our wills are captured and our emotions stirred to their depths. And something happens to our thinking. The doctrine of God takes on a new sharpness. We find in fact that our discovery of the uniting of infinite wrath and infinite love in the person of Christ provides the razor-edge to the Christian doctrine of God. We have discovered theism in all its purity. The moral difficulties of the Bible have in fact led us by a short cut into the heart of the modern debate about God, and we now find in our hands an unexpectedly powerful weapon with which to challenge all other presentations of the doctrine of God.[6]

Starting with 'the unusual, the odd and the seemingly inexplicable', we have found that our study has given a new clarity to the outline of the biblical picture of God's character. It has shown that 'the good theory, based upon phenomena that once seemed queer and out of the ordinary', can 'help us to understand the ordinary and the commonplace'. What at first appeared to be stumbling-blocks are proving to be stepping-stones to deeper faith. We have looked the problem of evil full in the face and we have thereby come to see God more clearly than ever before. And we know that we must either take him as he is, or not take him at all.

[6] In an Additional Study, *The Doctrine of the Good God* (p. 182), we have tried to show how biblical theism is related to other contemporary systems of thought. We believe that it towers above all other ways of thinking in its grandeur and in its power to satisfy both heart and mind.

10 THE GOD WITH WHOM WE HAVE TO DO

Simply as an intellectual edifice, biblical theism towers over every other system of human thought. It preserves in its fullness the omnipotence and the righteousness and the love of God, with no attribute detracting from the perfection of another. It preserves creation in all its richness and diversity and man in all his dignity and degradation. But God himself is not an intellectual system, he is a Person – the One with whom we have to do. The revelation of God gives only a small place to abstract propositions; God has made himself known rather by a myriad stories of action, actions recorded in the Bible and actions recorded on the pages of history.

This is the real God; he has not been thought up by philosophers, nor foisted on the world by some dynamic personality; bit by bit he has made himself known by deeds and by explanatory words. He is the only God; we must take him as he is or else we must inevitably find ourselves rejecting him, either by atheism or by creating a god out of our own imagination. Yet no thoughtful person, once he realizes what he is doing, can be content with a self-made god; if, therefore, in his heart he wishes to refuse God, he can only say: 'There is no God.' And the Bible (rightly) calls that man a fool.

Unsophisticated man, man when he is true to his human nature, knows intuitively that there is a God. He looks at the grandeur and delicacy and beauty of the world around him and he knows that it did not just happen. His instinct is to worship. In times of great joy or relief, his instinct is to give thanks. But if he does not want God, he must stifle that instinct and suppress his desire to adore his Maker and to utter his thanks. He must build up barriers to buttress his unbelief; he must rationalize his unbelief and create a sophisticated façade.

But God in his love does not let this happen easily. Rejection of God means pain and sorrow, which brings home to us our weakness and need and arouses in us the instinct to pray. Supposedly convinced atheists, who have never been taught to pray or had the habit of prayer, frequently find themselves praying when in acute danger or sorrow. Sometimes their prayer is a prayer of genuine repentance and faith, and their distress is the gateway to the new life. But those who resist the instinct to worship and the instinct to pray are in danger of being given up by God to the depraved reason and evil conduct of which Paul speaks so terribly in his letter to the Romans. He describes the fate of a God-rejecting society in these words: 'They are filled with every kind of injustice, mischief, rapacity, and malice; they are one mass of envy, murder, rivalry, treachery, and malevolence; whisperers and scandal-mongers, hateful to God, insolent, arrogant, and boastful; they invent new kinds of mischief, they show no loyalty to parents, no conscience, no fidelity to their plighted word; they are without natural affection and without pity. They know well enough the just decree of God, that those who behave like this deserve to die, and yet they do it; not only so, they actually applaud such practices.'[1] This is our world, the real world; he is the real God.

To read the Bible seriously and to open one's eyes to the chronicle of history is to be awed and terrified. God has declared himself the Judge of sinners and his judgments crowd the pages of the Bible and shout at us in every segment of human life. His temporal judgments are *seen* in individuals and in society and in the whole human race. We see ourselves rushing headlong to destruction – and that not merely to a destruction which is temporal, but to one which is final and eternal. We are given no hope of reprieve so long as we persist in our rebellion against God.

Yet once we have turned to the God of the Bible, to the real

[1] Rom. 1:28–32. This quotation, and most of those which follow, are from the *New English Bible*.

God, our terror should turn to trust. Because the real God, who has made himself known as Creator of all things, has power and wisdom and love beyond our imagining. The forces of evil, it is true, are appalling (even as depicted in the book of Revelation they are not overdrawn) and they strike chill into our hearts. In today's world we seem to be helpless pawns manipulated by gigantic economic and political forces, and we know that callous violence and sadistic cruelty are not far below the surface. We have hints too of occult powers, all the more terrible for being unseen and for being nakedly Satanic in their promotion of evil. Yet God has allowed us in these days to see the limitless extent of *his* power by opening up vista upon vista of the created universe. Brute power in the hands of evil is frightening, but what of the brute power in the hands of God?

Our ancestors were justly awed by the forces of storm and earthquake. We have come to know in turn of the super-nova, the quasar and of places in the cosmos apparently of greater densities than those of the so-called elementary particles. The super-nova is a star which experiences a terrific explosion, suddenly becoming very bright and then over a period of years fading away again. The density of matter in the star at the beginning of the explosion can be calculated – a matchbox-full would weigh about 1,000 million tons. But now we know the quasar, whose energies are many billions of times greater. The pressure required to produce the energies of a quasar would be produced by taking the earth and squeezing its 6,000 million million million tons to the size of a golf ball. And there are energies greater still. In terms of sheer power, it is absurd not to trust the real God.

But the real God too has eternal wisdom. Far from diminishing our conception of God, geology has stretched it. It is good to go, for instance, to the Avon Gorge and look at the great stratified layers of exposed limestone hundreds of feet thick, and meditate. For millions of years the dying sea-creatures left their chalky remains on the ocean-floor; these were compacted under pressure to form rock, which was eventually raised above sea-level by earth movements. God apparently took some thousands of millions of years to prepare the earth for man. His plans are utterly unhurried; we should not fret.

And how marvellous in their complexity and economy of structure are the things that he has brought into being. Much has been known about the larger structures, such as the eye and the ear, for some generations. Even they are almost incredibly ingenious mechanisms, which it is very, very hard to believe developed by chance. But what of DNA, that beautiful and seemingly absurdly simple double helix, which is found in every cell of every living creature? DNA contains the genetic 'instructions' which direct the growth of an organism. Francis Crick, the Nobel prizewinner, says that if this genetic code were to be written out in English it would occupy about 500 large books, which means 'instructions' perhaps a hundred times the length of the complete works of Shakespeare in every cell. If all the molecules of DNA were taken from one human body and were laid end to end, they would stretch a distance comparable to the diameter of the solar system.[2] 'The fool' may dismiss this as just one of those things which happen to be. The one who believes in God sees it as inescapable evidence of God's limitless wisdom. He who designed such a world and who so unhurriedly prepared it for man's coming can be trusted – trusted to make no mistakes in his care for us.

But the real God too has love – love which may be seen as objectively and concretely as his power and his wisdom; not now in the marvels of creation, but in the marvel of the life and death of the Incarnate Son. For the answer to the question: 'What is God like?' is this: 'God is like Jesus' – for he who has seen Jesus has seen the Father. This book has laid great stress, one-sided stress, on the severity of God. And this has been done deliberately, because the Christian faith has been rendered incredible by its sentimentalizing. God has been made senile, Jesus has been made sickly, Love has been made vapid. It was necessary to expose the fallacy and disinfect the pious image in order to try to see the real God, the God with whom we have to do.

Jesus, as we have already reminded ourselves, was a lover of

[2] Francis Crick, *Of Molecules and Men* (University of Washington Press, 1966), pp. 58 f.

the Old Testament, a denouncer of human wickedness, a prophet of political disaster, a preacher of hell fire and a trainer of fiery preachers. Is then all this tradition of the kindness of Jesus an illusion? Was the real Jesus an unbalanced fanatic, deserving his inevitable disastrous end? On the contrary, Jesus was kind as well as severe – kind in an utterly unsentimental way, which combined depth of feeling with total self-giving. He pre-eminently showed the kindness of God to the world, for he taught God's love, he taught his followers to love and he demonstrated love by deeds and words and demeanour, and supremely by accepting his vocation to shed his blood for the remission of the sins of his enemies.

He did not in fact *say* very much about the love of God. The great New Testament passages on the love of God are to be found mostly in the Epistles, since it was only after the meaning of the cross had dawned upon the apostles' minds that they could begin to fathom something of love's depths. It is John in his first Epistle who declares that God is love, and the golden statement that 'God so loved the world that he gave his only Son' is apparently the Evangelist's comment rather than that of Jesus himself.[3] Superficially Jesus seems more concerned with sharpening the ethical demand and rousing a sinful people to the danger of their sins than with preaching the love of God. Yet behind it all there is the assumption that God is the perfect Father, who does indeed discipline his children, but disciplines them out of loving care for their welfare. There is no hint of dichotomy between his correction and his caring: one is the expression of the other.

God is pictured as the one who knows and the one who cares and the one who gives. He who knows the number of our hairs and cares for the fallen sparrow, will care for us and give us all we need. He is kind to the undeserving and ungrateful and selfish. He is like the shepherd who left the ninety-nine and searched for his one lost sheep till he found it and then brought it home with joy. He is like the father who daily waited and watched for his wastrel son, and then when he saw him in the distance ran to him and flung his arms round him and kissed him and called on everyone to celebrate the happy day.

[3] 1 Jn. 4:8; Jn. 3:16.

God is pictured as loving in a special way those who love Christ.[4]

Jesus not only taught God's love for men, he also taught his disciples to love their fellows. He taught gentleness, mercy, forgiveness, the turning of the other cheek; he urged them to leave self behind and take up the cross; he forbad the judging spirit, the calling down of fire on those who rejected him, the use of the sword to prevent his arrest; they were not to hate, but were to love even their enemies; he set up the good Samaritan as their example.

Jesus not only taught these things, but was uniquely successful in practising what he preached. He showed what love meant in action. Far from being the unbalanced fanatic, he had humility and quietness of spirit, and he showed a profound concern for people – both for people in the mass and for an endless stream of individuals. Not a hint emerges anywhere in the Gospels that he failed to live up to his own exacting standards. He spent himself on behalf of those who were ill; at times he was weary, at times he was too busy to eat; he cared for women and for children and for the outcasts of society; he comforted the bereaved and welcomed the over-loaded. Direct and specific references to his love are rare in the Gospels, but occasionally his love for particular people is mentioned – there was one follower who called himself 'the disciple whom Jesus loved'; his love for 'his own' is brought out especially in the discourses of John (he was the Good Shepherd who laid down his life for his sheep); he is said to have loved Martha and Mary and Lazarus; he looked upon the rich man who was not willing to part with his riches and loved him; during his final hours of agony he cared for his mother, for the penitent thief and for those who crucified him.

Yet in spite of the restraint of the Gospels, we get glimpses of the depth of the compassion which welled up in Jesus' soul. 'The sight of the people moved him to pity: they were like sheep without a shepherd, harassed and helpless.' 'When he came ashore, he saw a great crowd; and his heart went out to them.' 'I feel sorry for all these people'; 'Jesus was deeply

[4] Lk. 12:30; Mt. 10:29-31; 7:9-11; 20:1-15; Lk. 6:35; 15:3-7, 11-32; Jn. 16:27; 17:23.

moved'; 'looking up to heaven, he sighed'; 'he sighed heavily and was deeply moved . . . Jesus wept.'[5]

Jesus was moved to tears by the needs and sorrows and sins of those he came to seek and save, and his pain of spirit increased as the cross drew near. All the Gospels see the ministry of Jesus as a conscious acceptance of his vocation to death – a death which was indeed physically agonizing, but which was first and foremost a sacrificial, atoning death, bearing the sins of the world, in which he experienced the ultimate in spiritual agony. This vocation he was fiercely tempted to refuse during his forty days in the Judean wilderness, and to this vocation he had to set his face as a flint throughout his ministry, right through to the bloody sweat of Gethsemane and the cry of dereliction from the cross. This is where the New Testament sees the love of Jesus in all its depth. He who made the worlds, he whose glory is the theme-song of heaven, became a slave and humbled himself to that dire death in love for a thankless, rebel race of men.

His feelings found utterance when he cried: 'I have a baptism to undergo, and what constraint am I under until the ordeal is over!' 'When he came in sight of the city, he wept over it and said, "If only you had known, on this great day, the way that leads to peace! But no; it is hidden from your sight. For a time will come upon you, when your enemies will set up siege-works against you; they will encircle you and hem you in at every point; they will bring you to the ground, you and your children within your walls, and not leave you one stone standing on another, because you did not recognize God's moment when it came."' 'O Jerusalem, Jerusalem, the city that murders the prophets and stones the messengers sent to her! How often have I longed to gather your children, as a hen gathers her brood under her wings; but you would not let me.' 'When the time came he took his place at table, and the apostles with him; and he said to them, "How I have longed to eat this Passover with you before my death!"' In the garden 'anguish and dismay came over him, and he said to them, "My heart is ready to break with grief. Stop here, and stay awake with me." He went on a little, fell on his face in prayer, and said, "My

[5] Mt. 9:36; Mk. 6:34; 8:2; Mt. 20:34; Mk. 7:34; Jn. 11:33–35.

Father, if it is possible, let this cup pass me by. Yet not as I will, but as thou wilt." [6]

What is God like? He is like Jesus. Jesus was God Incarnate. The depth of God's love is seen when we see the cost of the Saviour's inexorable warfare against sin. The message rings out with solemnity, yet warmth: there is no salvation while men cling to their sins, but only a certain fearful looking for of judgment, yet Christ *longs* to gather his chicks under his wings. 'Come to me, all who labour and are heavy laden, and I will give you rest. Take my yoke upon you, and learn from me; for I am gentle and lowly in heart, and you will find rest for your souls. For my yoke is easy, and my burden is light.' 'Him who comes to me I will not cast out.' [7]

It becomes clear now that our initial questioning of God's goodness arose from an imperfect idea of goodness. It was altogether too shallow a concept to match up to the terrors and glories and compassion of the God who is. Instead of allowing the Bible to mould our notion of goodness, we let our false standard of goodness become a standard whereby to criticize the Bible. In doing so we lost the purity of our doctrine of God, and blunted the razor-edge of theism. We lost something of that awe and fear of the Lord which is the beginning of true wisdom and worship, and which is the necessary prelude to a realization of the depths of God's love.

Bonhoeffer, writing from prison, said:

> The day will come when men will be called again to utter the word of God with such power as will change and renew the world. It will be a new language, which will horrify men, and yet overwhelm them by its power. [8]

Does not the theme of this book horrify us, and yet at the same time convince our minds that it is the authentic teaching of Christ, the authentic word of God? However much we need to find contemporary words to express it, however much we need a visitation of the Spirit to feel it, we need no new message; the

---

[6] Lk. 12:50; 19:41–44; Mt. 23:37; Lk. 22:14 f.; Mt. 26:37–39. An anguish of spirit amounting to a willingness to be damned for the saving of others is also seen in Paul in Rom. 9:1–3 and in Moses at Ex. 32:32.

[7] Mt. 11:28–30, RSV; Jn. 6:37, RSV.

[8] D. Bonhoeffer, *Letters and Papers from Prison* (London, 1953), p. 160.

message is there in the Bible for the simplest to read, telling us that God is, that God rules, that God has revealed himself in word and deed, that God has shown us the depths of his severity and unfathomable kindness in and through Jesus Christ. This is the mighty, saving Good News which our sinning, suffering, sorrowing world *must* hear. It is this Christ whom we proclaim when we say:

Look at the goodness of God!

THE DOCTRINE
OF THE GOOD GOD

This book has been concerned mainly with phenomena in the Bible and only incidentally with modern currents of thought. But in the process of looking at some of the difficult things in the Bible, we have found ourselves immersed in the purest and richest form of what we believe to be the greatest system of thought that man has ever contemplated: theism. It has brought us into the heart of the modern debate about God. It would seem helpful to try to show the relation of the biblical doctrine of God to other schools of thought, both for the further clarification of the doctrine itself and also to demonstrate its relevance to present-day discussions. What follows is of course only an elementary guide to a vast and very deep subject.

THE PERSONAL GOD OF THE BIBLE

The Bible presents us with a personal God, who is Creator and Sustainer, Revealer and Inspirer, Governor and Judge, Lover and Saviour. God *created* the world. It is entirely dependent on him, but he is entirely independent of it. God is in no way to be identified with his world. Yet he is everywhere, and the creation exists only by his will. He orders everything in it 'according to the counsel of his will'.

Moreover, he created not merely things, but people. And the people whom he created he addresses in their own language. As C. H. Dodd says: 'The whole idea of revelation in the Old Testament is determined by the analogy of the word spoken and heard.'[1] Not only does the Spirit of God inspire the prophet as he declares his 'Thus saith the Lord', but he guides the writers of the Scriptures. Nearly a thousand pages of words are written: words of God, words about God, words about the people of God or about the works of God. And what was begun in the Old Testament is continued in the New. Thus biblical theism presents us with a speaking God, who cannot lie, whose every word is truth, who has *really* spoken. He is not some elusive inspirer of good thoughts which have been put into words by fallible men, words for which God can conveniently avoid responsibility. He is a Person of infinite wisdom who has spoken in human words many times during the course of biblical history; he has spoken through men and he has spoken through his Son, and he acknowledges their words in Scripture as his own.

God is seen as a Person also when he judges and when he saves. When God speaks to man, Person to person, he reveals his divine nature, and he gives man laws for the conduct of his life, promising him blessing for obedience and cursing for disobedience. God and sin are not merely uncomfortable partners, they are utterly irreconcilable, and the advent of sin meant man's total ruin. Man had no means of atoning for his sin, and no power (or even desire) to remedy the defects of his nature which the first sin had caused. He stood condemned under God's wrath, a rebel unable to save himself. He needed atonement, he needed a new status, he needed a new nature. It was upon men in such a state, guilty, hostile, helpless, that God set his love. It was a love infinite in its compassion and individual in its application. The very love with which the Father had loved the Son from all eternity was to lay hold upon those whom the Father had given to the Son. 'For God so loved the world that he gave his only Son, that whoever believes in him should not perish but have eternal life.'[2] In the hearts of men unable to fit themselves for God, God implanted his own life-giving word, giving them the power to repent of their sins and by faith to receive him. Salvation was not by good works. They

---

[1] Eph. 1:11. C. H. Dodd, *Interpretation of the Fourth Gospel* (Cambridge, 1953), p. 263.
[2] Jn. 17:2, 26; 3:16.

had no good works to offer. Their best deeds were all short of the divine standard. Salvation could be received only by faith. This is the doctrine of grace: sinners, all undeserving, simply accept the gift of God. Thenceforward, with his love in their hearts, they live for him out of pure gratitude.

ANTINOMIES

Biblical doctrine has the remarkable quality of being at one and the same time profoundly mysterious and pellucidly clear. At each point there are unfathomable 'antinomies' (that is, complementary truths which the human mind cannot reconcile), yet both sides of the picture stand out with intense clarity. There is on the one hand the Creator, and on the other the creation, which is not part of God, nor made of any substance external to God, but 'created out of nothing'. God is transcendent and God is immanent. There is one God and three Persons. Christ is both perfect God and perfect Man. There is divine predestination and human freedom. There is corporate solidarity and individual responsibility. Our study has emphasized yet another of these antinomies: the holiness of God and the love of God. God's holiness has been revealed as something terrible beyond human imagining. God is good in a manner quite outside our experience. God's goodness is a blazing, consuming, awe-inspiring thing, unlike the best that we know among men. It is when we see the Creator standing over against his creation, distinct from it, yet controlling every particle of it; loving his children with infinite love, yet hating the evil with infinite hatred, that we see theism in all its glory. Any form of Christianity which begins to confuse Creator and creature, or which begins to forget the severity of God's wrath, is departing from the truth and is detracting from the glory of God.

This system of antinomies to which the Bible leads us is nothing that the Christian need be ashamed of. It is not some coward's castle into which the Christian retreats when attacked, or a lazy man's let-out in which thinking is no longer necessary. On the contrary, the harder the Christian studies the clearer it becomes that to the human mind these antinomies are absolute. They belong to the nature of things as they are.

They govern the structure of his thought. It is true that a philosopher will probably soon tie a Christian in knots when he asks him to clarify his concepts. But equally one philosopher will soon tie a fellow-philosopher in knots, if he is rash enough to attempt to expound a coherent philosophy. As Bertrand Russell says, 'No one has yet succeeded in inventing a philosophy at once credible and self-consistent.'[3] The Christian believes that the Trinity-in-Unity is ultimate, and that in the creation we cannot dispense with either the One or the Many. The Christian is neither a monist nor a pluralist. When asked to clarify his concepts, he will say: 'The Bible appears to teach. . . .' He will go as far as the Bible seems to take him, even if it means following two different lines of thought which he cannot reconcile. It is, as we have seen, this unflinching pursuit of both the kindness and the severity of God that gives the razor-edge to biblical theism.

BLUNTING THE WORD OF GOD

a. Syncretism with pagan religion
All theological error is due in some way or other to the misuse of the Word of God, whether by addition or subtraction or distortion. Traditions of men are always in danger of blunting the Word of God. The church of both Old and New Covenants has been tempted in her weaker moments to apostasy, that is, to depart entirely from the faith she professes. But in her stronger moments she has always had to face a subtler danger, the temptation to syncretism. She has been tempted to add to her revealed faith ideas and practices which are man-made. The human and the divine are given equal status, and eventually the revelation is distorted beyond recognition. It was so under the Old Covenant in ancient Israel. At times the people lapsed into gross polytheism and practised magic arts in such a way that the Lord was virtually forgotten. But at other times, as when Jeroboam set up his calves in Dan and Bethel, the Lord was worshipped with the aid of idolatrous symbols. 'The sins of Jeroboam, which he sinned and which he made Israel to sin' form a refrain in the first book of Kings. The beginnings of idolatry soon led to a syncretism with Baal worship, till by the

[3] B. Russell, *History of Western Philosophy* (London, 1954), p. 637.

time of Elijah the worship of the Lord had become well-nigh submerged. It was so in the Dark Ages, when pagans poured into the church without a change of heart and they brought with them a strange medley of beliefs and practices which were baptized with the thinnest veneer of Christianity. Their very idols were sometimes retained, though re-named after Christian saints to whom were allocated the different functions of the old gods. The old polytheistic methods of prayer were continued almost undisguised. Ideas of merit and magic, together with elements of pagan philosophy and pagan mysticism, combined effectively to mask the simplicity of the New Testament doctrine. The attempt to regain and to retain the purity of the gospel has been a continuous struggle ever since.

b. Compromise with materialism: deism, the semi-chaos, impersonal judgment

Materialism does not seem to offer a very promising basis for a syncretistic marriage with Christianity. Yet certain deformations of Christianity have come from this source. The classical example is eighteenth-century deism, which regarded the world as a sort of machine, made by God with its own physical and moral laws and then left on its own to serve as a training-ground for human character. In deism we no longer have the God who 'accomplishes all things according to the counsel of his own will', whose hand is upon every particle in the universe, and who has personal dealings in grace and judgment with every person that lives. The Bible makes clear, it is true, that he has given to all his creatures their own individual natures and that, being true 'second causes', men's thoughts and deeds are their own thoughts and deeds, not God's. Yet God's perfect control of his world ensures that even wicked deeds take their place in his perfect plan. Amos could say: 'Does evil befall a city, unless the Lord has done it?' Amos does not of course mean that God is the author of sin, but that the evil consequences of Israel's iniquity are willed by God. Of the greatest crime in history, Peter could say, 'This Jesus, delivered up according to the definite plan and foreknowledge of God, you crucified and killed by the hands of lawless men.'[4] Theism

4 Am. 3:6; Acts 2:23.

never removes God by a hair's-breadth from anything in his world. It is with God as a Person, as the supreme Person, that we have to do.

It is thus a serious departure from the truth to regard God as the Creator of a semi-chaos. God's world is a cosmos, every particle of which he sustains and controls. Again it is a serious departure from the truth to regard judgment as impersonal. It is uncomfortable to sinful people to live continually under the all-seeing eye of the all-knowing Judge. Therefore Christians have been tempted to soft-pedal the theme of judgment. The theme of hell has been quietly omitted, and the wrath of God has been de-personalized.[5] The wrath of God is thought of as the outworking of a deistic machine, in which God is not immediately and personally involved. But it is because wrath is personal that mercy is personal.

[5] It has been said with some measure of truth that the theme of hell disappeared from our pulpits a hundred years ago, and that the theme of heaven followed fifty years later. The view that the wrath of God is impersonal is a serious error in C. H. Dodd's exposition of the Epistle to the Romans (Moffatt Commentary, London, 1932, pp. 20 ff.). Having reduced the wrath of God simply to a traditional way of expressing the dire consequences which naturally result from wrongdoing, there is no longer any personal wrath to propitiate. Substantially the same line is taken by G. H. C. MacGregor, 'The Concept of the Wrath of God in the N.T.', *N.T. Studies*, 7, pp. 101 ff.; A. T. Hanson, *The Wrath of the Lamb* (London, 1957); D. E. H. Whiteley, *The Theology of St. Paul* (Oxford, 1964), pp. 61 ff. The contrary view is stated by G. Stählin, *Wrath* (Bible Key Words from Kittel's *Theologisches Wörterbuch zum Neuen Testament*, London, 1964); R. V. G. Tasker, *The Biblical Doctrine of the Wrath of God* (London, 1951); L. Morris, *The Apostolic Preaching of the Cross* (London, 1955), pp. 129 ff., 161 ff. On the wrath of God in the Old Testament see S. Erlandsson, 'The Wrath of YHWH', *Tyndale Bulletin* 23 (1972), pp. 111 ff.

Though this is a most important debate, we must guard against an overpolarization of the issues. We must, it is true, never allow that God deals with any person in an impersonal way, but neither must we make his love and his wrath exact equivalents. The personal delight with which Jesus will say 'Come, you blessed' to those who love him, will not be matched by any delight when he says 'Depart, you cursed' to those who have rejected him. In biblical thought God and the redeemed rejoice when God's name is vindicated by his judgments, but there is no rejoicing either over sin or over its painful consequences. The hallelujahs in heaven over the fall of Babylon are rejoicings at the overthrow of an evil system (Rev. 18; 19), not over the suffering of individuals. All our thoughts about the vengeance of God or the wrath of God must be completely purged of the impure connotation which is characteristic of human vengeance and which is seldom wholly absent from human anger.

c. Diminished authority of Scripture: philosophy replaces theology

Another temptation has been to lower the authority of Scripture. The Christian can easily forget the insufficiency of his unaided reason and the need for total submission to the mind of God. He imagines that he can safely think his own independent thoughts, whereas in fact he will think correctly only if he thinks God's thoughts after him. If he forsakes his submission to holy Scripture, he is back in the empirical swamp. Scripture (and of course the world around us) is strewn with difficulties great and small. It is not clear at first sight whether these difficulties are in fact capable of harmonization or are the result of genuine contradictions. The anti-Christian, or the immature Christian who has not learnt much of his own ignorance, may be inclined to say, 'It is obvious to any honest man that there is a contradiction here.' He has no doubts about the sufficiency of his own reason in such a matter. The immature Christian has unwittingly discarded his Christian spectacles and has resumed his old empiricist spectacles. At first it seems to give great freedom. He feels that he can be completely 'honest'. He has not got to harmonize difficulties. He can frankly reject Old Testament passages which seem sub-Christian in tone. And so begins for him the disintegration of the whole biblical revelation.

What has happened in the church at large during the past century has been recapitulated again and again in the experience of individual Christians. A Christian may start with a rejection of a few items of the Old Testament; he then proceeds to the New; and finally he finds himself at loggerheads with the teaching of Christ. The diligent pursuit of these methods has resulted in the vast literature of disintegrating biblical criticism, which now dominates the teaching of the Bible in most of Christendom.[6] Attempts at reintegration have been going on continuously. But reintegration without a change of basic principles only means the dominance of some man-made philosophy. The tale of modern theology is one long story of the successive capitulation of theology to each new

[6] Biblical criticism as such is not of course wrong or harmful, but can be a useful tool. It goes astray, however, when it forgets the primacy of revelation. For a constructive treatment see G. E. Ladd, *The New Testament and Criticism* (London, 1967).

fashionable philosophy.[7] A weak theology is soon digested by the philosophy which it set out to digest. Each attempted re-integration is unstable. If reason (even unwittingly) is made our god, the result will inevitably be disintegration. But if reason is seen to be creaturely and sinful and in need of long and patient teaching, it will be found to be an instrument of integration, bringing together the seemingly disparate elements of Scripture and giving meaning to the world.

d. Pantheism

The legacy of the empirical approach has been an almost complete breakdown of trust in the Bible. A book as long as the Bible, under critical fire at literally tens of thousands of points, seems an intolerable incubus for the church to bear. It is not surprising, therefore, that many have looked in a quite different direction in search of a sure foundation. There has been a remarkable revival of interest in mysticism and in the pantheistic philosophy which normally goes with it.

Pantheism is by no means easy to explain. Like materialism, it seeks to describe the world in terms of a single principle. To many, materialism seems to be an upside-down proceeding, trying to explain the higher in terms of the lower. Matter, it is argued, must be explained in terms of spirit, and not *vice versa*. Could we but recognize it, Spirit surely is everywhere, is in everything, is everything. Pantheism in its most consistent form says, All-that-is is God. The whole world of existence is a unity; no distinctions have any ultimate validity; they are passing manifestations of the One. A moment's reflection will show at once that this is a diabolical doctrine. If God is identified with the world, God is identified with evil as well as with good. It means not merely that the beauties of Nature are God, but equally that the wicked and the ugly are also God.

[7] See H. R. Mackintosh, *Types of Modern Theology* (London, 1937). For the influence of philosophy on Anglicanism, see L. B. Smedes, *The Incarnation: Trends in Modern Anglican Thought* (Kampen, c. 1953). Smedes' examination of the teaching of Gore, Temple, Moberly, Weston, Thornton, Relton, Quick, Dix, Ramsey, Mascall, *etc.* is most illuminating. To my mind it is one of the important theological works of this century. A small edition was published in the Netherlands for a doctoral thesis, but this went rapidly out of print. Its reprint would be a service to theology.

A leader in the modern revival of Hinduism is reported to have said at a Congress of Religions that it is blasphemy to call men sinners – they are gods. He said: 'When I see a young mother bending over her child I bow before the image of God our Mother. When I see a harlot leaning down from her balcony, I bow before her also.' If good and evil are both identified with God, it means finally that good and evil are identified with one another. To have abolished the distinctions between good and evil, right and wrong, truth and error, beauty and ugliness, must surely be the Devil's final triumph.

Theism stands over against this in sharpest contrast. The world is not to be identified with God. Creature and Creator are totally distinct. To behold the beauties of Nature is to see, not God, but that which God made. To behold the good deeds of men is to see, not God, but that which God loves – a right use of his good gifts. To behold the wicked deeds of men is to see, not God, but that which is hateful to God – the misuse of his good gifts. The God of theism is a God who loves and hates; and since he is an infinite Being, a God who loves good with an infinite love and hates evil with an infinite hatred. In the terror of the loving Lord is seen the razor-edge of theism.

Now it is perfectly true that few men are thorough-going and consistent pantheists – the doctrine is too palpably absurd and too obviously dangerous. But pantheism in various less consistent forms has a strong hold on the modern world. It underlies several popular cults, including Christian Science, Theosophy, much of Yoga and of Spiritualism. Interest in the pantheistic religions of the East continues to grow. Zen Buddhism is but one element in this 'Eastern Invasion' of the West.[8] Pantheistic ideas have a great appeal to many intellectuals. A number of philosophers whose influence is still felt were more or less pantheistic in tendency, including such as Spinoza, Hegel and the idealists, Bergson and Whitehead. Cruder representations of pantheism are to be seen in the demand for an Impersonal God voiced by Bernard Shaw (as, for instance, in *Back to Methuselah*), H. G. Wells and the

[8] W. Braden, *The Private Sea: LSD and the Search for God* (Bantam Books, New York, 1967) gives a racy, but penetrating, account of the impact of this type of thinking on our culture.

Huxleys. Less clear-cut, but probably more influential, are the asides and cogitations of a host of contemporary novelists and poets.

e. Christian pantheizing

But even more serious than the pantheism of the non-Christian intellectuals is the pantheizing that has taken place within the Christian church, where attempts have been made to synthesize pantheism with biblical theism. In 1963 a book was published which 'appears to have sold more quickly than any new book of serious theology in the history of the world'.[9] Published in the middle of March, more than 350,000 copies of *Honest to God* were in print before the end of the year. In it John Robinson, an Anglican bishop, startled the world by bluntly asking the question whether it was not time for the Christian church to abandon theism. The bishop, a competent New Testament scholar who regarded himself as a biblical theologian, entitled his crucial chapter: 'End of Theism?' It was difficult to escape the conclusion that in his mind a struggle was going on between the personal God of his upbringing and the impersonal God of pantheism – with the latter gaining the upper hand.[1] Formally he gave a lucid exposition on straight pantheistic lines which would be entirely acceptable to many Hindu philosophers. The argument of this present book answers the bishop's question about the end of theism with a firm negative. What is required in the

[9] J. A. T. Robinson and D. L. Edwards, *The Honest to God Debate* (London, 1963), p. 7.
[1] Later on, he declared himself to be a pan-en-theist. Panentheism affirms that God is in everything, but omits or fails to give due weight to God's transcendence. God's Being (it is held) includes the world, but is not exhausted by it; evil is taken up into God and so is transformed. There seems to be some justification for thinking that Christian pantheizers argue on pantheistic premises and then smuggle in the God of love without rational justification. He is a 'God of the gaps'. In theism, however, transcendence and immanence are held together as antinomies without reduction. Teilhard de Chardin, in his attempt to wed an evolutionary philosophy (indebted to Bergson) with Christian orthodoxy, seems, in spite of his popularity both inside the Roman communion and without, to end up distinctly pantheizing. So do the process theologians, like C. Hartshorne and W. N. Pittenger, who lean heavily upon Whitehead. T. J. J. Altizer's version of the Death of God theology seems to abandon transcendence altogether.

Christian church is not an abandonment of theism, but its sharper and bolder reassertion.

It is hard to take seriously the idea (so widely canvassed) that our twentieth-century understanding of the universe necessitates the abandonment of the Bible's view of God. Both Jewish and Christian theology have always been quite clear that there are two proper answers to the question, 'Where is God?' One is: 'In heaven.' The other is: 'Everywhere.' God is both transcendent and immanent. God is not localized anywhere within the universe nor, in any literal sense, outside it. As Solomon said, 'The highest heaven cannot contain thee.' Or, as the psalm puts it,

> 'Whither shall I go from thy Spirit?
>   Or whither shall I flee from thy presence?
> If I ascend to heaven, thou art there!
>   If I make my bed in Sheol, thou art there!'[2]

The localized image of God is a necessity for the space-bound human mind when thinking of a personal God, but the Creator of the universe is everywhere within the world he made. The advent of the Space Age has no bearing whatever on the great issue: Is God distinct from the universe? Theism and pantheism are mortal enemies which cannot be synthesized. One or the other must win the day.

f. Mysticism

Attempts to synthesize pantheism with biblical theism have been made by Christian mystics. Many of the mystics in different periods of the church's history have come to an impersonal conception of the Divine Being; indeed it is a characteristic of a certain type of piety that it strives for a mystical union with the Absolute of a kind scarcely distinguishable from the avowedly pantheistic mystical experience of the Buddhist. It is a false spirituality which believes that it can dispense with the highest exercise of the intellect, and it is a false mysticism which believes that the impersonal is higher than the personal. Many earnest seekers after a deeper spiritual life need to be forewarned of the danger of devotion which is

1 Ki. 8:27; Ps. 139:7 f.

not nourished by intensive and comprehensive study of the Bible, which keeps the intellect stretched and alert, and which continually refreshes the imagination with a vivid and personal vision of the God there revealed.

g. *Weakened sacramental doctrine*

This same tendency is also found in certain types of sacramental teaching. Salvation is thought of, not in terms of sin and propitiation, but merely in terms of the incorporation of mankind into the eternal self-offering of Christ through the sacraments. Christ came forth from God, gathered mankind to himself by virtue of incarnation, and carried men back to God through their union with him in his Body, the church. There is often a suspicion of sacramental magic in this doctrine. Salvation is effected simply by an external rite, and membership of an earthly society is synonymous with spiritual union with Christ. But, more serious still, the death of Christ becomes merely an incident in his total self-offering. The weight falls on the metaphysical marvel of incarnation, not on the moral marvel of substitution. It was indeed a wonderful thing that the Creator should deign to join himself to those whom he had created, but that he should be made sin, and should be forsaken by his Father for us, is a wonder that passes understanding. In the New Testament, Christ became man in order that he might die. Death was the purpose of his coming and not merely an incident in the process of the incorporation of the church into Christ. This doctrine, again, tends to by-pass the need for repentance and a change of heart. It is sufficient to get into the ark and lead a respectable life, and the church will take the sinner to glory. Yet this is not the biblical doctrine. The sacraments are signs which point the sinner to Christ, bidding him to repent and to seek the washing away of his sins in the Saviour's blood. And when he has turned to him, they are seals of the covenant to assure him that the promises of the gospel are true and are meant for him. They are effective means of grace, but in no sense automatic. To the one who has not repented, they do not bring salvation; they bring increased condemnation. Outward membership of the church and external respectability provide no right of access to a holy

God. A doctrine which minimizes the need for the atoning blood of the Saviour and the moral change of the sinner blunts the edge of biblical theism.

h. Liberalism

This same tendency finds expression also in so-called liberalism or modernism. Liberalism is not pantheism, but it too is pantheizing in trend. It tends to obscure the doctrine of the personality of God and to mitigate the seriousness of sin, and it renders unnecessary a supernatural salvation. Perhaps the tendency can be most clearly illustrated by the modernist doctrine of the Universal Fatherhood of God. The New Testament speaks of all men as being the offspring of God in the sense that they are all created and sustained by him,[3] but it speaks of sonship of God in the proper sense as being the product of a supernatural work of creation wrought in man by the Spirit of God. To be a son of God, one must *become* a son; to enter the family of God, one must be adopted; to see the kingdom of God, one must be born again. Sonship is by the narrow door of repentance from sin and of faith in the One who came to deliver from sin. The Universal Fatherhood doctrine, on the other hand, usually represents man as being a child of God by nature. Made in the image of God, he is God-like. He has simply to live as though God were his Father and all men his brothers, and he will naturally develop into 'the measure of the stature of the fullness of Christ'. The dangerous inferences which can so readily and naturally be drawn from this doctrine are easily seen. We say with good reason, 'Like father, like son', which means that in using the father–son relationship to describe the kinship between God and the natural man, we are at least suggesting that by looking at man we may see what God is like. Heaven forbid! The ways of man, ancient, medieval and modern, are far more suggestive of the Devil – as indeed Christ himself on one occasion plainly said. He said to the Jews, 'You are of your father the devil.' He spoke of his contemporaries as 'you who are evil', and he traced the wicked deeds of men to the wickedness of their

[3] Acts 17:24–31.

hearts; 'From within, out of the heart of man, come evil thoughts, fornication, theft, murder.'[4]

The fullest revelation of the way of salvation is necessarily reserved till after the death and resurrection and exaltation of Christ, but all the main items of New Testament doctrine are unmistakably present in embryo even in the Synoptic Gospels. People are divided by Christ into just two classes, with only two possible destinies. Forgiveness of sins requires the blood of the covenant sacrifice and the offering of the ransom-life. Entry into the kingdom necessitates conversion and new birth. It is the Holy Spirit who effects renewal, and from the renewed man must come repentance and faith, faith directed towards Christ himself. Forgiveness manifests itself in devotion and obedience and it issues in eternal bliss.

So then once again it is the teaching of Christ which gives us the decisive guidance. His teaching is all of a piece – to him the Father is supremely personal, and his doctrine of God is the purest theism, as is shown by his endorsement of the Old Testament, by his teaching on judgment and by his teaching on salvation. But in this respect his teaching is also all of a piece with the rest of the Bible. And the teaching of the Bible is all of a piece with the teaching of Providence. Christ, the Bible, Providence, all point in the same direction, showing us both the kindness and severity of God; or, to sum it up in a single word, showing us the goodness of God.

[4] Jn. 8:44; Lk. 11:13; Mk. 7:21.

EVIL IN THE
WORLD OF NATURE

The fact of suffering in the animal world has seemed to some thinkers the greatest of all objections to Christian belief, because even if human sufferings can be explained by human sin, those of animals (which are incapable of sin) cannot be so explained.

Animal suffering is of course part of a wider problem of evil in nature, since there are disasters (*e.g.* through earthquake and storm) and diseases (in plants, animals and men) to be explained. Broadly speaking there are three ways of accounting for our imperfect world. To the atheist there is no problem. The atheistic view is that the whole is the product of the interplay of blind forces, which are non-moral and which often happen to be unpleasant in their operation. For the theist there are two possibilities. The theistic evolutionary view is that the whole is the product of the interplay of natural forces, together with a divine activity which guides the evolutionary process in its upward course. The divine activity does not eliminate the unpleasant features of the evolutionary process, though it can be expected to result in perfection eventually. The creationist view is that the world owes its origin to one or more direct acts of flawless creation and that all subsequent disharmony has been due to the misplacement of components which are in themselves good.

On the creationist view, earthquakes (which are part of the mountain-building process) are good things. Harm comes when man, out of touch with his Maker, is in the wrong place at the wrong time. Man in touch with his Maker, being in the right place at the right time, enjoys divine protection, so that Jesus could safely sleep in the storm. The earth is an awesome and magnificent home for man, but it is far too dangerous for him to venture forth from Eden on his own. Fire, water, electricity are beneficial things in the right place, but disastrous in the wrong. R. E. D. Clark in his chapter on Evil in *The Universe: Plan or Accident?*[1] argues that disease producing protozoa, bacteria and viruses come in the same category. These were not specially created to torture man and beast or to create diseases in plants. In some cases it is demonstrable that microorganisms have been transferred from their normal habitat,

---

[1] R. E. D. Clark, *The Universe: Plan or Accident?* (3rd ed., London, 1961), pp. 206 ff. I am particularly indebted in this note to chapter 16, in which many of the points are more fully developed.

Arthur Jones, in a note on 'The Goodness of Parasitism' in *Faith and Thought* 100 (1972/3), pp. 10 ff., calls attention to two articles: G. Rees, 'Pathogenesis of Adult Cestodes', *Helminthological Abstracts*, 1967, 36, pp. 1–23 (quotation from p. 2); D. R. Lincicome, 1971, 'The Goodness of Parasitism: a New Hypothesis', in *Aspects of the Biology of Symbiosis*, ed. T. C. Cheng, pp. 139–227 (quotation from p. 224). He says: 'Many Christians (e.g. Clark) have argued that the virulence of such organisms is due to disturbance of the normal relationships between different creatures and between these creatures and their environment. The evidence for this view has long been strong, but two recent articles make it as near coercive as it will probably ever be. The authors of both articles agree that a parasite does not normally harm its host: in fact its effect is usually beneficial. Rees concludes that, "Parasitic worms are, naturally, inherently non-pathogenic" and he cites evidence of, e.g., their bactericidal properties. Lincicome concurs and supplements a thorough survey with extensive experimental evidence supporting the goodness of parasitism, especially in relation to metabolic balance. He concludes that parasitism is "a metabolic ecological association of two organisms, the basis of which is chemical and the function of which is fundamentally one of molecular exchanges of social, ecological, and evolutionary values".'

He then says that parasites are apparently only pathogenic for one or other of the following reasons:

1. Excessive numbers enter the host causing damage by the act of entering.
2. Superinfestation occurs resulting in damage after entry.
3. The host's diet is inadequate.
4. The host is already suffering from disease.
5. The host is mutant.
6. The parasite is mutant.
7. They have been introduced into the wrong host.
8. They are in the wrong host organ.
9. The host is psychologically or spiritually unbalanced.
10. The environment is abnormal.

where they are beneficial (or at worst harmless), to an alien
habitat where they are harmful. To regard a diseased organism
as a wonderful living mechanism in which something has gone
wrong seems as sensible as thinking of it as one organism
suffering modification at the hands of others in a continuing,
mindless interplay of natural forces. But this is not the place to
attempt to weigh the merits of theistic evolution and special
creation.

Since no man can actually enter into the experience of an
animal, many of our deductions are bound to be speculative.
This renders arguments against the benignity of nature precarious, but it also renders arguments in its favour precarious
as well. It is necessary to remind ourselves that the Christian
does not in any case profess to prove the truth of what has been
given him by revelation. His is the humbler task of showing
that the case against the revelation has not been demonstrated.

It is not his task to prove that the world of nature is in a state
of perfection, except in so far as it has been spoilt by fallen
man. In its teaching about the Devil and demonic powers the
Bible clearly implies a fall before the Fall of man, and there is
no need to believe that the idyllic vision of the leopard lying
down with the kid reflects the situation immediately prior to
man's Fall. Nor is it necessary to believe that thorns and thistles
were first created after the Fall. The thorns and thistles indicate
rather that fallen man has found difficulty in managing his
environment since he forfeited God's blessing. In some sense
the whole creation groans under the oppression of evil and
awaits the day when man's redemption is complete and the
powers of darkness are finally overthrown.[2]

Nor is it his task to explain away animal pain. As we have
seen in the case of man, the pain reflex is essentially protective
and beneficial and becomes destructive only in its extreme
forms. Pain becomes a problem only when it seems over-
prolonged or over-severe. There is reason to think that extreme
sensations of pain and experiences of suffering may be rare or
even non-existent among animals. In the case of animals the
distinction between pain and suffering is particularly important. Physical pain is an experience in the body which, at

[2] Is. 11:6–9; Gn. 3:18; Rom. 8:22 f.

least in the case of human beings, often causes mental suffering. But, as we have seen, not only can a given degree of pain cause very varying degrees of suffering according to a person's state of mind – in a state of acute apprehension it may seem excruciating, while in a state of excitement it may go unnoticed – but most human suffering is in fact caused by non-physical factors, such as 'fear, anxiety, remorse, envy, humiliation, a sense of injustice, the death of someone loved, unrequited affection, personal estrangement, boredom, and frustration of many sorts'.[3] With the lower animals these factors do not operate at all, and even with the higher animals comparatively little. It is true that a few species wilt for a while when bereaved, but seldom for long.[4] There is no reason to think that animals have a time-consciousness or even imagination like ours, so that they are almost 'immune to the distinctively human forms of suffering, which depend upon our capacity imaginatively to anticipate the future'.[3] Active pain-reflexes do not therefore necessarily mean suffering.

Or again, there is the so-called 'threat' behaviour in animals. The sort of weeding-out process involved in pecking orders or dominant male systems can certainly be argued to have selective value, but it is worth noting that such processes are the exception rather than the rule. Most members of a species do *not* fight one another. They may engage in highly ritualized displays that we call 'threat' on the basis of human experience, but they rarely result in any damage to either party. It would certainly be wrong to assert that the 'defeated' animal in a threat display exhibits 'fright'.

We simply cannot enter into the experience of a fly caught in a spider's web. To think of predator and prey as if they had human personalities is to make revolting something which is non-moral, and may well be to invent suffering which does not exist. Animal behaviour which to human imagination may look cruel and ruthless may in fact be wholesome and hygienic, as when the strong members of the herd kill off the sick, or

[3] J. Hick, *Evil and the God of Love* (London, 1966), pp. 329, 350. His chapter 15 on 'Pain' is a valuable discussion of pain and suffering, human and animal.
[4] R. E. D. Clark, *The Universe: Plan or Accident?*, pp. 215 f.

when the vultures and hyenas polish off a carcase. When a human being tortures one of the lower animals for pleasure, the worst harm is done to the tormentor, not to the tormented.

Further, one needs to beware of attributing to animals the morals of human beings. The weasel is not vicious. Like all other animals he is a food-getter, who happens to be endowed with alertness, resource, good appetite and daring. He may be destructive in a man-made chicken-run where hens are artificially herded together, but he is not a 'murderer' with 'an insane blood lust'. Nor is he the terror of the neighbourhood. It is difficult to exaggerate the harm that has been done to our understanding of the world by the philosophical misuse of the principle of natural selection. Natural selection, whereby the least well-adapted are eliminated and beneficial mutations may be preserved, is a process which keeps a species healthy and in harmony with its environment. But to liken this to the struggle for existence in a gladiatorial show or in a totally soulless capitalist society is simply to misread nature. This is a legacy which we have inherited from the early days of the evolution debate.

Darwin himself made a good deal of play with this idea of cruel struggle, but it was T. H. Huxley who had the greatest influence in propagating it. Kenneth Walker writes:

> There is much to be said in favour of Raven's view that Huxley's insistence on the cruelty and amorality of nature was due to the fact that although he was a brilliant scientist, he had a strong distaste for field work and consequently seldom made personal observations of nature. Huxley had none of the field naturalist's delight in the study and observation of the actual living organism, but preferred, as did his great contemporary Owen, to shut himself up in the laboratory and the dissecting room. With no observations of his own to act as a corrective he readily fell into the error of believing nature to be utterly brutal and callous. This caused him considerable distress for he was an ethical idealist as well as a scientific realist and the two sides of his character were often in conflict.
>
> The animal world was soon pictured as a pitiless arena in which half-starved individuals carried on an inexorable struggle for food with complete disregard to all their fellows. Even Huxley, who in many ways was the ablest of Darwin's exponents, took this view and proclaimed that the animal world was on the same level as a gladiatorial show. He declared that the struggle was so pitiless

that there was no need, as in gladiatorial struggles, for any spectator to turn his thumb down, for no quarter was ever given.

The weakest and stupidest went to the wall, while the toughest and shrewdest, those who were best fitted to cope with their circumstances, but not the best in another way, survived.[5]

A. R. Wallace, who shares with Darwin the honour of having propounded the theory of natural selection, moved in a quite different direction. His views merit quotation at length:

Now that the war of nature is better known, it has been dwelt upon by many writers as presenting so vast an amount of cruelty and pain as to be revolting to our instincts of humanity . . . Even so thoughtful a writer as Professor Huxley adopts similar views . . . He speaks of the myriads of generations of herbivorous animals which 'have been tormented and devoured by carnivores'; of the carnivores and herbivores alike 'subject to all the miseries incidental to old age, disease, and over-multiplication', and of the 'more or less enduring suffering' which is the meed of both vanquished and victor . . .

There is, I think, good reason to believe that all this is greatly exaggerated; that the supposed 'torments' and 'miseries' of animals have little real existence, but are the reflection of the imagined sensations of cultivated men and women in similar circumstances; and that the amount of actual suffering caused by the struggle for existence among animals is altogether insignificant. Let us, therefore, endeavour to ascertain what are the real facts on which these tremendous accusations are founded.

In the first place, we must remember that animals are entirely spared the pain we suffer in the anticipation of death – a pain far greater, in most cases, than the reality. This leads, probably, to an almost perpetual enjoyment of their lives; since their constant watchfulness against danger, and even their actual flight from an enemy, will be the enjoyable exercise of the powers and faculties they possess, unmixed with any serious dread. There is, in the next place, much evidence to show that violent deaths, if not too prolonged, are painless and easy; even in the case of man, whose nervous system is in all probability much more susceptible to pain than that of most animals.[6]

The experience of Livingstone when he was seized by a lion is a well-known case in point:

He shook me as a terrior dog does a rat. The shock produced a stupor similar to that which seems to be felt by a mouse after the

[5] K. M. Walker, *Meaning and Purpose* (London, 1944), pp. 46, 44.
[6] A. R. Wallace, *Darwinism* (London, 1889), pp. 36–40.

first shake of the cat. It caused a sort of dreaminess, in which there was no sense of pain nor feeling of terror, though quite conscious of all that was happening.

R. E. D. Clark makes the same point:

In battle, severe pain is the exception rather than the rule. In World War II, two hundred and fifteen recently wounded men were questioned: less than a quarter had 'bad pain'; the rest moderate, slight or none.[7]

In times of danger there is an immediate hormonal response which acts as an analgesic as well as a quickener of responses. The same hormone is produced by all the higher animals. Wallace proceeds:

Neither do those (animals) which die of cold or hunger suffer much. Cold is generally severest at night and has a tendency to produce sleep and painless extinction. Hunger, on the other hand, is hardly felt during periods of excitement, and when food is scarce the excitement of seeking for it is at its greatest. It is probable, also, that when hunger presses, most animals will devour anything to stay their hunger, and will die of gradual exhaustion and weakness not necessarily painful, if they do not fall an earlier prey to some enemy or to cold.

He then speaks of the positive enjoyment of animals:

As a rule they come into existence at a time of year when food is most plentiful and the climate most suitable, that is in the spring of the temperate zone and at the commencement of the dry season in the tropics. They grow vigorously, being supplied with abundance of food; and when they reach maturity their lives are a continual round of healthy excitement and exercise, alternating with complete repose.
On the whole, then, we conclude that the popular idea of the struggle for existence entailing misery and pain on the animal world is the very reverse of the truth. What it really brings about is the maximum of life and the enjoyment of life with the minimum of suffering and pain. Given the necessity of death and reproduction – and without these there could have been no progressive development of the organic world, – it is difficult even to imagine a system by which a greater balance of happiness could have been secured. And this view was evidently that of Darwin himself, who thus concludes his chapter on the struggle for existence: 'When we

[7] D. Livingstone, *Travels and Researches in South Africa* (Harmsworth Library, London, 1905), p. 4. (The spelling and grammar are as printed in this edition.) R. E. D. Clark, *op. cit.*, p. 215.

reflect on this struggle, we may console ourselves with the full belief that the war of nature is not incessant, that no fear is felt, that death is generally prompt, and that the vigorous, the healthy, and the happy survive and multiply.'

This perhaps slightly underplays the harsher aspect of nature, and it needs also to be remembered that the same qualities which prevent animals knowing the depths of suffering presumably prevent them knowing the more sublime joys; yet enjoyment of life at the animal level is certainly real. V. Barclay quotes an interesting example of the utter unconsciousness of death in the animal world:

> While the fish, chiefly herrings (*Sardinella sajax*), were massed in the calm transparent water beneath the dock, a sea-lion appeared and glided about directly below us, making a clear path over and over again through the schools. As the lobo bore swiftly down upon the fishes, the latter would dart aside as if terror-stricken, but, astonishing as it may seem, they became quiet no less abruptly the instant that the enemy has passed, and they showed not the slightest tendency towards deserting the locality. To those who wax sentimental over the universal cruelty of nature, the scene would have been a convincing lesson. Ruthlessness in nature is not necessarily cruel. It is obvious that the herrings in the Chincha Strait, although from one point of view intended by nature to furnish the subsistence of the sea-lion, did NOT live in fear of their relentless persecutor. It is equally clear that those fishes which had achieved the most hair-breadth escapes from the lobo cherished no unhappy memories of their danger, not even from the briefest period.[8]

This is not only true of the lower animals, but also of the most highly developed. A big game hunter, Frank Melland, who went to an area hitherto unvisited by men with guns, recounts how, after he had shot an elephant, the four or five other elephants in the group 'simply stared at him when he fell, and though they retreated a few yards when I came up, they drew near again, quite close, when we were cutting him up and watched the whole operation! They had no fear.'[9]

---

[8] V. Barclay, *Darwin is Not for Children* (London, 1950), pp. 85 f., to whom I am indebted for a number of illustrations. The above quotation is said to come from R. C. Murphy, *Logbook for Grace* (1948), but I have not been able to trace this.

[9] F. Melland, *Elephants in Africa* (London, 1938), pp. 14 f.

There was no instinctive dismay at death itself; the smell of blood did not even cause a reflex.

What needs to be observed is that most of the *demonstrable* suffering in the animal world is due to man. For instance, untold millions of free and apparently happy creatures have been caught in gins and have suffered something analogous to crucifixion – surviving in great pain for perhaps a week. One can hope that such a death (the equivalent of which must occasionally occur in nature when a solitary animal suffers an accident) is not quite as dreadful as it looks; but with the higher animals the deliberate infliction of such a degree of pain in the interests of vanity and greed cannot be justified.

Or again, to quote R. E. D. Clark: 'In a few short decades we have seen whole continents drying up as a result of man-caused soil erosion; we have seen the creation of a million square miles of new deserts with many millions more well on the way.' Thirst is probably the worst type of common animal suffering. But water was normally abundant in nature, until man the desert-maker came upon the scene. In Southern Africa 'as a result of careless agriculture and the determination to keep more cattle than the land could support, erosion set in on a nation-wide scale. The level of the great lakes fell, the smaller ones disappeared, humid forests with their trickling streams became parched grasslands and often, even, desert.'[1] E. N. Marais in his book *My Friends the Baboons* describes how until about 1860 the wild baboon in Africa fed upon plants and insects. 'It has since acquired the knowledge, under the pressure of drought and famine, that food is to be found in the animals kept by man . . . It discovered that nourishing milk was to be found in the stomachs of lambs.' It became a catcher of lambs first in Cape Province and then 'this evil spread slowly northwards until nowadays it is a regular habit right up to the Vaal River'. In due course the baboons turned to other domestic animals as well.[2]

It has been the sin of man, more than any other factor, which has sown discord in the world of nature, not only causing animal suffering and the destruction of plant life, but

[1] R. E. D. Clark, *op. cit.*, pp. 212 f.
[2] E. N. Marais, *My Friends the Baboons* (London, 1939), pp. 2 f.

which now patently threatens mankind with self-destruction. Man's rape of the earth is a hideous and frightening story. Man was intended to live in partnership with the rest of creation, giving to it what he had to give and receiving from it what it had to give in return. But instead of trying humbly to learn God's laws and obey them, he arrogantly set out to exploit the world and to exploit his fellow-man. He little understood what irreversible forces he was setting in motion. His wars hastened the dissemination of micro-organisms from one area to another, decimating and enfeebling whole populations. In spite of his marvellous technological aids, he has brought famine to larger and larger areas of the world. Not content with making deserts of the land, he has poured his pollutions into the seas, which seem now to be, slowly but surely, dying. To all appearances the final result will be a Gadarene plunge to destruction.

Demonstrable suffering is at its worst when animals are in closest touch with man.[3] The anxieties felt by captive animals when approached by a cruel master are simply not paralleled in nature, nor are the worst features of factory farming or vivisection. Animals in their natural habitat experience fear, but it is a wholesome sort of fear. Among ourselves there is a fine dividing-line between fear which gives a great thrill (as in motor racing or in the seeing of an exciting film) and the fear which is too much and leaves mental wounds. A healthy animal's escape when hunted may well produce an exhilaration akin to that experienced by a daring young man who brings off a dangerous escapade. There is no reason to think that the alarm calls of birds mean a spoilt day for them. Life in the animal world is full of interest, at least until man comes on the scene. Man alone can make it boring, when he deprives a creature of its freedom and puts it in a zoo.

---

[3] An increased capacity for suffering seems to be developed by animals that are integrated into a human community. C. S. Lewis, *The Problem of Pain* (London, 1940), pp. 126 f., argues that the tame animal, which owes so much of its real self to its master, is pre-eminently occupying the place for which it was made.

INDEX OF BIBLICAL REFERENCES

AUTHOR INDEX

SUBJECT INDEX